The State and the Globa.

The State and the Global Ecological Crisis

Edited by
John Barry and Robyn Eckersley

The MIT Press
Cambridge, Massachusetts
London, England

MIT Press books may be purchased at special quantity discounts for business or sales promotional use. For information, please e-mail <special_sales@mitpress .mit.edu> or write to Special Sales Department, The MIT Press, 5 Cambridge Center, Cambridge, MA 02142.

This book was set in Sabon by Achorn Graphic Services. Printed on recycled paper and bound in the United States of America.

Library of Congress Cataloging-in-Publication Data

The state and the global ecological crisis / edited by John Barry and Robyn Eckersley.
  p. cm.
  Includes bibliographical references and index.
  ISBN 0-262-02581-7 (alk. paper)—ISBN 0-262-52435-X (pbk.: alk. paper)
  1. Environmental policy. 2. International relations—Environmental aspects. 3. International economic relations—Environmental aspects.   I. Barry, John, 1966–   II. Eckersley, Robyn, 1958–

GE170.S72 2005
363.7'0526—dc22   2004062133

For Eva, Dearbhla, and Saoirse

Contents

An Introduction to Reinstating the State

The modern environmental movement has long been ambivalent in its attitude toward the state and the state system. This division may be traced, in part, to the contradictory role that states have played in facilitating both environmental degradation and environmental protection. Standing at the intersection between domestic, international, and global pressures, the state is the preeminent institution with the requisite political authority and steering capacity to tackle ecological problems through multilateral agreements and domestic regulation. Yet the modern state can also be singled out as being wholly or partly responsible for driving environmental degradation, either through its military activities or through the various ways in which it has traditionally sought to assert bureaucratic control or foster national economic development and nation building. More recently, this economic imperative has taken on an increasingly global and more intensely competitive character that has threatened to thwart or overshadow some of the more promising domestic and multilateral initiatives that have emerged since ecological problems rose to global prominence in the 1960s. On the one hand, the raft of new specialized environmental functions and responsibilities that many states acquired in the latter half of the twentieth century carried intimations of an emerging ecological state. On the other hand, the ideological ascendance of neoliberalism has derailed this development by calling forth "the competition state," the primary tasks of which are to attract increasingly mobile capital and to make economic activities in the state more competitive in global terms. The growing critical debates on economic globalization, governance, and the state suggest that the modern state is losing its autonomy, steering capacity, and political legitimacy in the face of rapid technological change and global competitive pressures. Despite the juridical equality of states within the United Nations system, there is an extraordinary variability in state forms, from so-called failed states to unrivaled superpowers like the United States. The former appear incapable of addressing the ecological challenge, and the latter appear unwilling. None of these developments augur well for the development of effective ecological governance by states and the state system.

Against the background of these developments, this book provides a revisionist intervention in the debates about the state and the global ecological crisis. Its primary audience is scholars, students, and activists interested in national and global environmental politics who consider the state to be a lost cause or who are deeply pessimistic about the prospects for state-based governance systems to redress the global ecological crisis. This current of pessimism has been particularly strong in ecoanarchist, bioregional, antiglobalization, and ecorealist literatures and movements, and it is also an implicit premise in the burgeoning new field of global political ecology.

While we accept that there are many good reasons to be pessimistic about the ecological potential of states, our concern is that such pessimism too often becomes an excuse for political resignation to the idea of a weakened and ineffectual state, and to the idea that ecological degradation is inevitable. The animating idea of this book is to question this political resignation, to highlight the uneven and deeply contested role and character of the state in orchestrating and responding to economic and environmental pressures, and to explore some of the more hopeful signs and opportunities for ecological progress on the part of states at both the domestic and transnational levels. Our ultimate concerns are to discover to what extent it might be possible to "reinstate the state" as a facilitator of progressive environmental change rather than environmental destruction, to redress what we believe is a somewhat lopsided and unduly negative critique of the state by many radical political ecologists and radical environmental activists, and to develop a more nuanced and even-handed understanding of the ecological and democratic potential of states. However, questions concerning whether a nondominating state is feasible and conceivable, and the general legitimacy and future potential of the state, are also of major concern to political theorists and those concerned with progressive politics generally.

Our scholarly intervention, then, is essentially a *strategic* one: to high-light and interrogate the multiple and sometimes fragmented dimensions of the state, both domestically and internationally, and to pinpoint where possible some promising sites of engagement and renewal. The contributors to this volume all proceed from a critical perspective and, despite their differences, are united in their effort to develop constructive insights for institutional and environmental policy reform, based on a critical assessment of the capacity and democratic potential of states as both individual governance structures and units in a broader structure of regional and international multilateral governance. Given our strategic concern to draw out the positive possibilities of the greening of the state in a global context, we deliberately avoided imposing a tight analytical template on the contributors. Restricting the focus to, say, the juridical/constitutional state, or to the economy and the state or the state system, or to the state's administrative or security apparatus would have foreclosed possible avenues of constructive inquiry by our contributors and defeated our purpose. Thus our collection is illustrative rather than exhaustive of the potential for state-based ecological renewal. We also wanted the volume to reflect a diversity of (broadly critical and constructive) understandings of the state that extend to scholarship in the fields of domestic policy, comparative politics, political economy (including international political economy), international relations, development studies, and political theory.

Our purpose is not to discount other potential avenues of ecological reform beyond the state, such as grassroots community environmental initiatives, the development of green consumerism and green investment, environmental best practice on the part of businesses, or the development of alternative codes of practice on the part of transnational environmental nongovernmental organizations (NGOs). Rather, we are concerned to explore how states might better facilitate these and other initiatives (including hybrid state-nonstate initiatives) as part of a more concerted effort to orchestrate local and global ecological sustainability. So, while our primary focus of attention is the state, we also explore what might be called synergistic connections between state and nonstate actors, and how they might be promoted by states acting both individually and collectively.

We do not want to be starry-eyed about the green potential of the modern state, and we acknowledge the significant political and structural barriers to its realization. But it would be a great pity if environmental activists and NGOs were to turn their backs on what still remains the primary and most pervasive form of political governance in the world today. Despite the changes wrought by globalization, democratic states still have more steering capacity and legitimacy to regulate the activities of corporations and other social agents along ecologically sustainable lines in more systematic ways than any nonstate alternative. Democratic states therefore emerge as the preeminent (although not necessarily exclusive) institution to assume the role of protecting public environmental goods such as human health, ecosystem integrity, biodiversity, and the global commons. This notion is somewhat reminiscent of the Hegelian notion of the state as the embodiment of public reason and ethics. This is a far cry from the liberal idea of the state as a neutral umpire, the anarchist idea of the state as an inherently oppressive institution, or the orthodox Marxist idea of the state as an instrument of the ruling class. Of course, states themselves are neither unitary entities nor moral subjects. They do not stand above civil society but rather are deeply fragmented entities that are enmeshed with civil society and the economy. And notions of public environmental goods remain deeply contested. It is therefore helpful to think of the state, nationally, as a "container of social processes," providing a set of a set of facilities "through which society can exercise some leverage upon itself."[1] Internationally, states act as the most significant nodes in a complex network of governance that depends on the legal systems of states. This book explores to what extent the ecological potential of states has been realized, how it might be realized, and what political and institutional changes might be necessary to move closer toward this green democratic regulatory ideal.

Most books on the role of the state in environmental management and governance have focused on domestic policy or on regional/global policy and international regimes. This book offers a dual focus in order to direct attention to the kinds of mutually reinforcing ideas and practices that might produce (or impede) environmentally responsible practices in general. With these considerations in mind, we bring together domestically focused work in green political theory, environmental policy, and comparative politics with environmentally focused scholarship in international relations, international political economy, and regionalization to explore the existing and potential role of the state in securing environmental protection. Given the highly contested and culturally specific character of environmental values and goals, we have not sought to pin down the meanings of *environmentally responsible, green,* or *ecological state* in advance of the discussion. Rather, we have left this to the contributors to explore in the context of their own case studies and conceptual analyses.

Part I of the volume comprises contributions that focus primarily on domestic environmental management by the state. These essays look at the relationship between the state, the economy, the environment, and civil society from different angles and employ different levels of abstraction. Chapter 1 opens with a broad historical overview of the emergence of the ecological state; the rest of the chapters in part I cover both single and comparative case studies that together explore the interrelationship between the state, governments, sustainable development, ecological modernization, environmental democracy, and environmental justice. These chapters provide concrete examples of promising developments (or missed opportunities), explain why potential developments were not realized, and provide an empirical grounding for broader theoretical claims about the limitations and unique capabilities and potential of the state to redress the ecological crisis. Together they offer sober yet constructive insights into the kinds of institutional and policy changes required to bring environmental considerations to the core of the state's function (James Meadowcroft); to integrate economic and environmental policymaking (Matthew Paterson and John Barry, Peter Christoff); to reach a broader understanding of environmental justice, democracy, citizenship, or policymaking from the perspective of social movements and local communities (Christian Hunold and John Dryzek, David Schlosberg, Raymond Bryant and Karen Lawrence). Given that our concern has been to identify some of the leading green developments, the selection of case studies is necessarily skewed toward developed states. However, the selection nonetheless contains a balance of cases from Europe, North America, and Australia, and the inclusion of the case study on the Philippine state provides an interesting window into what is reputed to be one of the leading states promoting sustainable development in the developing world. Although the United States, as the world's only superpower, has failed to provide any environmental leadership on the international stage, many local developments within the

United States, such as the environmental justice movement (explored by Schlosberg), have served as an inspiration for other jurisdictions.

In chapter 1, James Meadowcroft explores to what extent the experience of the welfare state in the twentieth century sheds light on the emergence and future trajectory of the ecological state. Since the 1950s the idea of a welfare state has been commonly invoked to describe a state that accepts significant responsibility for delivering social services to its population (while continuing to preside over a market-mediated and private-property-based economic system). The growing salience of environmental problems at the close of the twentieth century prompted Meadowcroft to speculate about the possible development of an ecological state—a state that takes on the task of ecological protection as one of its foremost and essential regulatory functions. He explains that such a state would be concerned with both ecological crisis avoidance and ecological welfare–enhancing activities in order to ensure a social development trajectory that remains within the boundaries of sustainability. As with the welfare state, these ecological activities would not exhaust the functions and roles of the ecological state, nor could the full range of functions and roles of the state be deduced from this set of environmental commitments.

Meadowcroft also explores a broader range of significant parallels between the welfare state and the emerging ecological state, such as the extension of state authority to new areas of life, the need to rectify failures in markets and voluntary action, the attempt to change patterns of economic interaction, the continual adjusting of regulatory practices, and the management of complex and deeply contested normative understandings. However, there are also significant differences, not the least of which are the different political pressures and social agents that have produced the welfare and ecological states, the different assumptions about the significance and character of economic growth, the different forms of intervention, and the different links with democracy. On this last point, Meadowcroft suggests that the welfare state, at least in its initial stages, was more intimately linked with democratization than its ecological counterpart. Nonetheless, the poor ecological record of nondemocratic states suggests that there is still an important link between democracy and the ecological state—a point that Meadowcraft explored at length in earlier work with William Lafferty.[2] Ultimately, Meadowcroft suggests, the development of the ecological state will be a more protracted and messy affair than the development of the welfare state, and the results will probably be more uneven and less stable.

Against the backdrop of Meadowcroft's broad generic analysis of the ecological state (which draws primarily on the experience of OECD states), the rest of the chapters in part I provide more fine-grained analyses of particular states (and governments) that concentrate on, to borrow Meadowcroft's language, the "protracted and messy business" of moving toward sustainability in particular regions in response to particular political and economic pressures.

In chapter 2, Peter Christoff draws attention to the potential variety of ecological states, not all of which give priority to ecological concerns according to Meadowcroft's more generic schema. Chistoff shows that in the Australian case, certain environmental welfare measures were enacted before the development of social welfare measures. He also suggests that in the current Australian context, there is a trend of increasing national environmental expenditure against a backdrop of aggressive neoliberal, market-oriented economic reforms. His case study clearly cautions against any teleological assumption that the green state is a natural progression from the welfare state, or that environmental protection necessarily contracts when neoliberal governments come to power (although it may).

Christoff's chapter indicates that claims that economic globalization has caused a "retreat of the state" are overstated when viewed in relation to environmental matters because environmental problems encourage the rise of environmental welfare, reflected in state-based or state-directed ameliorative and preventative programs and budgets. Nonetheless, this development must still be understood in the context of the dismantling of state functions in other policy domains, which have exacerbated internal contradictions in the state related to revenue raising and policy implementation.

In demonstrating the lack of any necessary or intimate connection between social welfare and environmental policies, Christoff is able to offer a typology of environmental states, ranging from the green state (with high levels of environmental protection and social welfare) to the neoliberal state (with low levels of environmental protection and social welfare). In between, he distinguishes various permutations based on different environmental/ecological and social combinations, such as the environmental welfare state and the ecofascist state. This typology provides a very useful framework for further comparative research into the potential of different states to tackle the sustainability challenge.

Matthew Paterson and John Barry, in chapter 3, scrutinize the constraints and opportunities facing the British state under New Labour in developing a more ecologically sustainable economy. They show how the election of New Labour in 1997 (and reelection in 2001) created the possibility that the economic strategy of the British state could be transformed from the neoliberalism that had prevailed under the Conservative party. In particular, Prime Minister Tony Blair's ideological rhetoric of the Third Way, which stood between neoliberalism and old-style social democracy, appeared to open up a new discursive space for modernizing the British economy along ecological lines. However, Barry and Paterson argue, while New Labour has on occasion endorsed environmental protection and environmental modernization, environmental concerns have still remained peripheral to the economic core of the New Labour project, particularly in the key areas of transport, energy policy, and climate change, genetically modified food. New Labour's economic strategy seeks fiscal conservatism; a commitment to the unconstrained movement of goods and capital; improved labor productivity (via strategies designed to promote education, training, skill development, and welfare-to-work); and measures to promote the new knowledge economy (focusing on biotechnology and information technology). Paterson and Barry argue that New Labour's professed commitment to the environment is largely undermined by this overarching accumulation strategy, which leaves no real room for integrating ecologically informed strategies in the areas of transport, energy, and climate change, and technology policy. In sum, whereas a narrow focus on environmental policy developments in Britain might suggest not inconsiderable progress, they show how a political economy framework can expose basic contradictions in economic and environmental policy. This analysis therefore concurs with that of Christoff: that any concerted greening of the state and society requires a fundamental recasting of economic policy (not just environmental policy).

Christian Hunold and John Dryzek (Chapter 4) seek to understand the relationship between the state, the economy, and civil society from a somewhat different angle by shifting the focus to the practical, strategic question confronting the green movement: whether to work with or outside the state. In making these strategic choices, they argue, context is everything and comparative history can provide a source of insight to guide choices between state-based and non-state-based strategies. This argument is developed by means of a creative synthesis of political theory and a comparative historical analysis of four very different kinds of contemporary state (United States, Norway, Germany, and United Kingdom). They suggest that all states are constrained by accumulation and legitimation imperatives, and that therefore environmentalists have a better chance of achieving their goals if environmental protection can be understood as part of these imperatives (via ecological modernization or risk-associated legitimation crises) rather than as goals that are in tension with these imperatives. Yet, they also show, different states have different orientations toward new social movements, and these orientations help to explain the character of the environmental movement and the critical independence of the public sphere. In particular, they classify the United States as passive inclusive (or pluralist); the Norwegian state as active inclusive (or expansive corporatist); the German state as passive exclusive (or legal corporatist) and the United Kingdom (of the Thatcher era, 1979–1990) as active exclusive (or authoritarian liberal). These different orientations toward civil society explain why the United States was an environmental pioneer around 1970, why it was then eclipsed by Norway, and why Germany has now taken the lead in seriously incorporating environmental concerns into the core of the state. Ironically, while the incorporation of environmental NGOs into the policy-making process by the active inclusive Norwegian state facilitated weak ecological modernization, it also served to weaken the radicalism of the Norwegian environmental movement and the critical independence of the public sphere, which they argue is necessary for strong ecological modernization. In contrast, a long history of passive exclusion in Germany produced a vibrant environmental movement and an oppositional public sphere that eventually enabled stronger ecological modernization than Norway's from the late 1980s. In all, this suggests that whatever else happens, maintaining a vibrant and independent public sphere is probably the best way of achieving strong ecological modernization in the long run.

In chapter 5, David Schlosberg also underscores the importance of a critical and independent environmental movement in his examination of the role of the U.S. state in responding to the varied demands of the environmental justice movement. He argues that while exposing and redressing the inequitable distribution of environmental goods and bads is a major focus of movements for environmental justice, demands for environmental justice go well beyond strictly distributional issues. He shows that in order to achieve environmental justice, states must not only make progress in distributional terms but also take seriously claims for cultural recognition and political participation by excluded groups. He shows that most of the institutional responses by the state to the environmental justice movement have focused on distributional issues. The most significant initiative to go beyond this focus has been the National Environmental Justice Advisory Committee established early in the Clinton administration. While this committee afforded many excluded community groups around the country the opportunity to voice their concerns, in the end it remained true to its title and was merely advisory. Schlosberg's core argument is that environmental justice can only be achieved when the state addresses all three elements of justice— distribution, recognition, and participation. It is noteworthy that he applies these arguments not only to marginal and excluded groups in society but also to nonhuman nature, showing how this is possible without the need to demonstrate any subjectivity in nature. In the case of both social and ethnic groups and nonhuman species and communities, he argues, the source of environmental and ecological injustice is lack of recognition or disrespect on the part of social and political norms and institutions, which can give rise to harm to the bodily integrity of those who are not recognized or not respected. He argues that a state cognizant of the importance of all three dimensions of justice would be responsive to the full range of repercussions of the modernization process. Such a state would facilitate reflexive or ecological modernization and thereby rectify the problem of environmental legitimacy in terms of public safety and democratic inclusion. Schlosberg points to a range of new experiments in democratic environmental decision making that are connected to people and place, which he takes as illustrative of the sorts of symbolic and procedural changes that are required to achieve environmental justice for humans and ecological justice for nonhuman nature.

In chapter 6, Raymond Bryant and Karen Lawrence direct attention to the special challenges facing developing countries, which typically includes the legacies of colonialism, poverty, and corruption. Yet they show how the Philippine state has undergone a series of transformations that have shifted its reputation from one of the most environmentally destructive states in the developing world (famous for its "crony capitalism" under President Marcos), to one of the leading lights in sustainable development in the South. This transformation, which began with the People's Power Revolution of 1986 that toppled President Marcos and saw to the election of President Aquino, was the first step in a major overhaul of a bureaucracy that had hitherto presided over environmentally destructive behavior. President Aquino's successor, President Ramos, carried forward the momentum with the creation in 1992 of the Philippine Council for Sustainable Development and the Philippine Agenda 21, and several environmental NGO leaders were appointed to bureaucratic positions. However, this transformation cannot be solely attributed to domestic forces. The international discourse of sustainable development set in train by the Brundtland Report, along with the flow of conditional foreign aid money for protected areas and a debt-for-nature swap by the World Wide Fund for Nature, played major roles in galvanizing internal reforms.

Nonetheless, Bryant and Lawrence show, the Philippine experiment cannot be declared an unmitigated success. Contradictory development initiatives, continuing external debt (exacerbated by the Asian financial crisis of 1997), and the persistence of elite political clans have partially thwarted the effectiveness of the reforms. Through their detailed case study of a community-resource-based initiative in one of the Philippine biodiversity hotspots, Malampaya Sound in the Palawan region, they highlight the uneven articulation of the Philippine green agenda. They also highlight what they call the complex political choreography that is required to avoid externally imposed conservation and to coordinate the activities and understandings of local, regional, and national tiers of government, entrenched rival economic interests, local populations, and environmental NGOs. While continued outside support from donors, scholars, and the NGO sector is necessary to the greening of the Philippine state, they write, the ultimate success of state sustainable development strategy is crucially dependent upon making the concerns and participation of local people central to any environmental reforms. This chapter provides important insights for all developing countries that seek to make the move from coercion to conservation in ways that promote the welfare of local people.

Part II of this volume shifts attention to the role of the state in facilitating global, transnational, and regional environmental governance. This part includes an examination of regional environmental developments in the European Union (Hayward), new directions in global environmental governance (Eckersley, Conca, Slaughter, Vogler), including new hybrid forms of governance involving the state as but one player, and multilateral environmental initiatives and the greening of the constitutive discourses of sovereignty. All these chapters, in various ways, seek to offer alternative ways of framing and understanding transnational economic and environmental developments and new ways of thinking about the regulative ideals of international environmental governance. Common to all these contributions is a concern to move beyond the overdrawn opposition between state-centric and non-state-centric approaches to understanding global environmental politics and to search for ways in which the state can facilitate the democratic governance of different layers of political community in ways that are commensurate with the reach of particular ecological problems. This entails building on, rather than rejecting, the insights of mainstream international relations theory while also critically engaging with the alternative literatures in radical political ecology and political theory.

The fundamental role, purpose, and commitments of states are laid down not only in their constitutions but also by the constellation of shared norms and practices arising from multilateral engagement. Of course, not all states live up to their domestic and international commitments, but for those that do take their commitments seriously, the question arises as to whether constitutionally entrenched environmental rights would make a difference. In chapter 7, Tim Hayward shows that the European Union (EU) provides a unique context for examining this question. Members of the European Union are bound by a range of transnational (i.e., European) norms, and although they have a margin of discretion in determining their manner of implementation, they are nonetheless obliged to implement them. Most notably, the Treaty of Union signed at Maastricht provides that Community policy shall be based, inter alia, on the precautionary principle and the polluter pays principle. This federal structure tends toward convergence and harmonization of laws, along with a reasonable presumption that such laws will be implemented—a presumption that cannot be made with the same confidence in relation to purely domestic constitutional commitments.

Against this background, Hayward explores whether a fundamental substantive right to an adequate environment would enhance the main environmental rights currently enjoyed by citizens under European Community law. After surveying existing European Community environmental law, he finds that in those circumstances when rights can be inferred from environmental directives and even environmental policy statements, these do make a significant difference. He also shows that there is considerable environmental potential in existing substantive human rights in the European Convention of Human Rights and the EU Social Charter. However, he singles out as the most significant development in the EU the 1998 Aarhus Convention, which creates wide-ranging environmental procedural rights to information, participation, and access to justice for the citizens of all member states in relation to environmental decision making *anywhere* in the region.

However, Hayward concludes, procedural rights do not go far enough to counteract the prevailing presumption in favor of development and that the addition of substantive environmental rights with constitutional force in the EU would make a difference, serving as an important vehicle for the consolidation and expansion of transnational environmental norms. But there is a sting in the tail to this otherwise promising analysis. Hayward considers that the prospects for this move are not imminent, and the more general transnational diffusion of environmental rights cannot easily be extended to non-European states, especially where capacity is weak and the rule of law precarious.

The developments explored by Hayward form part of the basis of Robyn Eckersley's argument that the greening of the nation-state is already under way, and that there is considerable potential for this process to continue. In chapter 8 she argues that critical political ecology, which is grounded in both critical and constructivist theory, is better placed to understand the history and future green potential of states than mainstream international relations theory (notably neorealism and neoliberal institutionalism) or more radical Marxist-inspired approaches.

While acknowledging the ways in which the state system and global capitalism have together worked to promote environmental destruction, she shows how environmental multilateralism and strategies of ecological modernization have together promoted environmental protection in ways that are transforming the constitutive discourses of sovereignty (the right to develop, security and rights discourses) in a greener direction. She also argues—against those who see the state as fundamentally compromised and therefore a lost cause—that states will remain key nodes in environmental governance and that the effectiveness of nonstate modes of governance still requires the support of states. More generally, Eckersley suggests, it is now possible to glimpse the emergence of transnational states that engage in less exclusionary practices of sovereignty and act as local agents of transboundary democracy and the common ecological good. However, the further development of this trajectory requires, at the very minimum, that democracy become a defining, rather than merely contingent, feature of states. More important, it requires that liberal democracy give way to a more ecologically responsive democracy that is able to broaden traditional conceptions of citizenship, identity, and community and lead to the practice of inclusive rather than exclusive sovereignty. The Aarhus Convention provides a concrete example of a movement in this direction.

Whereas Eckersley emphasizes what states (at their best) might do, Ken Conca emphasizes the ways in which states have been variously decentered and recentered in new hybridized models of environmental governance that involve a wide array of state and nonstate actors. In chapter 9, Conca draws attention to the space between the familiar conceptual poles of formal interstate treaties and a world civic politics that transcends the state. He argues that the question of the state's governing power in an ecologically interdependent world has generated a poorly focused debate. A central problem is that both statist and antistatist perspectives have tended to focus on separate institutional domains of governance. Those who emphasize states-in-charge and the adaptive maturation of sovereignty tend to draw their accounts from the realm of interstate collective bargaining, which highlights the capacity of states to create (or resist) international environmental regimes. Observers who see a vibrant civil society usurping the authority of obsolete, dysfunctional states have focused instead on the transnationalization of entrenched popular struggles, where contestations against state authority are a central part of the political dynamic and where states therefore appear less authoritative by definition. Conca suggests that we think of interstate regimes and transnational social movements as the opposite ends of a spectrum of possibilities that includes more complex, hybrid mechanisms of global environmental governance that have emerged in the past decade or two.

For a wide array of environmental problems—particularly those physically localized but globally cumulative problems concerning the management of forests, watersheds, soils, coastlines, and wetlands—Conca shows that environmental governance is indeed growing increasingly transnationalized. Moreover, these new hybrid forms of governance occur at the *intersection* of several influences: international law, transnational advocacy networking, market relations, the activities of expert networks, and increasingly processes that seek to mediate stakeholder conflict. Using the examples of the World Commission on Dams and protected-areas governance, he shows how the roles of states are not so much displaced as decentered and then sometimes recentered and reconstructed in ways that contest and then reconstitute authority, understood as the marriage of power and legitimacy. Conca argues that understanding what states can and cannot do in these more complex but increasingly common settings is crucial if we are to understand the full scope of the problem of reworking state power to create effective and accountable forms of global environmental protection.

Steven Slaughter moves the discussion to a more overt normative level in exploring alternative foundations for global environmental governance. In chapter 10 he builds bridges between domestic and international political theory by defending the neo-Roman legacy of republicanism as a superior foundation for global governance than either traditional liberalism or neoliberalism. He argues that the contemporary institutions of environmental governance are framed by, and made to subservient to, the institutions of economic governance, which promote global capitalism and produce environmental risks and harm as part of normal practice. Here Slaughter singles out the liberal norm of noninterference as serving to legitimatize this general institutional reluctance to interfere in the freedom of property rights. Drawing on the work of both domestic and international political theorists (such as Philip Pettit and Nicholas Onuf), he contends that republicanism provides a more appropriate foundation for both state and international governance because it is primarily concerned to prevent nondomination rather than uphold the liberal idea of noninterference. In an argument that provides a significant departure from the claims of radical political ecology, he explicitly adopts a statecentric perspective, emphasizes the constitutive relationship between nondomination and the state, and argues that it is primarily the transparent, publicly governed, and nonarbitrary law of the state that constitutes liberty as nondomination. In short, Slaughter maintains that the protective, regulatory, and empowering functions of the state can be deployed to enable nondomination and thereby prevent capitalism from trumping the liberty of citizens. While this humanist norm does not, on its face, suggest green values, he shows how it can work to prevent ecological domination (including ecological vulnerability), which entails preventing the displacement of ecological costs in space and time that is institutionalized under contemporary neoliberal global economic governance. Although republicanism defends the importance of particularist political communities, Slaughter nonetheless defends the republican state and the republican society of states as both individually and collectively outward rather than inward looking. This follows from the fact that, in an increasingly global context, states must act collectively to achieve the conditions that enable states, as individual units in a larger governance system, to defend their public (environmental) good and the liberty of their citizens (understood as nondomination).

In chapter 11, John Vogler rounds out the discussion of the state and global governance by critically exploring contested views about the benefits of interstate environmental cooperation. In a line of inquiry similar to Conca's, he draws out the contrasting analyses of international cooperation by mainstream neoliberal institutionalism and radical political ecology and then draws out four significant criticisms made by the latter of the former. In particular, he shows how radical political ecology seeks to destabilize the conventional assumptions and complacency of mainstream regime theory by attacking its ontological and epistemological assumptions, exposing the limitations of a mere problem-solving approach and highlighting the ineffectiveness of many environmental treaties in terms of environmental outcomes. These theorists argue that the dissipation of time and energy in international environmental diplomacy is actually counterproductive and that effective political action for sustainability must occur at other levels that bypass state structures. However, in the course of exploring these criticisms of mainstream approaches, Vogler also argues that radical critiques sometimes fail to acknowledge the important functions of international cooperation, which include norm creation, the generation and dissemination of scientific knowledge, capacity building, and the provision of a multilateral regulatory framework. Whereas radical political ecology takes it as axiomatic that states in the North and the South are trapped in different ways within the structures of contemporary global capitalism, Vogler gives credence to the alternative view that states still have the capacity to orchestrate collective responses to environmental problems. Indeed, he argues that once we move away from a priori claims about the state, it is possible to find evidence in support of the claim that states have been able to reinvent and reconstruct themselves in response to new challenges, most notably in the European Union. Vogler points out that state capture in the North or state incapacity in the South is not an inevitable by-product of economic globalization; that states, on occasion, can act independently of the interests of capital; and that states can provide a much stronger bulwark against the exercise of corporate power than the new political actors in global civil society.

Vogler's conclusions resonate strongly with Conca's in arguing that what is required is not wholesale rejection of the possibility of effective state action, but a more precise view of the legitimacy and functions of international cooperation in relation to governance at regional, national, and local levels. This also involves setting state governments alongside other international actors such as the European Union and a whole range of NGOs.

In concluding chapter the editors seek to draw out the more general insights provided by the contributors, locate these insights in the context of recent work in green theory, and highlight some of major obstacles to the development of greener states and a greener state system.

Notes

1. Lacey (1991, 2). Lacey's quotes are taken from Poggi (1982, 351).
2. Lafferty and Meadowcroft, eds. (1996).

I

The State and Domestic Environmental Governance

1

From Welfare State to Ecostate

James Meadowcroft

Over the course of the twentieth century the provision of welfare services became an essential focus for government activity in the advanced industrial countries. Since the 1950s the notion of the welfare state has been invoked commonly to describe a state that, while continuing to preside over a market-mediated and private-property-based economic system, accepts significant responsibility for ensuring the delivery of social services to its population. The emergence of specialized structures of environmental governance is a more recent phenomenon. But the growing salience of environmental problems has led some analysts to speculate about the possible genesis of an ecological state, a state that places ecological considerations at the core of its activity.[1] The purpose of this chapter is to consider the extent to which twentieth-century experiences with the welfare state shed light on the potential and the limits of such an ecological state.

Setting up the Discussion

The idea of the welfare state assumes many guises in contemporary political argument.[2] For the comparison undertaken here, it is convenient to adopt a broad definition, associating the expression with significant state involvement in the regulation and supply of welfare services within the framework of an essentially free enterprise economy. In this context welfare-oriented intervention constitutes—and is acknowledged to constitute legitimately—an essential sphere of action for the public power. The welfare state describes a set of arrangements that emerged during the twentieth century and that despite recent retrenchment and reform continues to exist in one form or another in all developed industrial societies. It refers to government programes dealing with pensions, unemployment insurance, health care, family benefits, and so on; to the bureaucracies managing such interventions; and to the politico-ideological justification of these practices. Such an understanding differs from three other common usages of the expression: the identification of the welfare state with the state structure as a whole or with the entire fabric of the existing socioeconomic formation (in other words, invoking the term as a proxy for capitalist state or contemporary capitalism); a specific set of economic and social policies applied in the developed countries between the 1950s and 1970s (sometimes referred to as the Keynesian welfare state); and the particularly comprehensive welfare variant found in countries such as Sweden and Norway, which is often taken as the most complete expression of the welfare state ideal (the social democratic welfare state). As employed in this chapter, the notion of the welfare state is less comprehensive than suggested in the first usage, for it embraces only those elements of the politico-administrative order functionally implicated in welfare provision. But it is more temporally and geographically inclusive than implied by the other two usages, for it continues to be applicable to conditions across the developed world.

With respect to the ecological state, the understanding is similarly broad. The term is associated with a significant governmental focus on managing environmental burdens. It describes arrangements that may be taking shape in the developed countries today, where ecologically oriented intervention comes to constitute—and is generally acknowledged to constitute legitimately—an essential responsibility of the public power. It denotes government programs dedicated to controlling environmental impacts and adjusting patterns of socioecological interaction to avoid ecological risks and enhance ecological values, to the institutions charged with such activity, and to the politico-ideological legitimation of such practice. In the conventional idiom, an ecological state would be one committed to sustainable development,[3] to securing a social development trajectory that remains within the frontiers of environmental sustainability. As defined in this way, the ecological state implies something more than traditional environmental policy, which emerged in developed countries from the late 1960s, and was largely understood as a post hoc adjunct of "normal" economic and administrative activity. It is predicated on a recognition that environmental systems are critical to long-term social welfare and that their protection and enhancement require conscious and continual adjustment by the public power. And yet an ecological state does not necessarily imply a thoroughgoing ecocentric political orientation, which posits as an overriding political goal the defense of natural systems and environmental values for their own sake.[4] Since the notion of an ecological state is somewhat novel, it is worth considering a little further at this point. First, some understanding of limits is implicit in the idea of an ecological state. Ensuring that environmental impacts do not breach such limits, and so undermine the foundations for human economic and social well-being, would be an essential objective of an ecological state. Yet this does not exhaust its potential remit. Society and nature interact on many levels, and the state can (and in fact already does) act to realize a variety of ecologically related ends. In other words, the institutions of an ecological state could secure environment-related benefits—enhancing human welfare or the welfare of other species and ecosystems—*above and beyond* that minimum needed to avoid socioecological catastrophe. Indeed, because of the complexity of the normative judgments involved in assessing social welfare, it is impossible in practice entirely to separate these crisis avoidance and welfare enhancing dimensions.[5]

To assume such a role an ecological state would require the capacity to

- Monitor the state of the environment, map patterns of socioecological interaction, and anticipate future developments
- Take decisions relating to the assessment of risk, the definition of preferred environmental outcomes, the reconciliation of environmental objectives with other individual and societal goals, and the distribution of social costs
- Deploy effective steering strategies and policy instruments
- Finance and legitimate its activities

Moreover, since ecological and political boundaries do not coincide, and many potentially acute environmental problems concern the global commons, an ecological state also would need to

- Act in both the domestic and the international realms

From the way *welfare state* and *ecological state* have been defined here it should be clear that neither expression is taken to exhaust the essential characteristics of a state to which they are applied. A state dubbed a welfare state might also be described as a democratic state, a regulatory state, a developmental state, and so on, depending on its actual features and the perspective from which it is being assessed. The same is true of an ecological state: its being (so to speak) would not be summed up in its ecologicality; nor could all its features be deduced from its ecological character.

Before proceeding, it is worth pausing to make explicit four assumptions that underpin the argument developed here. The first is that states still matter, that they remain the critical foci of political power in the modern world. In particular, it is accepted that for the foreseeable future states will continue to play a pivotal role in both the organization of welfare and protection of the environment. Clearly, if one were convinced that globalization or localization had already decisively eroded the action potential of the state, there would be little point in pursuing the comparison mooted here. The second assumption is that through the agency of the state it is possible to make significant headway in managing environmental burdens. In other words, the state in and of itself is not understood to be the problem but potentially part of the solution. Again, if one accepted (as do many radical ecologists) that the abolition of states and the modern state system were a precondition to addressing the environmental challenge, then there would be little to learn from the comparison discussed here. The third assumption is that it is possible for an ecological state to emerge (much like the welfare state before it) though a process of incremental reform, without necessitating the sudden and radical overthrow of the existing political and economic order. Thus the sort of ecological state considered here is one that remains enmeshed with the dominant political and economic institutions we know today. Finally, it is accepted that some movement toward the creation of ecological states has in fact taken place in developed countries over the past fifteen years. The continued accretion of state responsibility in the environmental domain and the significant shift from the mid-1980s in the prevailing environmental governance paradigm are taken as indications of this development. Certainly initiatives to integrate the environment with core state concerns taken in some of the smaller European countries that served as environmental pioneers in the 1990s, such as Sweden, Denmark, and the Netherlands, point in this direction.[6]

Parallels between the Ecological State and the Welfare State

There are a number of underlying similarities between the welfare and ecological states. Both formations *involve an extension of state authority to new areas of social life*, or at least a systematization and intensification of preexisting interventions. Politicians become preoccupied with problems that concerned their predecessors only marginally; specialized agencies are established to administer new programs; the state bureaucracy grows to perform additional functions; and the expenditure of public funds rises in the new domain. The story of the development of the welfare state during the first half of the twentieth century and its rapid extension after World War II has often been told.[7] With respect to the genesis of an ecological state, clearly there has been a remarkable extension of the governmental role in environmental management during the last three decades of the twentieth century.[8]

The welfare and ecological states both *constitute a response to a perceived failure of markets and voluntary action.* Government is drawn into the new domain because problems are judged not to have been addressed adequately by other social institutions. The welfare state has been understood to provide a safety net, a national minimum, a collective insurance fund, and supplementary citizenship benefits. It serves as a distributional complement to market and voluntary mechanisms: redistributing among individuals at different points in their lives; between the healthy and the infirm; between the employed and unemployed; between families with and without dependent children; and between the more and the less affluent.

In the case of the ecological state, the propensity of economic agents to impose negative environmental externalities on other actors, the overexploitation of (potentially renewable) common pool resources, and the concern that grave harm might be done to environments necessary to human welfare justify an increasingly active environmental management function. In other words, it is accepted that markets and voluntary efforts cannot secure long-term ecological viability in the absence of active steering by the state. To some extent this can be understood as an issue of appropriate scale, of restricting environmental impacts within the assimilative capacities of natural systems.[9] But there are also issues of collective social choice: all social and collective goods are not compatible, and in an ecological state political mechanisms are used to choose some patterns of goods over others.[10] Moreover, there is a redistributive dimension here— redistributing impacts among those who generate and experience the effects of pollution, among those in different regions, occupations, and income strata, and across generations.

Another common feature of the welfare and ecological states is that born *alter patterns of "normal" economic interaction but operate within significant economic and political constraints.* By mandating certain courses of action and by absorbing and redirecting social income, the state alters patterns of choice confronting individuals and firms, modifies the operation of markets and the character of property rights, and has a substantial impact upon the pace and direction of economic development. With respect to the welfare state, the provision of monetary benefits, the expansion of public-sector expenditure and employment, and the direct management of certain economic sectors (for example, health care) potentially affect wage levels, the labor supply, conditions of employment, collective bargaining, individual and corporate tax rates, company profitability, international competitiveness, foreign investment, and the state budgetary position. With respect to the ecological state, pollution abatement standards, planning restrictions, and nature conservation initiatives alter the costs faced by businesses and consumers. Taxes and subsidies encourage or discourage consumption of specific resources, energy, or materials efficiencies, and the selection of specific technological paths. Again, there are consequences for the viability of specific enterprises, processes, and sectors, and potential obstacles to inward investment or international competitiveness.

The resultant development trajectory differs from that which otherwise would have prevailed. A direct consequence of these impacts on "normal" economic interaction is that established entitlements are disturbed and opposition inevitably erupts from actors who feel their interests are prejudiced by reform. Once programs are established, however, they can create powerful new interests (within the bureaucracy and society more generally) which defend the new initiatives but may render subsequent reform difficult.

Operating as they do within the framework of established economic and political relationships, both states face significant constraints: above all, sympathetic political coalitions must be maintained, and the fiscal foundations of the state must not be undermined. In short, intervention to rectify identifiable (welfare- or ecologically linked) problems must not disrupt the ongoing functioning of the economic and political systems.

The welfare and ecological states both *represent a continuing adjustment of governmental activity to long-term processes of economic, social, and political development*. In the case of welfare this relates to themes such as industrialization, urbanization, and a changing class structure, and to shifts in family, fertility, and life expectancy. In the case of the environment it relates to evolving patterns of production and consumption, shifting land use and settlement practices, rising population levels, and scientific and technological advance. In a sense, both realms of state activity emerge through a process of experimentation as political systems try to adjust to manage new problems related to the continued technological, economic, and social transformation of the modern world. Of course, the problems the welfare and ecological states are intended to address are not just givens but are defined by social actors in the course of social interaction and political struggle.

The welfare and ecological states both *have complex and contested normative associations*. In the case of the welfare state arguments have classically revolved around issues of justice (the entitlement of specific groups or the whole citizenry to certain levels of benefit or to a social obligation to eradicate poverty); equality (that extreme differences of wealth and income are undesirable); expediency (that the state is a convenient vehicle for providing collective benefits); efficiency (that the nation needs a fit population for defense or industrial competitiveness); stability (the fear of social unrest or working-class revolt); and citizenship (that in a free political union all are entitled to social rights). With respect to the ecological state these concepts can also be applied. Thus justice and equality, for example, can be related to future generations, the distribution of environment-related burdens among rich and poor, and the treatment of nonhuman nature. More typically, arguments are related to enhancing human health and welfare (the environment contributes to our well-being in many ways); maintaining economic prosperity (the environment provides a foundation for economic activity); prudence, precaution, uncertainty, and avoidance of serious risk (care now could avoid unpleasant consequences in the future); and the inherent worth of the nonhuman natural world.

In both cases different strands of argument are deployed at different times to support different programs and to win over different constituencies. After all, it is a hallmark of successful political reform that it can be endorsed by various groups for various reasons. On the other hand, different mixes of these normative elements can be used to justify *alternative* approaches to welfare provision or environmental protection: they constitute a basis on which contrasting interpretations of each of these states can be constructed.

Elements of Contrast or Ambiguity

While there are parallels between the welfare state and the ecological state, there are also apparent divergences.

First, with respect to the genesis of the welfare state much is usually made *of the role of the working class, the trade union movement, and social democratic parties.* In contrast, no class, movement, or political party could be said to stand in precisely the same relationship to the ecological state. Environmental movements and green parties draw diffuse support from various strata, and their claims are not obviously rooted in the immediate material interests of the bulk of the population. Some would suggest this makes the genesis of an ecological state unlikely. Indeed, it could be argued that the forces that were most significant in building the welfare state represent an obstacle to the ecological state—workers, trade unions, and social democrats can be suspicious of any project that threatens material living standards, jobs, and economic growth. Data on green parties, which shows they draw their support disproportionately from educated voters, could be introduced to substantiate such a claim.

Yet the link between the working class, trade unions, social democracy, and the welfare state is more problematic than often assumed. Some analysts dispute that pressure from below was the decisive element in the birth of the welfare state; in some contexts trade unions are known to have opposed the introduction of state-sponsored welfare programs (fearing a weakening bond with their members or cooptation by the state); and in many countries the most significant reforms were actually introduced by governments of the right. Still, one can overplay this argument, for even if benevolent technocrats, opportunist politicians, or crafty conservatives actually introduced the programs, working-class and reforming activism propelled welfare issues onto the public agenda, and the desire to win votes, diffuse protest, and undercut electoral rivals all clearly played some role.

But is the absence of a parallel social force so problematic for the ecological state? To date environmental movements and green parties have done an impressive job of moving issues onto the public agenda; specific groups experience the effects of particular problems, but the entire population is potentially affected by some environmental burdens; these impacts are material (not just postmaterial), affecting standards of living, health, and welfare; there are economic sectors that now have an economic interest in societal greening; and while some environmental issues will only bite in the long term, many are already apparent.

This emphasizes the importance of ideas in mobilizing support and crafting particular proposals for social reform. After all, the story of the emergence of the welfare state is not one of the blind operation of social or economic forces but of the (contested) social definition of problems and the design of arguments and policy options to mobilize support and engineer reform.[11]

Second, the welfare state has always been seen as *a complement to a growing economy.* Programs such as unemployment insurance were designed to mitigate the effects of an economic downturn, but it was accepted that vigorous economic growth was necessary to provide jobs for those able to work as well as resources to fund state programs. Even neoconservative governments of the 1980s, which declined to specify full employment as a policy goal, considered growth essential. But would an ecological state not have an entirely different attitude toward growth? If the expanding scale of economic activity generates environmental degradation, would an ecological state not try to slow down the hectic pace, placing ecological well being above economic gain?

Not necessarily. Certainly there is a need for change in the *quality* of growth.[12] Given a finite biosphere, material throughput—resource consumption and waste deposition—cannot grow for ever. But there are no a priori limits to development, if this term is associated with human progress in the broadest sense (including moral advance as well as material prosperity), or even to earthbound economic growth, if one is talking about the growth of monetary aggregates such as profits or GNP. What is required is a *decoupling* of economic performance from *material* impacts, so that social welfare could rise even though resource inputs and waste levels fall. Of course, the notion of decoupling is not straightforward and must be considered in relation to thorny issues relating to population, technology, consumption, and distribution.

Nevertheless, at the simple level the contrast between the welfare state as growth-dependent and the ecostate as growth-averse does not hold up. On the other hand, certain forms of growth are to be rejected. And this puts the underlying difference in focus. The institutions of the welfare state have been largely indifferent to the character of national economic growth (as long as it occurs), but for the ecological state the character of this growth is an essential concern. Of course, governments have always had ideas about what sort of economic development is desirable, and they intervene to promote favored sectors (traditionally heavy industry, defense production, and infrastructure projects, and more recently telecommunications, computing, and biotech). But this has not been of direct concern to the institutions of the welfare state.

The welfare state does have some effect on patterns of consumption by redistributing income (different recipients spend in different ways) and by providing and rationing services (health care, for example), but its impact on production is essentially indirect (demand and labor market effects). On the other hand, the ecological state must be concerned explicitly with *keeping patterns of consumption and production within ecological limits*. Indeed, one of its greatest challenges is to determine an appropriate portfolio of policy instruments to accomplish this while leaving individuals, groups, and the state (in its other incarnations) the freedom and resources to pursue other ends.

Third, as it emerged over the course of the twentieth century the welfare state was essentially *a national creation*. There was cross-national policy transfer; international agreements were structured to avoid poisoning domestic welfare initiatives; and there was even a modest internationalist component to welfare regimes—a sort of spillover of social programs into the domain of development assistance. But (*pax* the European Union), welfare policy has remained primarily in the national arena. In contrast, a nationally oriented ecostate seems almost a contradiction in terms. Many environmental problems, such as climate change, require an internationally coordinated response. Moreover, North/South issues are central to meeting the global environmental challenge in a way that they were not to a nationally oriented welfare regime.

The difference here is essential, for the aims of an ecological state could only be secured through joint action with other states—action to protect the global environment, to reduce environmental burdens imposed by developed states so that nations of the South would have environmental room to develop, and to assist development efforts in the South. Thus the ecological state needs to act on two fronts (internal and external) and to coordinate domestic and foreign policy initiatives to an extent unknown by the essentially nationally focused welfare state of the twentieth century.

This internationalization of policy changes the dynamic of debate and decision making, and although it enables collective action, it also restricts national freedom of maneuver. Over time, international environmental governance institutions may play an increasingly ascendant role in managing global issues such as climate change. Yet for the foreseeable future states (and quasi-states like the European Union) remain the key (although not the only) actors in the international arena: they mediate between the international and domestic realms; they determine and enforce policy within their national territories; and they make and carry through (or fail to carry through) commitments made at the international level. Of course, the increasing density of international interchange also has consequences for welfare regimes, and policymakers are now continually assessing domestic welfare programmes in light of international developments.

Fourth, since the two states are concerned with different sorts of problem, the *forms of intervention* they entail are likely to be different. The welfare state operates by absorbing income from individuals and businesses, and spending on transfer payments and the direct provision of benefits (health care, social housing, and so on). In most countries the majority of citizens are consumers of welfare services, and (whether they are conscious of it or not) have regular contact with the welfare state, especially through the pension, health, and family allowance systems, and a minority experience more systematic (and intrusive) contact though programs such as unemployment and disability allowances. Taxation, income transfers, and service provision lie at the heart of the welfare state, although this is accompanied by a dense framework of legislation and administrative rules, and increasingly complex delivery mechanisms. In contrast, environmental policy relies on a mixed portfolio of regulations and prohibitions, normative injunctions, taxes and subsidies, and negotiated agreements. Only a small proportion of state expenditure relates to environmental governance, although this is growing. For the most part instruments are targeted at producers rather than consumers, although fuel taxes and public education campaigns are obvious exceptions here.

Interestingly, both state forms require appropriate forms of social planning. For welfare policy this relates service provision to economic policy and to the evolution of demographic, labor market, and social circumstances. For environmental policy it relates management strategies to economic conditions and the evolution of environmental burdens and natural systems. In each case the linking of such planning processes to the state budget cycle is crucial.

Fifth, *the welfare state appears to have a more direct link with democratization* than does its ecological cousin. Historians of the welfare state emphasize that its emergence shadowed the transition to universal suffrage. As access to the franchise expanded, politics and politicians were obliged to address concerns of new voters, and to the extent that the economic security of the population was uncertain, the politics of welfare came to the fore. Ideas of citizenship explicitly link democracy to welfare: rights of political participation and social benefits are correlated with duties to use the vote responsibly, to be self-supporting if possible, and to contribute to the welfare of the community. But there are other types of linkage. Writing in the 1970s and 1980s, theorists of the fiscal crisis of the state hypothesized that democratic states were being driven toward administrative overload and budgetary crisis as politicians outbid each other with promises of ever more extravagant social benefits.[13] Here not just the genesis but also the subsequent crisis of the welfare state was tied to the realities of democratic politics. Claims about the middle-class character of much social expenditure also tie in with democracy, for at a time of relative individual prosperity and state fiscal retrenchment, the in-work majority is unwilling to see universal programs from which it benefits curtailed, while the programs targeted at vulnerable minorities (the unemployed, single parents, and so on) are gradually rolled back.[14]

Yet the link between welfare and democracy is more subtle than sometimes presented. In some contexts welfare measures were introduced as part of a strategy to delay democratization (consider Bismarck's welfare program). And the interest shown by some nondemocratic developing states in establishing welfare systems suggests the issue is also related to the functional requirements of an industrializing market economy.

Moreover, with respect to fiscal overload, democratic polities proved more flexible than many expected, and the parties of the right established that voters could be mobilized to support a rationalization of welfare provision.

Nevertheless, in historical terms democracy appears more intimately linked with the politics of welfare than with the politics of environmental protection. Or at least this initially held true in the older established democracies. Among countries that have undergone a recent democratic transition (states in eastern and central Europe, for example) the environmental movement was sometimes a crucial component of the anti-authoritarian coalition, and the transition to democracy led to rapid innovation and institutionalization in the environmental field. The comparatively poor environmental record of nondemocratic states suggests an underlying link between democracy and environmental protection. Democratic frameworks provide an opportunity for the organization of affected interests, the critique of established practices, and the articulation of alternative perspectives.[15] The press, opposition movements, and environmental campaigners can bring problems into the open, mobilize public opinion against abuses, and hold political and economic leaders to account. Indeed, in developed states the environmental critique and the continued reform of institutions of environmental governance have been associated with calls for (and some progress toward) the further democratization of societal decision making.[16] The extension of rights to environmental information, increased public consultation and participation in environmental affairs, greater openness by regulatory bodies, and a relative opening of formerly closed policy networks are examples of such movement.

Lessons from the Evolution of the Welfare State?

If we accept that there are intriguing parallels, then it is possible to enquire whether experience with the welfare state may provide further clues about the emergence of an ecological state. In this respect six characteristics of the welfare state appear particularly suggestive.

First, the welfare state developed over a comparatively long period. Although we tend to think of modern welfare institutions as a product of the second half of the twentieth century, the foundations for the welfare state were set in place in most developed countries before the First World War. By 1914 some form of industrial accident compensation was already operative in fifteen of seventeen developed countries, health insurance and old age pensions had been introduced in eleven, and unemployment compensation in five.[17] By 1939 industrial accident compensation schemes existed in all seventeen developed countries, health insurance was working in thirteen, and old age pensions and unemployment insurance programs had been adopted in sixteen. State social expenditure exceeded 3 percent of GNP in six countries by 1910. All seventeen states had passed the 3 percent mark by 1926, and all but Finland and Italy were spending more than 5 percent of GNP on social programs by 1939.

As the century progressed, welfare programs were extended, and across the OECD social expenditure continued to rise as a proportion of GNP until the mid-1980s. Of course, political debate about the advisability of government's taking a more active role in the provision of social benefits was under way through much of the nineteenth century. Thus, in the broadest sense, the evolution of the welfare state has already spanned more than a century. If we date the first innovations from the 1880s, and the widespread consolidation of mature systems from the 1930s or perhaps the 1950s, then the establishment of the welfare state appears to have taken between fifty and eighty years.

Second, during the evolution of welfare states, periods of rapid growth or innovation alternated with phases of consolidation or stagnation. The development of the welfare state was not smooth but uneven and episodic. Periods of legislative activity were followed by phases of administrative consolidation during which bureaucracies and expenditures rose in response to decisions taken earlier. Commitments were initially made to one segment of the population and then gradually extended to wider strata.[18] Population growth and aging, the extension of entitlements from specified trades to the entire working population, and the eventual linking of benefits to inflation or average earnings meant that expenditures on pensions increased dramatically over the decades following their initial introduction. Issues such as maternity benefits, family allowances, and day care were generally much later innovations. The exact timing of the various phases differed from country to country.

Third, as the welfare state developed, very different (national) patterns of welfare provision emerged. There are universal and targeted programs;

programs financed by dedicated contributions or from general taxation; benefits fixed at a minimal level or at a higher standard; flat rate and earnings-related benefits; and variation in the extent (or direction) of redistribution.[19] The simplest classification of welfare regimes might array them on a "generous versus stingy" or a "left versus right" continuum, related to the relative size of social expenditure, the scope of programs, and the degree of redistribution from rich to poor. On such scales the United States would stand at one extreme, Sweden and Norway at the other, with other counties arrayed between them. More sophisticated approaches include Esping-Andersen's well-know typology dividing welfare regimes according to the extent that they are "market-supporting" or "market-usurping."[20] This scheme suggests that welfare states can be classified into three basic forms: liberal welfare states (as in the United States or the United Kingdom), which are dominated by market logic, encourage private provision, and provide low benefit levels; conservative welfare states (as in France and Germany), which recognize social rights but maintain traditional hierarchy; and social democratic welfare states (as in Sweden and Norway), which de-commodify much of social life (emphasizing equality, citizenship, and high-quality state provision).

What is important for my purposes here is not the detail of these classificatory schemes (and many others have been suggested) but a recognition that broad differences exist among developed countries (and even among jurisdictions and programs within individual countries). (Of course, such differences matter to the life chances of claimants "on the ground," say, for a teenage mother in London or Stockholm, or an unemployed office worker with heart trouble in Miami or Montreal.)

Fourth, actually existing welfare states are composed of a patchwork of partially overlapping and sometimes contradictory laws, administrative rules, and programs. There are gaps and inconsistencies, and different groups of claimants are often treated in different ways. This is a reflection of the welfare state's growth as an accretion of distinct initiatives directed toward different objectives and constituencies. It is also a product of the political compromises that were required to introduce new initiatives and adjust existing programs.[21] Over time, a complex but only semicoherent patchwork of programs and agencies emerged. As a historical product the welfare state is only a very rough approximation of the normative models proposed by social reformers who campaigned to introduce benefits and by theorists who reflected on the nature of the welfare state.

Fifth, more than a century after the introduction of welfare programs, contrasting theories about the character and historical development of welfare states remain. Pierson (1998) suggested a basic distinction between approaches that see the welfare state as a functional response to industrialization, modernization, capitalism, and those that see it as a fundamentally contradictory development. Social democratic attitudes typify the first camp, whereas new right, Marxist, and neo-Marxist commentators represent the second. Such differences feed into varied perspectives on the future of the welfare state—whether it has undermined the conditions for its own existence or failed to adapt to changing circumstances, whether it should be maintained or dismantled, reformed or transcended. Novel perspectives (feminism, environmentalism, new social movements) offer additional interpretations. Thus closure is elusive, and even when there is some agreement about how welfare structures actually operate, there is no agreement on the meaning of this activity.

Sixth, welfare states are only relatively stable and continue to be subject to reform, readjustment, and retrenchment. Their creation cannot be understood as a once-and-for-all process like constructing a bridge, which once built requires only periodic maintenance until the day comes to pull it down. Although there was a brief period in the 1960s when some observers concluded that welfare states were approaching a mature and settled configuration, the economic turmoil of the 1970s and the budget deficits and economic restructuring of the 1980s soon made a mockery of this complacent assumption. The stability of welfare programs is relative rather than absolute.[22] On the other hand, fears of the imminent dismantling of the welfare state also proved exaggerated. Instead there has been a period of protracted reorganization continuing from the 1980s through to the present day.

What do these observations suggest for the possible evolution of the ecological state? If it follows a historical trajectory analogous to that of the welfare state, we could expect that *the emergence of the programs and structures of the ecological state will be spread over a comparatively long time frame*, at least half a century and probably more. Taking 1970 as the starting point, we have had three decades of innovation in environmental governance. Half a century of development would bring us to 2020, a period that coincides with the forward horizon of many first-generation strategic plans for the environment and with the approximate date for a Rio + 30 review.[23] This also marks the initial time frame presented in current Inter-governmental Panel on Climate Change adjustment scenarios, and a point (according to current estimates) by which conventional oil and gas production would have peaked.[24] Eighty years on from the 1970s would bring us to mid-century. To anticipate political change this far into the future is virtually impossible, but it represents a time scale over which significant economic and technological developments are possible. In some respects the initial environmental innovations of the 1970s spread more rapidly than did the earliest welfare measures of the 1880s. Presumably this relates to differences of historical conjuncture: by the later part of the twentieth century the rhythm of international interchange had increased, and the reflex to turn toward the state to resolve emerging problems was well entrenched.

Periods of innovation and periods of relative stagnation or consolidation in ecostate development will alternate, and changes in rhetoric may take time to feed through to operations on the ground. After the initial burst of legislative activity in the early 1970s governments gained experience operating regulatory agencies and attempting to manage discrete environmental burdens. A growing appreciation of the complexity and interrelated character of environmental problems led first to a proliferation of administrative rules and programs, and later to shifts in the environmental management paradigm. Increasingly this came to emphasize the need for continued attention across government, an integration of environment and economy in social decision making, the international coordination of policy, and recourse to a broader range of policy instruments.[25] The idea of sustainable development was linked to a longer-term, more integrated vision of managing environmental burdens and to a greater appreciation of connections between the environment, on one hand, and development, distributive justice, democracy, and participation, on the other.[26]

The flurry of legislative and administrative initiatives in the late 1980s and 1990s are still feeding through in terms of implementation and expenditure. Further rounds of institutional development will be required to address climate change issues that are already fixed on the political agenda, and this will imply adjustment in other sectoral domains. Issues of cross-sectoral policy coordination, long-term planning, and the monitoring of environmental loadings and policy impacts have not been resolved by the initiatives governments have undertaken so far, and further periods of innovation are to be expected.

Contrasting national approaches to environmental governance will coexist. Pioneering studies of comparative environmental policy in the 1970s already indicated that there were significant divergences in national styles of regulation.[27] Although recent work suggests that there is substantial cross-national policy diffusion and a certain convergence in structures and instruments of environmental governance,[28] the varied institutional, political, and ideational contexts of national polities and the differences of economic structure and ecological character imply that divergent approaches are certain to continue.

Important dimensions of variation in the contours of the ecostate in different countries are likely to include

- The balance between public or private initiatives in making and implementing policy
- The preferred basket of policy instruments—a mix of regulation, normative injunction, negotiation, and financial incentives across different policy sectors
- The trade-offs between central and regional or local decision making (especially important in federal states)
- The extent to which the state is involved in collective decisions about environmental futures above and beyond the minimum requirements of crisis avoidance
- The approach to the distributional consequences of environmental policy
- The linkages between national and international decision making
- The extent to which concern for the well-being of nonhuman natural entities informs policy

Ecostates will encompass an array of only partially integrated initiatives. Environmental governance regimes already display this feature: management is distributed among various administrative bodies, functions overlap but there are also gaps in coverage, and programs often operate at cross-purposes. Attempts to harmonize initiatives and to introduce more integrated approaches (integrated pollution control, one-stop permitting, environmental codes, more comprehensive planning, and so on) have had some success, but they also add additional layers of complexity. And as new problems are identified, and new actors become involved (at local, regional, national, and international levels), the fragmented character of environmental governance has continued to reassert itself. The idea that the ecological state will transcend such a disjointed and fragmented structure is likely to prove illusory.[29] Almost any dimension of social and economic development can potentially affect the environment. Environmental impacts are manifest at all scales, evolve over time, and shift with changes in human activity. Moreover, our understanding of ecological processes is necessarily limited.[30] In such a context, the fragmented character of the governmental response is more or less inevitable; indeed overlap and friction between programs can provide protective redundancies and enhanced opportunities for social learning.

Rival accounts of the development, functions, justification, and future of the ecostate will persist. Since the emergence of modern environmental discourse in the 1960s there has been continuing controversy over the definition of environmental problems, and the assessment of the extent to which contemporary institutions will have to be transformed to deal with such difficulties.[31] The development of an ecological state will not preclude such controversies. Technological, economic, and social development will raise a stream of questions about what environments are to be transformed or preserved, about humankind as part of (or as standing apart from) nature. Whether the programs and structures that are being established are capable of resolving environmental challenges, and whether the solutions on offer are actually desirable, will remain open questions. At any given point some are likely to hail the emergent institutions of the ecological state as the epitome of rational problem solving, while others will portray them as a reformist deception intended to preserve an inequitable or environmentally corrupt system. While some will argue that the new structures and practices have more or less cracked the problem, others will see them as just a first step toward a steady-state economy, or toward a scientifically managed planetary ecosphere, or on the human journey out into the solar system and beyond.

The ecological state will prove to be only relatively stable. We should anticipate that, like the welfare state, the ecological state will not achieve a permanent configuration. New understandings of the consequences of environmental loadings imposed by earlier activity; pressures from ongoing processes or from the unintended consequences of remedial initiatives; the changing rhythm and direction of technological and societal change; and shifts in the perception of risk, the understanding of human welfare, or the valuation of natural entities will all alter problem definition and the priorities of publics and governments. Even in a world where atmospheric concentrations of greenhouse gases had been stabilized, one could imagine many and varied threats to environmental integrity. For example, we stand today at the threshold of a biological revolution that will make possible the deliberate modification of all life forms, including the human genome. Only time will tell the consequences of this for humans and for the other species with which we share the planet.

Conclusion

This chapter has argued that interesting parallels can be drawn between the development of the welfare state during the twentieth century and the ecological state which today may be taking shape in the developed countries.[32] It has suggested that by reflecting on the practical experience of welfare states we may gain a useful historical perspective from which to contemplate the potential of an ecological state. Obviously there are major differences between the normative underpinnings and functional requirements of the two projects as well as between the historical periods during which they took form. Yet it has been argued that they have much in common. Above all, the discussion has emphasized that the emergence of an ecological state may be a more protracted and messy affair, with the results more patchy and unstable, than is sometimes assumed in discussions of environmental futures. In other words, the far-from-perfect welfare states of today are likely to herald the far-from-perfect ecological states of the future.

Notes

1. See for example, Dente (1988); Lafferty (2000); and Lundqvist (2001).
2. Pierson (1998).
3. World Commission on Environment and Development (1987); Lafferty and Langhelle, eds. (1999).
4. Eckersley (1992).
5. James Meadowcroft (1997).

6. For developments in these countries, see Anderson and Liefferink, eds. (1997). For a sophisticated assessment of the extent to which Swedish environmental policy respects ecological principles, see Lundqvist (2004).

7. Ashford (1986); Flora and Heidenheimer, eds. (1981); and Thane (1982).

8. Hanf and Jansen, eds. (1998); Lafferty and Meadowcroft, eds. (2000).

9. Daly (1991).

10. Jacobs (1999a).

11. Ashford (1986); Mishra (1990).

12. World Commission on Environment and Development (1987).

13. James O'Connor (1973); Offe (1984).

14. Pierson (1998).

15. Lafferty and Meadowcroft, eds. (1996).

16. Paehlke (1988).

17. Pierson (1998). The countries are Australia, Austria, Belgium, Canada, Denmark, Finland, France, Germany, Ireland, Italy, Netherlands, New Zealand, Norway, Sweden, Switzerland, United Kingdom, and United States.

18. Ashford (1986).

19. Pierson (1998).

20. Esping-Andersen (1990).

21. Ashford (1986).

22. Mishra (1990).

23. United Nations Conference on Environment and Development, Rio de Janeiro, June 3–14, 1992, <http://www.un.org/geninfo/bp/enviro.html>.

24. The Intergovernmental Panel on Climate Change (IPCC) was established by the World Meteorological Organization and United Nations Environment Programme to assess scientific, technical, and socioeconomic information relevant for the understanding of climate change, its potential impacts, and options for adaptation and mitigation. <http://www.ipec.ch/>.

25. Weale (1992); Glasbergen (1996); van Tatenhove, Arts and Leroy (2000).

26. Meadowcroft (1999a); Baker et al., eds. (1997).

27. Lundqvist (1980); Enloe (1975); and Downing and Hanf (1983).

28. Jänicke and Weidner, eds. (1997).

29. Meadowcroft (1999b).

30. Dryzek (1987).

31. Dryzek (1997); Benton and Rennie-Short (1999).

32. Space precludes examining here the interlinkage *between* welfare and environmental institutions. Ecological states are emerging today in countries that already possess welfare states, and this raises the question of possible tensions and affinities between the two forms.

2

Out of Chaos, a Shining Star?
Toward a Typology of Green States

Peter Christoff

Over the past thirty years both industrialized and industrializing states have shown an astonishingly uniform shift in their intentions, if not capacities, to deal with environmental problems. Indeed, few countries are now without an environmental ministry, or waste management and pollution abatement programs, or laws establishing nature reserves and protecting native flora and fauna. Most states have sought to give direction and impetus to ecological modernization through national green plans of varying levels of sophistication and implementation. Together, these changes have been articulated through the evolving international discourse of sustainable development, overwritten by the demands of international environmental regimes, and responsive to the new wave of global environmental issues. Are we seeing here the birth of the green state,[1] emerging—as Nietzsche might have put it—"out of chaos, a shining star"?

On the other hand, over roughly the same period, the institutional burdens and fiscal demands on the welfare state have grown, despite attempts at welfare capping by social democrats and welfare retrenchment by neoliberals. Given demographic projections and associated pressure for aged care and health services, these burdens are likely to continue to grow.[2] Environmental problems will add to them. So, what then might this green state or ecostate, look like in future, and what relationship does it have to the (social) welfare state?

Indeed, how useful is it to talk of the ecostate as such? Huber and Stephens have observed that since publication of Esping-Andersen's *The Three Worlds of Welfare Capitalism*[3] in 1990, "the dominant approach to the study of welfare states in advanced capitalist democracies has been to study variations in welfare state provisions through the typology of three or four types of 'welfare state regimes.' "[4]

In this chapter I suggest that it may be similarly useful to talk about different environmental state regimes, and I propose a typology to describe and categorize the different ways in which specific states have begun to handle environmental demands, and the possible alternative trajectories for welfare states responding to conflicting and compounding social and environmental pressures.

I also argue that it is problematic to speak of a simple historical progression or evolution from the (social) welfare state to the ecostate. For over a century, the state in general has evidenced a complex range of institutional responses to environmental concerns. These responses have emerged sometimes as part of, or sometimes parallel to, the rise of the social welfare state. I explore these issues through an analysis of Australian developments.

Saving Paradise

Just three months after the arrival of the First Fleet and the start of European colonization of Australia early in 1788, Philip Gidley King, Governor of the penal colony of Norfolk Island, issued Australia's first environmental regulation when he ordered his subjects "not to cut down or destroy" the island's plantain trees. This first attempt at resource conservation preceded growing awareness of the environmental limitations of the fledgling Antipodean colonies. Soil erosion and salinity were observed as early as the 1830s.[5] By the mid-1850s certain tree species had been entirely logged out, and the need for both forest and water conservation were frequently debated in Victoria and South Australia by the 1860s.[6]

As a result, during the latter part of the nineteenth century, Royal Commissions inquired into the impacts of land clearing for agriculture and of gold mining on colonial timber and water supplies. These inquiries led to the establishment of public bodies such as Water Boards, Forest Commissions, and Departments of Agriculture and Lands, and the proclamation of laws (or attempts at legislation)[7] to regulate logging, land clearing, and water use—activities central to Australia's burgeoning rural economy—in most Australian States by the start of the twentieth century. Richard Grove observes that similar resource conservation regimes were common among French and British colonies in the nineteenth century.[8]

The dissemination of new frontier-breaking techniques and inventions—new types of plough and, later, tractors, bulldozers, and chainsaws—resulted in settler societies' often experiencing similar environmental problems in tandem, as occurred with the Dust Bowl erosion crises that affected both the U.S. Midwest and semiarid Australia during the 1930s and 1940s. Unsurprisingly, from the 1860s onward, these common experiences and crises encouraged the rapid transnational transmission of ideas about resource conservation and regulation between scientists and administrators across the oceans. Indeed, some Australian laws were regarded as mere "crude copies" of contemporary U.S. legislation,[9] following a practice that continued well into the twentieth century. In all, the resulting transfers of species, technologies, techniques, and laws encouraged what might be called a common environmental sensibility and similar institutional frameworks.[10]

Separately, during the late nineteenth and early twentieth centuries, Australia's colonies and then States looked mainly to British regulatory innovations to ameliorate the effects of industrialization and urbanization on human health and welfare, and to counter local public concerns about sanitation and disease. During the mid- to late nineteenth century, Sydney and especially Melbourne experienced intense industrialization and rapid urbanization that in turn led to water shortages, dramatic failures in water and air quality, and the cholera and typhoid plagues that periodically threatened both settlements. Melbourne in the late nineteenth century was often described as standing "ankle deep in its own wastes."[11] The citizens of Sydney complained about the impact of raw sewage as it accumulated in the harbor, "rendering all business occupations upon its shores disgustingly offensive."[12]

As a result, late in the nineteenth century, public bodies based on British models were established in most Australian capital cities to limit pollution, regulate industry, manage urban open space, parks, and gardens, and provide or supervise the development of infrastructure for clean water, sewerage, and the disposal of domestic and industrial waste. Regulations governing industrial pollution of air and water were also devised at this time under various new health laws, then revised during the 1950s, and further refined and consolidated when environmental protection agencies—modeled on the 1969 U.S. EPA legislation and agency—were established in New South Wales, Victoria, and Western

Australia in the early 1970s and the remaining States during the early 1990s.[13] Together, these developments overwhelmingly reflected anthropocentric concern over the effects of environmental degradation on human well-being, or what Robyn Eckersley has called human welfare ecology.[14]

In addition, one can discover in Australia a third, parallel albeit subordinate, narrative of environmental history—this one relating to an aesthetic and moral concern for nature. This too is reflected in aspects of early state development and behavior. In *The Colonial Earth*, Bonyhady emphasizes that the regulatory prohibition of 1790, intended to protect the petrels of Norfolk Island, was inspired by something more than a merely utilitarian calculus. The birds were being slaughtered for their flesh and also taken for their eggs. Since, initially, "the birds were superabundant, there was no market for them, but there was a limited market for their eggs," birds found without eggs were sometimes released whereas those carrying eggs sometimes had their eggs cut out, leaving the still-live petrels "to become a nuisance round the hills."[15] Lieutenant Ralph Clark regarded this as "one of the Crueles[t] things which I think I Ever herd" and hoped "Some of them will be caught at this Cruel work for the Sake of making an example of them."[16] Laws soon enacted to stop such cruelty broadly reflected the new sentiments toward nature emergent in Europe during the period from 1500 to 1800 and then rising to the fore.[17]

And then there was the influence of widespread fascination with the natural wonders of the Antipodes. From the first moments of European discovery, artists painted, and visitors and settlers wrote about, its strange birds, fish, plants, natives, and landscapes. Bonyhady comments that "the invaders loved birds. Their letters, despatches and books attest to their delight in the 'astonishing variety' and 'uncommonly beautiful plumage' of Australia's novel species."[18] Between the late eighteenth and the early twentieth centuries, scientists and artists established and educated colonial and international interest in Australian species. In doing so, they created the cultural foundations for domestic political and legal action for the preservation of nature.[19] Fascination with this new but threatened realm spurred enactment of wildlife protection laws, which emerged in several phases. Before 1900 they concentrated on providing sporadic and ineffectual protection for hunted emblematic species.[20]

From about 1900 to 1920, reflecting greater public concern, statutes offered continuous but still ineffectual protection in limited areas. After the 1920s more comprehensive legislation was articulated, first at State level[21] and then, from 1972 onward, nationally, in response to environmentalist pressure.

Preservationist concerns also combined with and later overwhelmed the early push for the conservation of scenic sites and recreational areas. The National Park (later, Royal National Park) on the coast just south of Sydney was Australia's and the world's first officially designated national park. Proclaimed in 1879, fifteen years after the reservation of Yosemite in the United States, it was intended to provide "a national domain for rest and recreation . . . for the use of the public forever" and became, as Anderson puts it, "a sanctuary for the pale-faced Sydneyites fleeing the pollution—physical, mental, and social—of that densely packed city" rather than a sanctuary for natural flora and fauna.[22] By contrast, Victoria's Fern Tree Gully, a "much loved destination for excursionists since the 1860s"[23] was set aside in 1887 both as a recreational reserve and as a public park to protect its exotic vegetation, and Wilson's Promontory, also in Victoria, was (temporarily) reserved in 1898 under the Lands Act for a national park for public recreation and to preserve flora and fauna. This trend toward setting aside parks for both human welfare and nature conservation was also common in other States. From the 1930s on, the various bushwalking, wild life preservation, and forest conservation clubs began to display the features of a social movement (shared networks, unifying discursive framework, collective and sometimes coordinated approach to political action). By the 1970s their leading arguments for reservation were predominantly preservationist in intent, and by the 1990s Australia's national parks were being regarded, by environmentalists and governments alike, as a core component of a larger strategy for the protection of national biodiversity.

In all, the foundations of the environmental aspects of the Australian state—its European-style environmental institutions and agencies, established to conserve natural resources, limit pollution and disease, and preserve nature, and associated actions and expenditures—date almost from the moment of white settlement over two hundred years ago. It is this long history, substantially influenced by three or four waves of global environmental concern,[24] which underlies the rapid growth of additional

environmental institutions in Australia during the last part of the twentieth century.

Crisis and Reform

The last two decades have seen a period of exceptional innovation for
Australia's environmental institutions. In 1983 the newly elected Hawke
Labor government confronted both political and economic crises in
Australia. It inherited a deteriorating balance of payments, an elevated
budget deficit, and unprecedented levels of unemployment—problems
common to a number of other welfare states at this time. Faced with an
immediate flight of capital, Prime Minister Bob Hawke and his Treasurer
and successor Paul Keating floated the exchange rate, deregulated the
finance sector, and relaxed regulatory controls over transboundary capital movements (especially overseas borrowing). Throughout the remainder of the 1980s, Labor sought to enhance economic competitiveness and
hasten the integration of the national economy into international markets. It reduced tariff barriers by increasing the manufacturing sector's
exposure to import competition and selectively targeted manufacturing
industry sectors with incentives intended to promote export enhancement.[25] In retrospect, many of these steps merely weakened the Australian
state's capacity to direct and implement fiscal and industry policies.

The new Labor government also swiftly rewarded the environmental
movement. In the run-up to the 1983 election, the national Fraser coalition government had refused to protect the iconic, untamed, and World
Heritage–listed Franklin River from damming by Tasmania's State
government. It regarded this issue as a State matter under Australia's
Constitution. Labor, in opposition, vowed if elected to save the river. It
would empower itself to trump the Tasmanian government by enacting
Commonwealth legislation that reflected the requirements of the World
Heritage Convention. The environmental movement mounted an unprecedented national electoral campaign that delivered a crucial proportion of the vote and power to Labor. The Hawke government's first law
delivered on Labor's promise, and the Franklin was saved.

Each of these domestic developments—economic and environmental—
defined the national settings for green politics and policy during the latter
part of the decade. The international context for domestic environmental

politics also changed profoundly through the 1980s. The symbolic, political, and economic dimensions of conflicts between environmental preservation and economic development intensified, and by the close of the 1980s the environment had risen high on the Australian political agenda. Environmental conflict had generated legitimation crises for both State and national governments in relation to their facilitation of resource development and appeared to challenge their capacity for economic management by forcing "policy on the run." By 1990 a political conjuncture unique in Australian history offered opportunities for environmental institutional development. This conjuncture was composed of several elements.

First, the wave of international media attention and public concern over climate change and ozone depletion had further invigorated public awareness of domestic environmental issues in Australia. The collective membership of key Australian environmental nongovernmental organizations (NGOs) grew to unprecedented levels, enhancing the movement's financial and political strength accordingly. These developments were assisted by vigorous campaigns for the preservation of wilderness and against the intensification of industrial clearfelling and woodchipping of (primary or old-growth) native forests and the threat of mining in national parks. Such issues achieved national exposure through widespread media interest in photogenic conflicts over road work in the Daintree wet tropical rainforest in Queensland, logging in Tasmania's southern forests, and a bid to mine uranium at Coronation Hill in the proposed third stage of Kakadu National Park. Building on the experience and precedent of the Franklin campaign, the Australian movement sought to "nationalize" successive conflicts—to engage the national state in environmental governance by appealing to its capacity to employ emerging international environmental treaties (usually the World Heritage Convention) to overcome gaps in the Australian Constitution and the States' developmentalist bias.

Second, the Hawke government became increasingly electorally vulnerable following the 1984 and 1987 elections, with a decline in its primary vote and in its majority in the Lower House. This political trend increased its susceptibility to pressure from interest groups able to influence its electoral fortunes—a capacity that the environment movement had already evidenced. The then Minister for Environment and Labor power broker, Graham Richardson, devised a strategy to woo the green vote. As a result, the leading national environmental organization, the Australian Conservation Foundation, gained exceptional access to and leverage with Hawke and Richardson through its promise and capacity to deliver votes.

Third, the domestic politics of deregulation and global economic integration had unforeseen consequences: continuing decline in both the terms of trade (especially for rural commodities) and in the value of the Australian dollar generated a new balance-of-payments crisis and burgeoning national debt. These economic trends elevated the importance of mineral export revenues for the Australian economy and enhanced the political leverage of the mining industry.

This conjunctural moment, between 1989 and the end of 1991, produced an exceptional period of environmental institutional innovation. In 1989, in Australia's first Prime Ministerial Statement on the Environment, "Our Country, Our Future," Hawke outlined an agenda for institutional change for both green (or nature preservation) and, to a lesser extent, brown (urban, industrial, and pollution) issues.[26] Its measures included major national programs to restore native vegetation and to combat land degradation (the Decade of Landcare and the Billion Trees programs), the creation of a Commonwealth Environmental Protection Agency (EPA), and a national strategy for sustainable development.

Over the next three years the Hawke government also established a suite of other national strategies and measures that addressed politically charged issues and were, more rarely, supported by legislation. Australia was an eager signatory to the Framework Convention on Climate Change and announced a target for greenhouse gas reductions set at 1990 levels. National biodiversity, cleaner production, and waste minimization strategies were mooted. A national Resource Assessment Commission was formed to provide independent guidance in resource development policy to national government. That such institution building occurred while neoliberal retrenchment affected most other policy domains in Australia at this time is an apparent anomaly.

The most ambitious, problematic, and for the purposes of this chapter, illuminating of these initiatives was the proposal for an Antipodean green plan, a strategic framework for ecological sustainability on one continent. This strategy, which survived only from late 1992 to early 1997, was the product of arguably the most wide-ranging consultative policy initiative— or policy experiment—ever undertaken in Australia. Nine working groups covering industry sectors such as Agriculture, Energy, Forests, Mining, and Tourism were established in 1991. A year later they produced over five hundred recommendations intended to be the foundations of the national strategy. The National Strategy for Ecologically Sustainable Development (NSESD) was finalized by government agencies and endorsed in December 1992 by the Council of Australian Governments (COAG), the preeminent ministerial body for federal decision making. However, its relatively weak recommendations were merely paid lip service during subsequent implementation by the Commonwealth and States. The strategy—never protected in national law or revitalized through review (as occurred, by comparison, with the Dutch National Environment Policy Plan)—was abandoned in 1997, having proved, ultimately, neither strategic nor capable of delivering sustainability.[27]

Like several earlier, weaker attempts at green planning in Australia, the ESD strategy was thwarted in multiple ways. Its economic context—the deregulatory interventions of the early 1980s, the neoliberal redefinition of effective economic management as the containment of public-sector expenditures and debt and the production of surplus budgets, and resistance to sweeping strategic reforms such as the NSESD by politicians and bureaucrats in economic ministeries—militated against substantial ecologically oriented economic reform.

More directly, certain deeply embedded institutions, especially Australia's federal Constitution, played a profound and perhaps determining role in the strategy's fate. Insofar as the NSESD was oriented toward State implementation, it was fragmented horizontally and vertically between competing State-based actors empowered to protect their own narrow strategic interests. These problems were further compounded by the sway of bureaucratic rationality on the reception of the draft strategy: issue compartmentalization and problem decomposition marked the transformation of the working group reports into material that could be readily absorbed by existing bureaucratic structures. The fragmentation and dismantling of complex cross-agency proposals were thus almost inevitable.

Paradise Deferred

The alignment of factors that had enabled environmental issues and institutional reform to rise on the political agenda between 1989 and late

1991 collapsed soon afterwards. A new recession pushed formal unemployment in Australia to an all-time peak of over 12 percent. The discourse of economic crisis again dominated the media and political and policy debates, and media fatigue with the environment reduced the profile of green issues. Newly articulated political responses to critical global concerns such as climate change and ozone depletion convinced the general public that these were now being addressed effectively, and popular concern about the environment declined in relation to other issues. The conjunctural opportunity for significant environmental institutional transformation had been largely squandered. As environmental politics became increasingly marginalized, key national green policy experiments from the earlier period, including the ESD strategy, were wound down, the Resource Assessment Commission was closed, and the Commonwealth EPA reduced in size and then dismantled.

Meanwhile, other initiatives, such as an Inter-Governmental Agreement on the Environment (IGAE)[28] and the National Forests Policy Agreement (NFPA), were deliberately pursued because of their capacity to systematize and normalize environmental policy relations with the States. The IGAE defined a federal process for creating national environment protection measures and minimum, nationally uniform standards for air and water quality, toxic waste management, and so on, through mirror legislation enacted by all States, Territories, and the Commonwealth. The NFPA proposed the establishment of regional forest agreements based on accredited State assessment processes. These regional agreements were intended to finally resolve conflict over harvesting in native forests by reserving 15 percent of remaining forest ecosystems and releasing the remainder for logging—in effect providing those resource security arrangements the environmental movement had successfully rejected in the early 1990s. In other words, while on the one hand the integrative, *centralizing* green state–building initiatives of the ESD strategy were ignored, *federalist* processes were extended to rationalize, systematize and standardize environmental policymaking, resource management, and environmental conditions nationally *without* effecting a transfer of powers to central government.

As the 1990s progressed, the other major national strategic initiative of the earlier period—the National Greenhouse Response Strategy—was constrained and weakened by the counteraction of the fossil fuel industries and their champions within the national economic ministries and inside Cabinet. Arguments about the importance of fossil fuel exports for the national economy and of low fossil fuel–based energy costs to Australia's international competitive advantage dominated debate over a national carbon tax in 1994 and later underpinned the Australian government's stance seeking and winning additional CO_2 emissions capacity during the Kyoto Climate Change Protocol negotiations in 1997 while blocking endorsement of the Protocol itself.[29]

Last, a series of elections early in the 1990s saw the rise of conservative coalition governments in most States. Perhaps most significant here was Victoria's Kennett government, which pursued a radical neoliberal agenda to reduce State debt, privatize State services, reduce State regulatory capacity, and extend and enhance market activity. Between 1992 and 2000 the Victorian Department of Natural Resources and Environment experienced deep cuts to funding and staffing levels, and with two notable exceptions relating to catchment and coastal management, the Victorian Environment Minister dismantled critical environmental consultative and deliberative policy bodies. These moves hollowed out the environmental components of the State, substantially reducing its capacity to define strategic directions, undertake independent research and monitoring, form consensus and support, and develop and implement environmental policy.[30] This radical, ideologically driven pursuit of state minimalism underlined the extent to which three decades of environmental institution formation could be undone. However, the creation of local catchment boards and coastal councils provided an interesting and revealing contrast as it embedded neoliberal notions of mutual obligation in the environmental domain.

When the conservative Howard coalition government won the national election in 1996, it continued and strengthened the program of welfare state retrenchment initiated by Labor through the privatization of core public assets and cuts to state funding and employment. However, unlike the Kennett government in Victoria, it sought to *expand* its environmental role and capacity. Indeed, since 1996 significant growth in environmental capacity has occurred under this neoliberal national government. This growth has included the creation of the country's first *autonomous* Department of Environment (known as Environment Australia) and the establishment of several major cross-sectoral agencies and programs.

For instance, the Natural Heritage Trust was established in 1997 and is jointly administered by Environment Australia, and the Department of Agriculture, Fisheries and Forestry. Since its inception, it has received $A2.9 billion (to be spent over twelve years) to finance a broad range of national environmental rehabilitation projects under five key themes— land, rivers, coasts and marine, vegetation and biodiversity. The Australian Greenhouse Office, established in 1998, is the Australian government's leading agency in response to the challenge of climate change and has been touted as the world's first national agency devoted specifically to addressing climate change. In addition, in October 2000 the Prime Minister released the National Action Plan on Salinity and Water Quality in Australia (NAPSWQ), the first national initiative of its kind. The action plan is implemented through bilateral agreements between the Commonwealth and each State and Territory, with the Commonwealth allocating $A700 million over seven years to the plan, and the States and Territories an equal amount.

Overall there has been a profound increase in the level of national funding of environmental programs over the past decade and substantially since 1996. In 1992 total Commonwealth government expenditures on the environment totaled some $A100 million. By 2003 this had risen to $A1.965 billion, close to 1 percent of Gross National Product.[31]

Nevertheless there have been no attempts to articulate a new national green plan or to institutionalize sustainability planning. In addition, Australia has proved weak in its domestic legal recognition of its environmental treaty obligations. Successive national governments—first Labor and then coalition—have been politically reluctant to establish a strong foundation for environmental management in national laws, despite their constitutional capacity to do so. This is most clearly the case in the areas of biodiversity conservation, land clearing, and climate change. Furthermore, there has been a devolution of powers to the States, and a corresponding diminution of Commonwealth environmental authority during this period.[32] In part this trend reflects the point made earlier that there has been a reluctance among national governments to lead and to "tackle the States" on environmental issues. Even so, there has been a trend, based on the diffusion of power inherent in the original IGAE and the subsequent 1997 COAG agreement, toward more uniform environmental policies, processes, and standards across the national and State and Territory governments. Finally, the Howard coalition government's hostility toward and assault on environmental treaties and conventions—prominently including the Kyoto Protocol—has been a notable feature of its *international* stance on environmental cooperation.

Three summary observations may be made about the past two decades in Australian environmental politics. First, there has been an incremental but contradictory and uneven process of national consolidation of environmental functions. While since 1996 the Howard government has pursued its strong ideological commitment to reducing the influence of the state and the size of the public sector, the environmental portfolio has expanded materially. However, no attempts have been made to establish explicit national policy-coordinating mechanisms, and national consolidation around environmental and sustainability principles has been ad hoc, selective, and weak. Similarly, the integration of ecological considerations and related principles into economic and social policy, into public-sector activity, and into the broad workings of the economy has not occurred. For instance, although the principles of ESD were slowly incorporated into some national and State environmental and resource management legislation during the 1990s, systematic review of *all* laws and regulations to ensure their conformity with these principles—a move essential to achieving uniform guidance—has not been attempted. (Ironically, such an approach was used to deal with microeconomic reform.) Despite COAG reforms, the Australian state remains, in environmental terms, what Phillip Toyne once called "the reluctant nation"[33], in which federalist fragmentation still prevails where ecological matters are concerned.

Second, administrative, legal, and funding reforms remain vastly inadequate to meet current trends and emerging needs. Environmental conditions continue to deteriorate at an alarming rate. For instance, Australia has the world's worst national record for mammalian extinctions over the past three hundred years, and its biodiversity remains under extreme threat from the historical and ongoing effects of land clearing, the impacts of invasive species, and the pressures and effects of continuing inappropriate agricultural practices. Some sixteen hundred terrestrial species are listed as nationally threatened,[34] and a new wave of extinctions is expected over the next two decades. Overharvesting of surface water, particularly for irrigation, is rife, and land degradation is a major issue. Salinity is predicted to affect some 31.2 percent of cultivated land by 2050 if nothing is done beyond existing relief programs, and it will make the Murray River, Australia's largest and most important waterway in economic terms, unfit to drink in its lower reaches within three decades, leaving one State capital, Adelaide, without a major supply of fresh water. Recent reports indicate that effective action to halt the crises of land and water degradation alone could cost in the vicinity of $A65 billion over the next decade, of which the Australian Conservation Foundation and National Farmers Federation expect that $A37 billion should be public-sector funding.[35] Treasury has estimated the cost of repairing just the Murray-Darling Basin at $A30 billion.

Third, it is clear that, for social and economic as well as environmental reasons, pressures for environmental policy intervention are increasing. Media coverage of Australia's environmental crisis is again strengthening, and successive authoritative and alarming environmental research reports have gained significant exposure. Membership of key environmental groups is growing. The environment is rising again on the Australian political agenda.

Green State, Ecostate, or Environmental State?

I want now to set this specific environmental political history in a broader theoretical context. In the well-established debate over the nature and origins of the social welfare state, arguments have revolved around when individual welfare states came into being, what were the major factors behind their emergence, and whether any patterns are common across national examples. Similar questions may be asked about the sources, characteristics, trajectory, and likely success of the state's environmental provisions.

Marxists, neo-Marxists, and others have argued that the welfare state arose as a functional response to the logic and structural needs of capitalism. For instance, in emphasizing the welfare state's role in securing and fostering capital accumulation, Claus Offe has argued in this regard that two modes of state intervention—allocative and productive—may be identified.[36] The allocative mode refers to the state's regulatory (and strategic) capacity, which "creates and maintains the conditions of accumulation in a purely authoritative way" in both private and public sectors. By contrast, the productive mode describes state intervention in those areas of economic activity where the market has failed to provide the material conditions necessary for capital accumulation, because of the initial cost, risk, or low returns associated with investment. In Australia during much of the twentieth century, for instance, the state was heavily committed to the provision of health and education and also to "socialized production" through the direct provision of air, sea, and rail transport, dams, banking, and telecommunications services, in a large country with a low population.

Others, arguing that the welfare state was fashioned by and represents a victorious embodiment of the struggles of an emergent organized working class, and the rise of social citizenship and social democracy, place greater emphasis on forces in civil society. Despite historical differences between individual states, broadly speaking, the welfare state, through its provision of social pensions and public health, education, housing, and transport, has ameliorated the worst impacts of capitalism and improved the lot of those it assists as a result of these victories. (By contrast, neo-Marxists such as Offe and Habermas consider the welfare state to be an institutionalized response to the threats posed by social movements to capitalism, and therefore in significant part fashioned around and engaged in the legitimation of capital accumulation and in the pacification of dissent.) However, whether the emphasis is on struggle or resistance, there is agreement that differences in patterns of welfare provision exist and that these reflect the specific political and institutional histories of individual states. These may nevertheless be typified or classified in various ways, for instance, as by Esping-Andersen, who classified welfare regimes as market-supporting or market-usurping and welfare states as liberal, conservative, or social democratic.

It is essential to read the environment into these debates. For example, aspects of state environmental activity are clearly market-supporting and intended to assist capital reproduction. They may be considered, in Offe's sense, productive (providing funding or infrastructure like dams or logging roads, and state-funded research to boost primary production and expenditure on environmental amelioration in order to sustain the quality of natural resources as a factor of production) or allocative (regulating uniform access to, and stable conditions and quality of, natural resources). While facilitating economic growth and capital accumulation overall, the state's environmental interventions can be considered to be defensive and remedial (for instance, repairing land degradation that may threaten future farm productivity) or proactive (legislating or establishing reserves to conserve natural resources for the future, or implementing regulations that will limit future costs associated with environmental damage).

Clearly, what has been left out of the frame to this point is the state's ambivalent normative stance over the uses of nature. Increasingly the state is morally and materially divided against itself along a green fracture line, one evidenced in the combative stance taken by state environmental agencies versus their resource-exploiting counterparts in agriculture, mining, or energy. Institutionally, most advanced industrial states embody a series of historical compromises over conflicting demands in this realm. Indeed, departments of environment and environmental laws are in significant part the outcomes of contested interventions by green groups and ecological citizens.[37] Certain of these responses operate *despite* and *against* the imperative to capital accumulation by decommodifying nature, for instance, by "locking up valuable resources" as the timber and mining industries in Australia are so fond of saying, for the benefits of nonmaterial human needs and for nature.

Differing emphases on state functions and imperatives have also shaped narratives about the origins of specific welfare states. The establishment of a national social security scheme or of state-funded health and education; enactment of the first comprehensive national laws to regulate salaries, limit working hours, and improve conditions for labor; the first clear signs of an emergent policy debate about founding the national welfare state; or when a certain significant percentage of the national budget or of national GDP is devoted to social welfare expenditure may be taken as initiating or defining features of the welfare state.[38]

Foregrounding crucial legislative innovation, or the creation of foundational state agencies, or the establishment of critical funding arrangements, or the rise of specific discourses and their political champions, as signposts marking the start of the social or environmental characteristics of the welfare state will therefore define a different chronology and canvas for the historical trajectory and cultural and legal foundations of the environmental or green state. In what follows, I consider a range of these factors and use a broader rather than narrower template of functions to frame the historical canvas of the (social and environmental) welfare state.

Before I revisit my account of Australia's recent environmental political history, I want to introduce several conceptual distinctions. Clearly, the social welfare aspects of the state include state expenditure and capacity devoted to the provision of social security benefits and public health and education services. While there is considerable blurring at the point where one considers environmental matters with implications for human health, such as pollution regulation and amelioration, these *social welfare* aspects can, to an extent, be separated from the state's *environmental welfare* functions, where public expenditure, laws, and state capacity are devoted to environmental restoration and remediation, the provision of infrastructure to manage the exploitation of natural resources, and the prevention of environmental degradation. Accordingly, I refer to these elements separately as the "social welfare state" and the "environmental welfare state," although developments and characteristics in both policy domains predominantly relate to *human* welfare and are usually often found as *characteristics* of the one state.

In addition, I want to suggest a way to add definition to James Meadowcroft's vision (see chapter 1) of the ecostate in general, a term which for him encompasses a wide array of variations and initiatives, by distinguishing between possible types of neoliberal, social democratic, and other types of welfare state on the basis of their environmental characteristics.

The range of possible versions of ecostate suggests a typology that may assist in characterizing individual states in terms of the strength or weakness of their environmental welfare capacities and green (ecological sustainability or ecological modernization) provisions (see table 2.1).

Green states, were they to exist, would be characterized by the predominance of types of state activity aimed at strong ecological modernization. Here state activity would have, centrally, a driving and predominant moral purpose in directing social and economic activity toward ecologically sustainable (and socially just) outcomes. It would incorporate at its heart recognition of environmental constraints on material activity, and this would be reflected in institutional developments that substantially benefit nature in addition to or apart from human welfare. Significant

Table 2.1
Toward a Typology of Environmental States

Type of State	Characteristics	Examples
Green state	Strong ecomodernization through • High levels of state environmental capacity and intervention, and of integration of economic, social welfare, and environmental welfare policies • Strong cultural and political institutionalization of ecological values • High levels of ecocitizenship—state highly inclusive • High commitment to biocentric values • High commitment to human welfare environmentalism • Strong budgetary commitment to both human welfare environmental and ecocentric issues	Sweden, Netherlands
Environmental welfare state	Weak ecomodernization through • Moderate state environmental capacity and intervention • Weak institutionalization of ecological values, with human-oriented (social and environment) welfare, including resource conservation, predominant • Moderate levels of ecocitizenship—state moderately inclusive • Low commitment to biocentric values • High commitment to human welfare environmentalism • Moderate budgetary commitment to ecological issues	

Table 2.1 (continued)

Type of State	Characteristics	Examples
Social welfare state		Socialist Hungary
Neoliberal state		
Environmental neoliberal state	Very weak ecomodernization through • Weak state environmental capacity and intervention—strongly market-oriented • Weak institutionalization of environmental values • State concentration on resource conservation and environmental remediation • Low levels of ecocitizenship—exclusionary state • Low commitment to biocentric values • Moderate to high commitment to human welfare environmentalism • Weak to moderate budgetary commitment to social and environment welfare	Australia, United States
Ecofascist state	Strong ecomodernization through • Strong institutionalization of ecological values built around a neo-Malthusian outlook • High levels of state environmental capacity and actual intervention • Authoritarian political characteristics • Very low levels of ecocitizenship and democracy—state profoundly exclusionary • High commitment to biocentric values • Low commitment to human welfare environmentalism • (Possibly) strong budgetary commitment, especially to ecocentric issues/values	

state capacity for ecologically sustainable development would be evident in the following areas:

- *Consensus formation.* The state, in its activities, would be highly inclusive of civil society in institutions and processes for the deliberative consideration of programs for substantial ecologically bounded economic and social change.[39]
- *Strategic planning.* The state would provide the capacity for (or facilitate) long-term integrative social and economic planning aimed at ecological sustainability with horizons beyond those available or meaningful to actors in specific industry or social sectors.
- *Policy coordination and integration.* This would occur both within the state and across sectors of economic activity and civil society in ways that enabled and guaranteed effective ecological governance by ensuring that ecological concerns were effectively incorporated into all decision making.
- *Implementation.* The state would also ensure that resources were available for appropriate regulatory, monitoring, allocative, and productive tasks.[40]

These capacities would also necessarily be such as to enable the green state to participate effectively in various forms of international environmental governance.

By contrast, one may now talk of two types of welfare state. *Social welfare states* may be characterized by the predominance of well-developed state social welfare capacities and functions that ensure the reproduction and legitimization of capital accumulation, with major environmental problems or issues often barely recognized or disregarded as externalities. (Many socialist states fitted into this mold.) By contrast, *environmental welfare states* are distinguished by their developed capacity to engage in weak ecological modernization. These states predominantly engage in environmental activity that ensures the reproduction and legitimization of a "nature-blind" form of capital accumulation or which meets short-term human welfare requirements. However nonmaterial ecological considerations and longer-term environment-related human welfare requirements remain incidental to or subordinated to these functions.[41]

These types of state may in turn be set apart from two types of neoliberal states: *"Classical" neoliberal states*, which manifest weak state social and environmental welfare capacity and a strong bias toward market-oriented solutions in these and other policy domains, may be distinguished from *environmental neoliberal states*, which manifest weak state social welfare capacity and a strong bias toward market-oriented solutions to social welfare problems but have developed, in parallel, a moderate to strong environmental welfare capacity.

Last, for the sake of analytical completeness, it is possible to conceive of an *ecofascist state*, which places priority on ecological values at the expense of social welfare and human rights—one akin to those authoritarian states proposed by neo-Malthusians and ecosurvivalists in the early 1970s.

How, then, does Australian environmental political history look when analyzed using these terms? Several observations can point to clear contrasts between the growth of environmental and social welfare institutions. For a start, as table 2.2 suggests, there is no apparent close link between the rise of the Australian social welfare state and the appearance of the environmental welfare and ecological characteristics of this state. Colonial state education systems emerged during the late nineteenth century, and hospitals during the early twentieth century, developing an overlay of national educational and health funding assistance during the second half of the twentieth century. Between 1910 and 1945—mainly in response to the Great Depression of the 1930s—a nationally funded social security system displaced the voluntary religious and private charitable and relief schemes that emerged in the nineteenth century and that were consolidated by State acts in the early twentieth century.[42]

The first labor laws, the emancipation of the (male) working class, and the rise of social democracy were realized over the period 1890 to 1910.[43] The national welfare state, which was well recognized discursively by the 1940s and was also propelled into being by widespread bureaucratic and political support for Keynesian economic policies at this time, may be said to have become fully realizable only following creation of a stable national funding base in 1942.

By contrast, the foundations of the Australian environmental welfare state were established much earlier, during the early to mid-nineteenth century, via the colonial laws, commissions, and agencies mentioned earlier in this chapter. However, environmental welfare then went through several stages of change and intensification, only achieving national focus and organization after 1970 and becoming relatively coherent at this level only in the 1990s.

Table 2.2.
Rise of the Australian (Social and Environmental) Welfare State

	Social Welfare Measures	Environmental Welfare Measures	Ecological Measures
Foundational colonial and State legislation	1900 onward	1860s onward	Mid-1860s onward Legislation preserving species 1880s onwards National parks and nature reserves
Foundational national legislation	1900 onward	1972 onward	1972 onward
Creation of foundational colonial or State agencies	Late 19th century in education; 20th century in health	1880s onward	1970s
Creation of foundational national departments, agencies and institutions	1945	1970 First environment department as joint ministerial function 1998 First autonomous environment department	1996 Draft national biodiversity strategy; national endangered species legislation
Substantial funding at State-level	Mid-20th century	Early 1900s	Mid-1980s onward
Substantial national funding (over 1 percent of GDP)	1942	1996	
Emergence of major civil society champions of social or environmental welfare	1930s onward	Late 19th century onward	Mid-1970s onward

Although social and environmental welfare concerns were intertwined when confronting impacts of industrialization on the urban poor during the nineteenth century, other environmental institutional developments (such as nature reserves and national parks) were not dependent on the rise of class solidarity or social citizenship in the ways that the evolution of the social welfare state was. In addition, it is clear that environmental welfare and ecological state developments have coexisted during the past few decades, although the latter are exceptionally weakly developed and relatively recent in Australia.

Nevertheless, inevitably, environmental state developments have been affected by, but not always directly dependent on, the larger settings that influence other aspects of Australian social and economic policy. Accelerating economic globalization and increasing international market exposure during the 1980s and early 1990s resulted in higher unemployment, budgetary deficits, and national debt in Australia, and precipitated the rise of neoliberal political forces nationally. But the resultant partial retrenchment of the Australian social welfare state has been accompanied by "environmental regime growth," including increasing national environmental budgets and growth in state environmental capacity during this time.

The patterns of emergence and evolution in both the social and the environmental institutions of the Australian state, while indistinctly related, were themselves linked to transnational discourses in their separate fields. This is perhaps most evident in the environmental domain, where the transnational exchange of regulatory models for tackling pollution and resource management has been long established and where Australian national environmental developments have increasingly been propelled and disciplined by changes in global and international environmental governance. The relatively recent creation of global regimes relating to climate change, trade in wastes, biodiversity, and world heritage preservation, has led to a rapid convergence in national institutions and practices.

Indeed, the changes of the past two decades, and the current trends described for Australia, suggest that there is a growing tension between (at least) two possible characterizations of state trajectory in Australia. On the one hand, one sees the formation of an internationally oriented economistic "competition state" with loosely bound subnational/regional components each competing for its own version of global competitive advantage to which environmental characteristics adhere. On the other hand, it is possible to discern the outlines of a weak environmental welfare state forming around the dual problematics of environmental regulation and remediation for future social benefit and ecological protection. These politically contested trajectories coexist like feuding Siamese twins. The extent to which these trajectories are, ultimately, mutually exclusive and internally contradictory is unclear.

No doubt local resource opportunities, environmental context and intensifying environmental crises, and sociohistorical factors have provoked these Australian developments, but to what extent are these outcomes uniquely Australian? In general terms, these interpretations suggest several interrelated questions that a more comprehensive historical sociology of the environmental state or green state must confront.

First, when can we say that we *have* an environmental welfare state, or environmental neoliberal state, or a green state? Pierson[44] uses three criteria to mark the establishment of a social welfare state. These are the dates of introduction of social insurance and of the extension of social citizenship, and the growth of public expenditure on social welfare to over 3 percent of GNP.[45] Additional criteria, similar to those mentioned earlier and in table 2.2, could be employed to mark the existence of, for instance, an environmental welfare state, including the date significant public institutions and laws relating to pollution and the protection of nature were founded or enacted, and the growth of a significant public environmental budget (although it is clear that the level of public budget committed to the environment would have to be commensurate with national need rather than simply based on some simple hurdle requirement).

Using Pierson's criteria and other distinctions described earlier, Australia, it could be argued, now has autonomous and significant national and subnational environmental institutions and laws and a major national environmental remediation program (the Natural Heritage Trust). But its citizens, while now able to vote for a green party with a clearly defined ecological program, still do not have real legal standing on environmental matters, and so the criterion of full environmental (let alone ecological) citizenship is not met. Meanwhile, even if one considered total national expenditure (not just Commonwealth but also State and local government outlays) to include some very marginally environmental activities like waste disposal to total some $A 5 billion, this amount not only is less than 3 percent of Australian GNP but, more important, is well below the sum *needed* for environmental remediation and environmental infrastructural transformation, and less than that currently afforded in hidden subsidies to environmentally destructive activities such as fossil fuel exploitation and land clearing.[46] In all, while Australia during the early 1990s began developing features of a weak environmental welfare state, in the early 2000s it is probably more accurately classified an environmental neoliberal state, according to the typology offered in table 2.1.

Second, to what extent is the history of the emergence of the environmental welfare or green state *synchronous* with, or *dependent* and *founded* on, the development of the social welfare state—and if not, why not? In the Australian case, the historical relationship is clearly not straightforward. One can conclude that a significant and persistent disjuncture exists between developments in different parts of the Australian (welfare) state and also that it is impossible to argue that the Australian environmental state simply evolved out of the social welfare state. Nor can claims for simple historical succession—the evolution of a social welfare state into an environmental welfare state and then, possibly, a green state—be sustained. The argument for parallels in development between, first, one welfare state form (the social welfare state) and then the next (the ecostate), as suggested by Meadowcroft, may not hold up to close scrutiny.

Third, what forces drive the environmental welfare state's development, and how do these relate to the sources of the social welfare state? To what extent is the fate or *trajectory* of the various environmental or green states linked to or autonomous of that of the social welfare state? The Australian instance suggests that these links are indirect, complex, and politically charged and include the long institutional history of a state as much as its immediate circumstances. It is also clear that ecological crisis—about global issues such as climate change or domestic issues such as the fate of threatened forests or species—can influence political mobilization and action in ways that are not dependent on, that take the heat out of, that even draw attention away from, other (social or economic) policy issues.

Even if the state were capable of retreating from or even shedding its historically accrued responsibilities for certain allocative and productive functions—those relating to social reproduction—the intensification of (global) environmental crisis means the state is increasingly being pressed to perform a green welfare function by organizing and funding remediation, infrastructure provision, research and implementation, and regulating environmental degradation in the environmental domain. As the Australian example suggests, these costs, while still marginal now, are likely to become a profound political and economic burden in the future (given climate change). Although industrialized states have moved to deal with these demands in ways that are culturally and situation specific, and sometimes seemingly contradictory across states, there is also a divergence of environmental policy responses and institutional tendencies in this domain across the OECD.

In conclusion, I would suggest that claims for a teleological development from social welfare state to green state do not hold. Historically, some environmental characteristics of the state precede its social welfare aspects (at least in Australia), and there are also clear instances of states' being wound back from stronger to weaker positions on matters of ecological sustainability in recent political times. Yet even if the collective trajectory of states appeared to be toward strengthening national environmental capacity in response to intensifying environmental pressures—the argument underlying Meadowcroft's notion of the emerging ecostate—this development would require more nuanced description of the potentially very different types of environmental welfare state that might be emerging. For that reason, this chapter has sought to provide a better means to describe individual states and their environmental capacities, and to assess their future development not merely against institutional precedents but against present and future ecological trends and needs.

Notes

1. Throughout this chapter, I use *state* to refer to the concept in general and *State* to refer to Australia's subnational unit of government.

2. On whether this may constitute a serious crisis, see Kaufmann (2001).

3. Esping-Andersen (1990).

4. Huber and Stephens (2001, 107).

5. Robertson (1898).

6. Powell (1976, 60).

7. For instance, in *Environmental Management in Australia* (1976), Powell comments that "Forest Bills were introduced into the Victorian Parliament in 1879, 1881, 1887 and 1892 but none became law" (124). The first Victorian Forests Act was passed in 1907.

8. Richard Grove (1995).

9. Powell (1976, 130).

10. See also Grove (1995); Grove (1997); and Tyrell (1999).

11. See Dunstan (1984); Dunstan (1985).

12. Coward (1976, 9).

13. See Christoff (1999).

14. Eckersley (1992).

15. Bonyhady (2000, 30–31).

16. Cited in Bonyhady (2000, 31).

17. See Thomas (1983).

18. Bonyhady (2000, 14).

19. Moyal (1986); Finney (1993).

20. In 1861, Tasmania enacted a law preventing the taking of the black swan, the first statute to provide limited protection for a native species.

21. See Walker (1991); Harris (1956, ch. 1).

22. Esther Anderson (2000, 4).

23. Esther Anderson (2000, 52).

24. These waves occurred during the mid-nineteenth century (the rise of the resource conservation movement), the end of the nineteenth century (the movement for urban planning and sanitation, and the rise of species preservation), during the 1970s (antipollution and nature conservation movements, leading to departments of conservation, U.S.-style environmental protection agencies and national parks authorities, and a new emphasis on ecological preservation), and during the 1980s and early 1990s (in response to global threats—particularly climate change and ozone depletion—and leading to sustainability planning).

25. The effort was largely unsuccessful, resulting instead in a significant loss of employment in the textile, clothing, and footwear industries, where tariff reductions permitted competition with cheaper overseas goods and hastened transfer of manufacturing to offshore havens of low-cost labor.

26. This agenda represented a key component of the strategy crafted by Richardson to gain environmental group support in the 1990 election.

27. Productivity Commission (1999).

28. The Inter-Governmental Agreement on the Environment (IGAE) codified environmental powers between Commonwealth, State, and local government spheres and reinforced the States' power as environmental managers after almost

a decade of attrition. The IGAE was concluded in mid-1992 and reviewed and revised in 1997.

29. Christoff (1998a).

30. Christoff (1998b).

31. Department of Communications, Information Technology and the Arts (2004, 4).

32. This shift is most notably the result of the revision of Commonwealth environmental laws and the enactment of the omnibus Environmental Protection and Biodiversity Conservation Act of 1999.

33. Toyne (1994).

34. National Land and Water Resources Audit (2002, 55).

35. Australian Conservation Foundation/ National Farmers Federation (2001).

36. Offe (1975, 128).

37. Christoff (2000).

38. Ashford (1986); Thane (1982).

39. See also Dryzek, Downes et al. (2003).

40. See Janicke (1997); Christoff (1998b).

41. Christoff (1996).

42. "New South Wales had no equivalent of the English Poor Law, which imposed upon the State the duty of supporting all who were destitute," writes T. H. Kewley in *Social Security in Australia* (7). In fact, only the Colony of South Australia went on to develop such legislation. See also Watts (1987); Wilson, Thomson, and McMahon (1996).

43. Political emancipation did not occur in Australia until 1967, with the legal recognition of its indigenous inhabitants as citizens.

44. Pierson (1998, 106–107).

45. The arbitrary choice of 3 percent is not explained.

46. Christoff (2002).

3

Modernizing the British State: Ecological Contradictions in New Labour's Economic Strategy

Matthew Paterson and John Barry

Debates about the state and the environmental crisis tend to adopt a highly abstract account of what the state is, and engage in a deductive form of reasoning that attempts to show how the state is either compatible, or more usually incompatible, with principles of environmental sustainability. This is clearly the case with classic 1970s debates. The eco-authoritarians, in particular Ophuls and Hardin, argued that the state was constituted internationally through the institution of sovereignty in competitive relations with other states, which precluded sufficient coordination to resolve transboundary or common problems.[1] But they also argued that within the state there was insufficient authority or coordinating power to compel citizens/subjects to behave in ecologically rational ways. The state is conceptualized as an abstract entity analogous to an individual human being, following a tradition going back at least to Hobbes.

This conceptualization can be found in more recent debates. For example, we have engaged in such forms of reasoning in different ways.[2] In international relations, debates have taken off from the "tragedy of the commons" element in Hardin's arguments to turn on the question of whether international anarchy compels states to forms of interaction that both produce global environmental degradation and prevent sufficient cooperative efforts emerging to resolve such degradation.[3] Most writers in this debate reject the Hardin position by arguing that the possibilities of cooperation in anarchic systems to resolve commons, transboundary, and shared resources problems are considerable.[4] But they share the account of the state as an abstract, utility-maximizing entity, analogous to an individual as understood by rational choice theory.

In political theory the debates are a little more wide-ranging, but a prominent one has included arguments that the state is inevitably ecologically problematic because of its monopoly of violence and its centralizing tendencies, which disrupt ecologically sustainable practices. These set in train what Carter calls an "ecologically hazardous dynamic."[5] Critics argue that these tendencies are not necessary but historically contingent features of the state and that some features of the state, in particular its ability to authoritatively allocate and redistribute resources, are necessary features of a sustainable society.[6]

Our approach in this chapter is to question these abstract forms of reasoning by engaging in a concrete analysis of a historically and spatially specific state from a broadly critical political and economic perspective. This analysis involves looking at the particular social relations in which state managers engage to reproduce state power and the specific political projects that are superimposed on and help to reproduce and transform that state. We argue that it is more fruitful to examine the ways that states attempt to engage with ecological crises, to show the constraints and opportunities for developing more sustainable social and political forms, than to decide a priori that the state must be antiecological because it is sovereign and thus can ignore ecological concerns (or to reject that particular position, but on similarly abstract grounds).

This chapter therefore analyzes the way that the British state under the New Labour government has attempted to deal with ecological questions since the election of the Labour government in 1997. We do this through analyzing not only Labour's environmental policies, narrowly understood, but also by looking into how central aspects of Labour's political and economic strategy contain within them ecological contents in terms of channeling how British society uses resources, produces pollutants, or metabolizes nature in the broadest sense. Through this analysis we hope to show that the state, and projects through which states are reproduced and (occasionally) transformed by governments and external social forces, should be understood as contradictory in relation to the environmental crisis. Ultimately, we argue that the specific state form in Britain in the late twentieth and early twenty-first centuries is highly problematic in ecological terms. This should not necessarily be understood as a generalizable argument about the state but rather specifically traceable to central elements of government strategies through which states are reproduced. We highlight in particular here how globalization and flexible labor markets are central elements in New Labour strategy that work to under-mine the explicit environmental elements in Labour's policies.[7]

The Environment in New Labour's Strategy

In the run-up to the election in 1997, the Labour party made statements that were interpreted by commentators to mean that its environmental policies would be significantly different to those of the outgoing govern-ment. Consequently, expectations about New Labour's performance in environmental terms, while dampened (as New Labour worked tirelessly to diminish expectations *in general* among their core supporters before their election victory),[8] were nevertheless considerable. Many believed that the Labour government elected in 1997 would deliver significant shifts in key areas of policy affecting environmental performance. In par-ticular, optimism was felt in areas such as transport and its consequences, climate change (with Labour prepared to commit Britain to significantly more stringent CO_2 emissions targets than the Conservatives were, and to play a more active role in the international diplomacy on global warm-ing), energy policy more generally, and overseas environmental aid (with an "ethical" foreign policy).[9]

In addition, the government had seemed to understand the necessity of integrating environmental questions into the core business of government. Thus Prime Minister Tony Blair, shortly after the election, proclaimed that governments should "make the process of government green. The environ-ment must . . . be integrated into all our decisions, regardless of sector. They must be in at the start, not bolted on later."[10] Within New Labour discourse, environmental concerns were thus regarded as a classic instance of the need for "joined-up" government.[11] The government implemented a number of institutional reorganizations in line with these claims. Most notable were the creation of the superministry Department of the Environment, Transport and the Regions (DETR),[12] and a cross-departmental Sustainable Development Unit (SDU) designed to look at whether all departments practices were in line with overall objectives in this regard.[13] In other words, at least rhetorically, there was an under-standing of the interconnections between environmental policies and other aspects of government policy and of the need to think about government strategy as a whole in terms of its environmental consequences.

But fairly quickly such optimism subsided. Michael Jacobs, General Secretary of the Fabian Society and a well-known writer on environmental politics, wrote, in a pamphlet, *Environmental Modernization*, "It is evident that New Labour is not comfortable with the environment as a political issue."[14] Jacobs's pamphlet attempted to show why New Labour has failed to deal with various environmental policy areas adequately and how Labour could develop a much more ambitious set of environmental policies within its own Third Way framework.

Sticking to environmental policy narrowly construed, three policy arenas are worth exploring to illustrate these shortcomings: transport, energy/climate change policy, and genetically modified (GM) foods.

Transport

As Andrew Jordan suggests, transport could be taken as a test case both of the novelty of Third Way politics and of its environmental commitments.[15] For the former, it represents a classic balancing of rights and responsibilities characteristic of Third Way rhetoric. For the latter, "There is no better example of the need for better interdepartmental coordination than transport policy."[16] New Labour came into office in a context of significant problems concerning transport (road congestion, roads protests, chronic problems in the rail network) and a set of policies designed to deal with these problems. Many of these policies formed a significant part of environmentalists' optimism concerning the incoming government. They aimed to reduce car use, reduce CO_2 emissions from transport, and increase use and provision of public transport. These would not only meet New Labour's environmental commitments but would be dealt with in the context of the party's approach to "social exclusion."

One of the problems that became quickly apparent was that despite the attempts to portray labour policies as conflict-free, favoring everyone, conflicts within government surfaced rapidly. John Prescott, whose commitment in this area was relatively strong, was ostensibly in charge of transport policy as Secretary of State for the Department of Environment, Transport and the Regions (DETR). However, conflicts between Prescott and Blair surfaced early on, with the Prime Minister concerned that the agreed policies would alienate voters on whom the New Labour project was held to depend: "Middle England," or "Mondeo Man" (so dubbed because of the Ford car model many choose to drive). The latter label reveal much about the consumerist assumptions of Labour's electoral strategy, according to Jordan.[17] "Much to his [Prescott's] annoyance, Blair has intervened on more than one occasion to pacify the anxious car drivers of Middle England, personified by the archetypal 'Mondeo Man' who bore him to power in 1997."[18] These contradictions were exemplified in equivocations in government policy over road building, congestion charging, and fuel taxes.

Contradictions were also magnified in the government's response to the fuel protests of September-November 2000,[19] which revealed that the government's central purpose for high fuel taxes was to support levels of government spending rather than fuel economy improvements or emissions abatement. (The government claimed public services, particularly the health service, would be threatened if fuel taxes were cut.) But in the budget following the protests (in spring 2001), it also showed willing to articulate environmental concerns in the tax structure, accentuating differentials between regular fuels and the newly introduced ultralow sulfur fuels and between car tax levels for large- and small-engined cars. Nevertheless, the principal effect of the budget was seen as appeasing "Mondeo Man," whose political preferences were judged to have been expressed in the fuel protests.

As a consequence, while Labour transport policy has been noticeably different from that of the Conservatives, with increased spending on public transport, re-regulation of the privatized rail industry, and legislation facilitating congestion charging in city centers, it has been significantly less ambitious and less aggressively pursued than had been hoped. Key legislation facilitating the full creation of a Strategic Rail Authority and other measures was greatly delayed. The generalized commitment to reduce car use has not been followed up with specific targets against which to judge progress in this regard. As Toynbee and Walker conclude regarding measures to "green" urban transport, "Some local action, some good ideas but no overall sense of direction and scant willingness to offend motorists."[20]

Energy Policy and Climate Change

Another arena in which such contradictions emerged was energy policy. The Labour government committed the British state to aggressive reductions in CO_2 emissions of 20 percent by 2010.[21] This was a noticeably more stringent target than that adopted by the previous Conservative government. John Prescott played an important role in forging the deal at Kyoto in November-December 1999, which resulted in the first international legally binding targets on emissions of CO_2 and other greenhouse gases. But at the same time, the government pursued an energy policy (as well as a transport policy) that undermined the likelihood of achieving this target and thus the basis of Britain's professed leadership on climate change.

Mostly as part of its climate change program, unveiled in November 2000, New Labour introduced a number of specific measures in relation to climate change policy in order to meet both its unilateral and its multilaterally agreed target under Kyoto and the European Union (EU) bubble within the Kyoto agreement.[22] Perhaps the most important of these, and certainly the most controversial, was the climate change levy.

In his March 1999 budget Chancellor Gordon Brown announced that as of April 2001 a surcharge would be levied on the fossil fuel energy consumption of companies, designed to reduce the fossil fuel use by industry and creating incentives for it to become more energy-efficient. There followed a fierce, although not heavily publicized, campaign by manufacturing companies, particularly those engaged in energy-intensive production, against the levy. Companies argued that it would erode their competitiveness and harm exports. In response, the Treasury granted a number of concessions to businesses.

The government also introduced a number of other measures, including increased government funding for research and development and investment in renewable energy. Known as the New Carbon Trust, this was to channel up to £50 million a year toward developing low-carbon technology, partly funded from the climate change levy. A Kyoto Mechanisms Office was also established to encourage the private sector to invest in innovative energy projects abroad, to help tackle climate change, and to allow British business to seize new opportunities. Also in spring 2001 the government launched a national CO_2 emissions trading system, designed to allow emissions trading among domestic businesses, primarily in order to prepare them for international trading schemes under the Kyoto Protocol.[23]

There is widespread skepticism among environmental nongovernmental organizations (NGOs) and others that these measures will deliver the CO_2 reductions claimed for them.[24] Some claim that not enough resources have been devoted to the various projects, for example, the New Carbon Trust or transport fuel efficiency.[25] Others believe that the items formally called climate change policy are undermined by other elements in the government's economic strategy.[26] Contradictions may be found not only in transport policy but also in energy policy.

With the exception of a windfall tax on the profits of selected privatized utilities, and a moratorium on new gas-fired power stations (to protect jobs in the coal industry), new Labour largely continued the previous Conservative government's energy policy. The cornerstone of this has been the promotion of increased competition in energy supply with the declared intention of reducing prices for electricity and gas. The regulator for these utilities generally has acted to prevent increased prices even if these might help meet environmental goals, in order to protect consumer interests (defined as low prices). As a consequence, the energy intensity of the British economy has increased, and achieving targeted CO_2 emissions under the Kyoto Protocol to the UN Framework Convention on Climate Change and under the EU division of commitments to that Protocol has become more difficult. Projections in 2000 were that the United Kingdom would fail to meet its Kyoto commitment to reduce six selected greenhouse gas emissions by 12.5 percent by 2010 and would attain only a 10 percent reduction.[27]

Contradictions can be seen in the way the Department of Trade and Industry (DTI) resisted proposals to promote solar technologies while the DETR advocated such promotion.[28] As well, at no point in energy pricing debates have the ecological consequences of the government's commitment to low energy prices been noticed. As Jordan points out, some elements of Labour's energy policies work against each other: commitments to reduce energy consumption to slow climate change versus commitments to reduce energy prices (which will likely increase use).[29] Similarly, in debates about the price of new cars, Labour adopted the slogan "rip-off Britain," with the DTI promoting its new-found role as champion of consumer rights against the unscrupulous practices of car dealers. But nowhere in this debate was there any serious discussion of elements of environmental policies regarding the car that might bring to bear pricing mechanisms to reduce car use.[30]

Unlike in the transport case, however, there are signs of tension in the government's economic strategies that create openings for the pursuit of more aggressive environmental measures. Of particular importance is the apparent (if belated) realization by the DTI of the economic potential of renewable energy. In late 2000, New Labour started to promote photovoltaic solar energy as a "leading edge" technology, and thus as an economic opportunity for British industry, and in November 2001 the Policy Innovation Unit (an influential Cabinet Office think tank set up by Prime Minister Blair) produced a report, *Renewable Energy in the UK: Building for the Future of the Environment*, which urged more funding for renewable energy and proposed that 20 percent of Britain's energy needs be met by renewables by 2020.[31]

Genetically Modified Foods

Another area where environmental concerns were prevalent when New Labour came into office concerned genetically modified crops and food from issues. The environmental implications of GM are much more heavily contested than those of energy and Transport, so it is more complicated to make evaluative claims concerning the strength or otherwise of environmental policy in this field. Nevertheless, to the extent that the promotion and development of GM crops can be considered an antiecological measure, New Labour can be regarded as resisting the incorporation of an environmental agenda into its policies. As in the transport and energy cases, the central obstacle is the overall economic strategy adopted by the state under New Labour. Although concerns about GM foods were widespread among certain electoral constituencies whose support New Labour hoped to secure, economic considerations overrode these possible electoral threats.

A number of concerns about GM crops and food had been raised from the mid-1990s onward. The most commonly expressed were questions concerning the effects on health of consuming GM foods (especially salient in the wake of the panic over mad-cow disease). But environmental concerns regarding possible effects on biodiversity and the viability of organic farming methods as well as worries about the concentration of corporate power over the food chain played some role in public concerns also.

In general, however, Labour, on coming into office in 1997, was predisposed toward the biotechnology industry. It saw this sector as a leading high-technology growth sector that should be encouraged in order to promote the overall growth and competitiveness of the economy. While most public attention was on GM crops and food, the bulk of the biotechnology sector's interests are in medical and pharmaceutical uses, not involving crop production.[32] Thus there has been a substantial amount of equivocation by the government regarding GM crops. The public tensions over how to treat them have been reflected in tensions within the government, with Michael Meacher (Secretary of State for the Environment) being noticeably less in favor of GM crops than other ministers, and with the range of advisory bodies and government organs out of which official policy has emerged giving widely differing opinions on appropriate policy.[33]

As a consequence of these tensions, Labour's fundamental position is hard to pin down.[34] It remains opposed to the U.S. doctrine of "substantial equivalence," namely, that GM crops and foods should be regarded as substantially equivalent to non-GM products and that there is no need for a specific regulatory framework to deal with them. In this, Britain stands somewhere between the position of the United States and other EU countries that want a stricter set of regulatory schemes in place.[35] Prime Minister Tony Blair stated,

Contrary to the myth that somehow wicked multinationals and politicians have pressed us to be pro-GM, I am fully aware of the potential impact on biodiversity and people's concerns about health. I am neither pro nor anti. I simply say: let us evaluate the technology, test it, and then make a judgment; rather than ban it before we even look at it.[36]

New Labour placed a temporary moratorium on the commercial sale of GM crops for human consumption combined with a set of procedures based on the principle that each proposed new crop should be thoroughly tested in field trials before being licensed for sale.

But despite this apparent neutrality and caution, there is nevertheless a general predisposition toward the biotechnology sector, such that in individual controversies the government has tended to take positions favorable to the sector's interests. This can be clearly seen in Labour's manifesto for the 2001 general election.[37] Since about 2000 one of the main planks of this has come from Clare Short (the then Secretary of State for Overseas Development), arguing the case for GM foods on the grounds of alleviating world hunger, as part of her general arguments attacking anti-globalization protestors on the grounds that they aim to stunt Southern development.

At times, this rationale for GM technology is connected to environmental policy as part of a New Labour "ecological modernization" policy framework for the environment, whose basic principle is that policies aimed at ecological sustainability and economic growth are compatible rather than mutually exclusive.[38] Here, biotechnology is presented as an environmentally friendly form of economic activity and investment.

The central explanation for the problems environmentalists and others have had in persuading New Labour to reject GM crops and food has been the way in which such technologies have been articulated as part of an overall economic strategy. Biotechnologies, along with information technologies, have been understood by New Labour as the central growth sectors to be promoted by the government in order to promote the broader growth and competitiveness of the U.K. economy. Biotechnology is interpreted as a knowledge-based economic activity and thus as a perfect example of the type of industry that New Labour sees as crucial to Britain and Europe in the future. At the same time, the government is aware that while Britain is good at scientific invention, primary research, and discovery, in comparison to the United State it does not have the same success in terms of the commercial exploitation of British-based and funded science.[39] This promotion of the knowledge economy and biotechnology's role in it therefore reflects New Labour's globalization story.[40]

The Ecology of New Labour's Economic Strategy: Questioning Environmental Modernization

Michael Jacobs in his pamphlet *Environmental Modernization* has articulated the place (or rather lack of it) of environmental concerns in New Labour political discourse. Two questions are thrown up by Jacobs's account of why New Labour's environmental performance has been disappointing:[41] How well has New Labour understood the need to integrate environmental considerations into all areas of government policy? and how different is New Labour's economic strategy from the previous Conservative government's?

Jacobs argues that Labour can integrate a solid set of environmental policies into its current economic strategy without necessarily transforming the key aspects of that strategy itself. So he acknowledges the importance of such integration but implies that it is possible for governments to choose (or not) to integrate such policies with economic strategy. How these environmental policies are integral to economic strategy is thus not clear; they seem to be a bolt-on extra.

Jacobs attempts to provide a rationale by which New Labour can develop a set of environmental policies. He suggests that New Labour's environmental performance has been disappointing because environmental policies have been framed in a discourse—either green radicalism or sustainable development—to which Labour has traditionally been resistant. Nevertheless, New Labour made much of the improved environmental performance that would result from its election in 1997. Jacobs argues that once brought out of this discourse, a set of policies could be developed to deal with specific environmental problems within New Labour's own framework. His main point is that for environmental goals to be articulated by New Labour they must be framed to fit within New Labour's rhetoric and political project.

According to Jacobs, many environmental policies can simply be bolted on to Labour's economic strategy. He terms this environmental modernization, and while it is clear that this comes out of the ecological modernization approach of people like Hajer, the debt is only briefly acknowledged.[42] Jacobs's environmental modernization is heavily weighted toward a supply-side, technological (and state-bureaucratic-centered) interpretation, in which, through technological improvements in resource efficiency and matching improvements in labor productivity, we can have a growing economy without any resulting ecological problems.[43] So, for example, he discusses how in the context of general economic and industrial policy, the focus of Labour's strategy is to increase labor productivity. He suggests that the concept could be expanded to increasing environmental productivity, referring to decreases in the ratio of natural resource throughput to GDP.[44] He argues that the Sustainable Technologies Initiative established by New Labour could be a mechanism for promoting this (although he complains of its lack of funds and asserts the necessity of significant increases to achieve the environmental productivity gains).

According to Jacobs, in a number of other areas, such as health (focusing on the mad-cow disease debates), urban life (focusing on transport, particularly cars), and social exclusion, Labour could significantly improve its environmental performance without having to change its fundamental political economic approach.[45] This environmental modernization can be achieved through minor changes in taxation and regulatory measures designed to improve the environmental performance of the economy while contributing to New Labour's overall goal of a more general modernization and maintenance of conditions for improved (technology-and investment-led) economic growth.

But two things (at least) are unclear in Jacobs's account. First, why has New Labour not developed such an environmental modernization approach? Jacobs attributes this failure to hostility to environmentalism as an ideology, perhaps combined with a lack of political imagination. New Labour needs to be persuaded that it can integrate such policies within its overall approach. Thus, for Jacobs, this is purely a question of strategy and will, not (as we argue) a contradiction between environmental needs and economic goals. Jacobs believes that a narrative needs to be found to integrate environmental concerns into the New Labour modernization project without linking them to "environmentalism" and the green movement. The attitude of New Labour to "environmentalism" is revealing. Prime Minister Blair places the environmental movement, when it "stands in the way of progress" (protests against road building, free trade, or trials of GM crops), as part of the "forces of conservatism" allied against New Labour's modernization project.

Second, if we abandon the discourse of environmentalism, what is the normative basis for enacting environmental policies? At a number of points in Jacobs's text, the contradictions that come about from abandoning such a normative basis are apparent. For example, while discussing possible policies consistent with his approach, he discusses cars under the rubric of the quality of urban life. He applauds some of what the government has done in terms of enabling congestion charging in city centers but then goes on to say an environmental modernization approach could operate discursively to legitimize the development of many more ambitious policies and maximize their impact. In particular, he argues for policies that would make it possible for people in towns and cities not to use their cars but to travel by other means (public transport, cycling, walking).

But from his own analysis earlier in the work, this fails to exhaust (pardon the pun) the environmental impacts of the car. The implication is that the primary problem is urban congestion. He then comes up with a classic Third Way piece of rhetoric:

From the perspective of environmental modernization the crucial requirement here is to avoid the impression of being anti-car. There is no political mileage in this at all. Contrary to the claims of many environmentalists, cars have tremendous benefits, and people value them. . . . The issue is simply that in certain places, and at certain times, the number of cars on the road causes unacceptable congestion, and for this reason, in these places and times [city centers in daytime], car access will have to be constrained.[46]

The attempt to conceal conflict, to present politics as if it were simply a matter of finding a compromise, is a classic part of Third Way rhetoric, as emphasized in particular by Elliott and Atkinson.[47] One effect is to fail to please anyone, a central element in the origins of the fuel protests in September 2000.[48]

A wide range of other environmental problems associated with cars, alluded to elsewhere in Jacobs's text, is thus avoided here. Jacobs does qualify the point but deemphasizes it by relegating it to a subordinate clause: "Outside those times and places—particularly urban commuting and interurban motorway travel—there will be no restrictions, *though continuing efforts must be made to improve fuel efficiency and emissions*.[emphasis added].[49] But he has already shown that transport energy use, and thus emissions of CO_2 (and possibly other pollutants) are increasing across the OECD at the same rate as GDP. In other words, the benefits of efficiency gains (which have continued through the 1980s and 1990s despite historically low fuel prices), are recurrently negated by increases in overall distances traveled, in particular, by car. Thus a strategy to reduce overall use would seen crucial to achieving environmental goals (retardation of global warming, in this case), which only under the most wildly optimistic conditions could be met purely by efficiency gains.

Elsewhere in the pamphlet the failure of integrated thought is also apparent. Jacobs asserts (while discussing controversies over GM foods and the need to promote organic foods more effectively) that the DTI has become more a consumer advocate than a protector of industry interests. As evidence he points to the DTI's pressuring car manufacturers to lower car prices.[50] But he does not pick up on the contradiction in New Labour strategy:[51] On the one hand, New Labour claims to be trying in its transport strategy to promote lower car use. On the other hand, it is actively making it easier for people to buy cars.[52] In its transport documents and in John Prescott's speeches in this area, the argument has been that it is possible to have both higher rates of car ownership and lower levels of use. The evidence advanced has usually been a form of comparative statistics—other West European countries have higher rates of ownership with lower levels of use—but this is simplistic, failing to take into account the denser nature of continental cities and towns, which often makes urban car use (even more) irrational than in the UK.

With respect to whether New Labour's economic position is distinct from neoliberalism, Jacobs argues that the Third Way does constitute a position distinct from both neoliberalism and "old" Labour. The core of this distinctiveness, Jacobs believes, is the form of economic interventionism: an industrial policy that focuses not on "picking winners," as in the 1960s, but on the development of labor market skills and a set of infrastructural or regulatory systems designed to promote the "knowledge economy" as the engine of Britain's economic modernization. This is combined with "active labor market" policies (welfare to work, in particular) designed to improve the rate of new job creation and discipline the unemployed into taking those jobs that do exist. For Jacobs, there is no necessary contradiction between this strategy and pursuing environmental goals because a "knowledge economy" and "e-commerce" can deliver high rates of economic growth, employment, and competitive advantage while requiring less energy and material resources throughput.

An alternative explanation for Labour's disappointing environmental performance is that the core economic strategy of New Labour is in fact in basic contradiction to many of the environmental policies Jacobs and others wish to see enacted. Jacobs may have given far too rosy a view of New Labour's interventionism and difference from neoliberalism.[53] Indeed, a major debating point in both political and academic discourse is the degree to which New Labour has successfully fashioned a Third Way, a genuine alternative both to the Keynesian welfare state/social democracy of "old" Labour and to the neoliberalism of the previous Conservative governments. The most prominent popular work arguing that New Labour is in fact neoliberal is Larry Elliott and Dan Atkinson's *The Age of Insecurity*, and the most sophisticated academic account propounding this view is Colin Hay's *The Political Economy of New Labour*.[54] On the other side of the fence, one could point to Anthony

Giddens's *The Third Way* and *The Third Way and Its Critics* or Stephen Driver and Luke Martell's *New Labour*.[55]

Much of the debate seems to turn on interpretations of New Labour's "active labor markets" policies and attempts to devise supply-side measures in labor markets to improve employment rates as well as economic productivity. For Giddens or Driver and Martell, this is taken as evidence of a departure from neoliberalism, which (allegedly) left such elements to individuals and firms. For critics, however, this is in fact interpreted as evidence of a continued neoliberal approach: active investment in education, training, and promotion of labor force skills is in practice fairly minimal, and the "active labor market" policies amount to an intensification of policies already adopted by the Conservatives and reflect a neoliberal approach where the state is disciplining the unemployed into taking more active measures to find and take work.[56] Such policies, of course, now have a green spin in the introduction of "environmental task forces" as one of the options available to the unemployed.[57]

We are persuaded by this more critical view. To regard "active labor market" policies such as welfare-to-work as a departure from neoliberalism is to ignore the way in which neoliberalism is a fusion of authoritarian social conservatism and free market economics. Welfare-to-work policies come as much out of the former as the latter. Driver and Martell for example, focus only on the free market aspect and thus Portray welfare-to-work as a departure, from neoliberalism.

The economic strategy of New Labour can be summarized as follows. First, there is a continuation of basic macroeconomic policies emphasizing fiscal conservatism and aiming for low inflation targets. Public spending was reined in to meet previous targets set by the Conservatives. This is the basic hallmark of neoliberal management and is combined with a second element, a continued commitment to unrestrained global movements of goods and capital. Third, dealing with the new conditions that globalization is held to create is done by promoting flexible labor markets and emphasizing further improvements in labor productivity to provide a skilled workforce for multinational capital. Fourth (and this *is* a minor departure from strict neoliberalism), there is a more developmentalist approach to growth, with the state taking a more active role in promoting particular sectors, notably biotechnology and information technology, summed up as the "knowledge economy."

New Labour's economic strategy thus adds up to an accumulation strategy designed primarily to promote U.K. competitiveness within European and global markets. At the same time, the New Labour project has refashioned the redistributive aims of traditional Labour by stressing that wealth creation is prior and more important than wealth redistribution and the lessening of socioeconomic inequalities. This point is worth noting. Given its experience of eighteen years out of office, and the firm belief that Labour's economic policies were largely to blame for its five electoral defeats, New Labour's determination to reverse this popular sense of economic incompetence ("tax and spend" Labour) is absolutely central to its political project. This explains the painful transition within the Labour party away from an unelectable socialist platform (from disarmament to welfare to economic policy) toward a more electable and "less extreme" set of policies that are beholden to special interests, primarily the trades union movement. This process was begun by Neil Kinnock and Roy Hattersley in the 1980s, continued under John Smith, and completed by Tony Blair. It had at its core a political strategy based on a growing British economy's providing employment, wealth, and opportunity to all.[58] This focus on economic "competence" fitted the "pragmatic" postideological character of New Labour, where government was to be judged by the ends it produced (a growing economy, higher employment rate, effective health care, decent education, reliable and affordable transport system) and not the means chosen (private enterprise, public-private partnerships, Private Finance Initiatives).

Thus the failure to pursue a clear strategy regarding, for example, transport can be more easily understood when set against the backdrop of these general strategic and economic realignments within Labour. The political imperatives of appeasing "Mondeo Man" reflect an accumulation strategy predicated on car-led mobility. Flexible labor markets require flexible laborers, and the flexibility of the car in terms of mobility is key. Those voters dependent on the car thus become key elements in Labour's electoral strategy, and simultaneously key elements in Labour's economic strategy, which requires continued (if not accelerated) throughput and consumption of strategic economic goods, notably cars.[59]

Other examples are more equivocal, however. The failure to pursue renewable energy aggressively seems a key test case of the contradictions between New Labour's neoliberalism and its environmental policies, and of a simple failure to integrate environmental concerns into its modernization agenda. While new technologies in which Britain has a strategic edge have been a key element in New Labour's accumulation strategy, this has focused primarily on biotechnology and information technologies. New energy technologies, in particular solar photovoltaics, in which Britain had (in 1997 at least) a competitive edge and which seemed on the verge of major market breakthroughs, have received very little support, and thus the country has lost major market share in this field. Major producers, notably BP and Shell, have set up production of these technologies outside the United Kingdom.[60] Thus the integration of environmental policies (in this case, the energy side of its climate change policy) into economic strategy has failed dramatically. This is evidence of the way in which the core of New Labour still regards environmental concerns as a constraint rather than an opportunity.

Conclusion

The British state under New Labour management is thus ambivalent regarding the environmental crisis. On the one hand, New Labour wants to make highly positive statements about the environment, as highlighted by John Prescott's transport strategy, attempts to play a leadership role in climate change politics internationally, and the establishment of various environmental policy initiatives, task forces, policy reviews, committees, and reports from "sustainability indicators" to the climate change levy. On the other hand, central elements in New Labour's political and economic strategies undermine attempts to reduce the environmental impact of the British state and society. As Young puts it in his review of the nation's attempts to implement sustainable development, "Where there were conflicts with environmentalists, the neo-pluralist state invariably sided with business".[61]

One particular contradiction is worth spelling out in more detail. Globalization has also been a key element in New Labour's understanding of the structural situation within which the British state must operate, and thus of the ways in which state economic intervention needs to act to stimulate certain forms of behavior by firms and workers.[62] But globalization, or more precisely New Labour's understanding of this complex set of processes, acts as a discourse to shape such state intervention to benefit highly mobile transnational capital. It thus connects closely to Labour's attempt to shape a technology-led pattern of economic growth through the promotion of information technology and biotechnology firms. Both are understood as leading economic growth sectors that provide a means of improving the productivity and competitiveness of the U.K. economy, and specifically of attracting investment from sectors that will then have a high export content, contributing to nation's trade balance. This is a central explanation of the dynamics of policymaking concerning GM agriculture as well as policies promoting renewable energy.

Thus globalization, and specifically the economic imperative that New Labour understands globalization to create, helps to explain the fervor with which most within the Labour government have favored GM technologies and companies like Monsanto. This persist even in the face of public opposition to such technologies, which have caused the companies themselves (notably Monsanto) to modify their commitment to GM technologies.[63] Thus the ecologically modernizing British state under New Labour does not seem to fit the characteristics of Meadowcroft's ecostate (see chapter 1). Perhaps the British state under New Labour serves as an example of the tensions and contradictions faced by welfare states rhetorically attempting to become ecostates within a broadly neoliberal economic policy strategy aligned to a particular discourse and commitment to globalization.

The relation of the state to global environmental management needs to be analyzed in a manner that minimizes abstractions about what the state is, and that focuses on exploring the concrete patterns through which particular states produce and respond to environmental challenges. In this case study of the British state we hope to have shown the utility of adopting a less abstract/theoretical and a more sociological/political economy approach to the study of the state in its particularity and historical context. Such theoretical and ideologically driven debates about the state within green politics have hindered important debates about what the state within the context of the global ecological crisis *does* as opposed to what the state *is* or *should be*. Crucial here are the processes, dynamics, and constraints faced and (self) imposed on particular governments and political parties in power in the development of state economic strategies. In the New Labour case, we hope to have shown the importance of this, by highlighting some of the major ecological implications of the specific forms of U.K. policy interventions and economic strategies since 1997.

Notes

1. Ophuls (1977); Hardin (1966).
2. Barry (1999); Paterson (1996).
3. Hardin (1966).
4. For example, see Oran R. Young (1989); Oran R. Young (1994); Ostrom (1990); and Hass, Keohane, and Levy (1993). For a review, see Paterson (2000a, ch. 2).
5. Carter (1993); see also Bookchin (1980) and Bookchin (1982) for similar arguments.
6. Barry (1999, ch. 4).
7. We do not provide any general background on New Labour's politics in this chapter. For general accounts, see Hay (1999); Driver and Martall (1998); Toynbee and Walker (2001); Stuart White, ed. (2001); Ludlam and Smith, eds. (2000); and Coates and Lawler, eds. (2000).
8. See Hay (1999, ch. 3).
9. For example, see Jacobs (1999b); Jordan (2000); and Toynbee and Walker (2001).
10. As quoted in Jordan (2000, 257).
11. Jordan (2000, 258).
12. Renamed Department for Environment, Food and Rural Affairs in 2001 after the second New Labour electoral victory in May 2001.
13. Jordan (2000, 260–261).
14. Jacobs (1999b, 1).
15. Jordan (2000, 268–269).
16. Jordan (2000, 268).
17. Jordan (2000, 270); Hay (1999, 97).
18. Jordan (2000, 270).
19. In the second week of September 2000 networks of farmers and hauliers protesting against high fuel prices launched a series of pickets of British fuel depots that stopped most distribution of petrol within a few days. This was part of a wave of similar protests across Europe, which had begun in France in early September. For further analysis, see Doherty et al. (2002).
20. Toynbee and Walker (2001, 191).

21. Department for Environment, Food and Rural Affairs (2000).

22. Department for Environment, Food and Rural Affairs (2000).

23. Department for Environment, Food and Rural Affairs (2003).

24. See, for example, Friends of the Earth (2000); Jordan (2001); and Royal Commission on Environmental Pollution (2000).

25. Worldwide Fund for Nature (2001).

26. See also Jordan (2001, 251).

27. Jordan (2000, 272).

28. Polly Toynbee (1999).

29. Jordan (2000, 271–272).

30. The government was, of course, engaged in such pricing policies in its fiscal policy, with the introduction of differential road tax levels dependent on the size of engine. But the "joined-up government" was not evident in relation to these two debates, which were treated separately, and the knock-on ecological consequences of the reductions in car prices, which dwarf the differential increases produced by the changes to the road tax.

31. Department for Environment, Food and Rural Affairs (2000); Paterson (2001); Labour Party (2001); and Policy Innovation Unit (2001).

32. For example, of the 35,000–40,000 people employed in the U.K. biotechnology industry, only 3,000 are in agriculture, ("Parliamentary Answer for Mr Battle to Joan Whalley" 1999). Public opinion has been in support of medical uses of biotechnology even while it has been fiercely opposed to agricultural biotechnology (MORI 1999), and environmental groups have similarly not been hostile to medical uses. See, for example, Friends of the Earth (2001).

33. Compare, for example, the statements by the British Government Panel on Sustainable Development (2000) and the British Medical Association (1999), both of which were highly critical of the Government's Advisory Committee on Novel Foods and Processes.

34. This is reflected in the wildly differing interpretations of the government's position, ranging from the deeply critical, arguing the government is engaged in a conspiracy to force GM crops on an unwilling public (see Monbiot 2000a, ch. 7) to praise for the government's "cool politics in a hothouse of emotions" (Toynbee and Walker 2001, 196).

35. On differing regulatory styles in the EU and the United States over GM foods, see Dunlop (2000).

36. Blair (2000).

37. Labour Party (2001, 10–11).

38. Jacobs (1999b).

39. See, for example, Nuffield Council on Bioethics (1999, 43).

40. Hay (1999); Barry and Paterson (2004).

41. Jacobs (1999b).

42. Hajer (1995); Jacobs (1999b, 45).

43. See, for example, Barry (2003a); Barry (1999, ch. 5); Christoff (1996).

44. Jacobs (1999b, 30–31).

45. See generally Jacobs (1999b, 30–42).

46. Jacobs (1999b, 41).

47. Elliott and Atkinson (1999).

48. The concern with ensuring the electability of New Labour by minimizing those sections of the electorate threatened by its policies cannot be overemphasized. As Blair (2000) admitted in his speech to the Business and Environment conference, "There are at points real conflict between the immediate interests of consumption and the longer term interests of the environment; and to be frank, between the politicians' need to woo the electorate a well as lead them" (3).

49. Jacobs (1999b).

50. Jacobs (1999b, 37).

51. Of course, this is the whole point of the ecological/environmental modernization approach—to overcome or to render noncontradictory the imperatives of capital accumulation, exponential economic growth, and ecological sustainability.

52. We are not, of course, arguing that collusion by car manufacturers to keep prices high is a good thing. But given a choice of targets to attack for dodgy business practices, it seems indicative of the government's priorities that the car industry was chosen (along with, although not quite as ferociously, supermarkets).

53. See Colin Hay (1999).

54. Elliott and Atkinson (1999); Colin Hay (1999).

55. Giddens (1998); Giddens (2000); Driver and Martell (1998).

56. See Anne Gray (1998).

57. Elliott and Atkinson (1999, 138, 233).

58. We should emphasize that we reproduce the standard narrative here not because we believe in the "necessity" of this shift for the Labour Party but simply because this was the internal rationalization of the shift within the party. See Colin Hay (1999) for a detailed account of the internal debate within the party as well as a critique of the "necessity" of the shift. See Monbiot (2000a) for a more polemic critique.

59. A detailed analysis of this is beyond the scope of this chapter. But we would expect that a collation of quantitative data concerning changes in the numbers of households where one adult is traveling long distances to work and is required to be mobile in this fashion, combined with qualitative data on people's perceptions of their "need" to drive, would back this point up.

60. Toynbee (1999); Monbiot (2000b).

61. Stephen Young (2000, 270).

62. Colin Hay (1999); Colin Hay (2001); Colin Hay and Matthew Watson (1998).

63. For more on globalization, ecology, and New Labour, see Barry and Paterson (2004).

4

Green Political Strategy and the State: Combining Political Theory and Comparative History

Christian Hunold and John Dryzek

Universalism in Green Political Theory

All green theorists believe in the universal applicability of basic green values, to which we have no objection. And we doubt that any of them would explicitly deny that green political action—strategic and tactical choices—must respond to the broader political and institutional context. Yet few greens give any detailed account of how exactly strategy and tactics should be shaped by context. Advocacy for universal values outweighs attention to context in most green political theory. Hence green theory's sensitivity to context in principle turns into universalism in practice, thus diminishing the value of green political theory to guide action.

Some contextual variables are more important for greens to consider than others, and any attempt to consider *every* potentially significant contextual variable would be quixotic. But there is much fertile ground between casual concessions to context on the one hand and aimless empiricism on the other, and theory helps identify contextual factors that merit serious attention. The context we have in mind looks to variety across time and place within the contemporary era of environmental challenge to the dominant political economy. Our aim is to combine theoretical analysis with comparative history in order to provide precepts for guiding choices between state-based and non-state-based strategies for green activists.[1] This strategic question has long been one of the main axes of contention in green politics, most noisily in the Realo-Fundi debate in Germany. In this debate, the eventually victorious Realos argued for action through party politics and the institutions of government, whereas the Fundis believed in grassroots organizing, protest, and confrontation. Beyond antistate advocacy, it took green political theory a while to come to grips with the problematic surrounding the state, but this question is now at the center of theoretical debates.

Attention to context means attention to history, so we draw examples from our own comparative histories of environmentalism.[2] We do not have the space here to reproduce our full historical analysis of the interaction between the environmental movement and the state in different countries since 1970. So we outline the relationship between the state and social movements represented by each of the countries we have studied and then discuss what sort of strategy makes the most sense in each context by analyzing examples of environmental activism, focusing on the United States, Norway, and Germany, with occasional mention of the United Kingdom. We argue that sometimes it makes sense to be a statist, sometimes it makes sense to be an antistatist, and sometimes it makes sense to combine orientations within, apart from, and against the state. It all depends on the context.

The context that matters most to environmental movements is what sort of state they are trying to green. All states are alike in that state action is constrained by a number of imperatives, regardless of the specific preferences of the government of the day. However, in their orientation to civil society states differ in ways that have real consequences for the ability of environmentalists to link their aims to state imperatives. On one dimension, states can be inclusive or exclusive. Inclusive states welcome representation from a broad variety of interests, be they social movements, corporations, labor unions, or professional associations. Exclusive states restrict the access of interests, sometimes accepting only those of the state itself (such as administrative bureaucracies), sometimes reaching out only so far as the leadership of business associations or of labor federations. On a second dimension, states can be active or passive in how they organize representation. Combining the two dimensions yields four categories (table 4.1). A passively inclusive state accepts whatever interests civil society generates; the best example is the pluralism of the United States. An actively inclusive state intervenes in civil society to organize social interests and integrate them into government; the best example is Norway. A passively exclusive state provides few avenues for the influence of social interests but otherwise leaves them alone; the best example is Germany, whose traditionally corporatist government and Prussian-style bureaucracy allowed little representation from outside. An actively exclusive state intervenes to

Table 4.1
A Classification of States

	Inclusive	Exclusive
Active	Expansive corporatism: Norway	Authoritarian liberalism: UK 1979–1990 onward
Passive	Pluralism: U.S.	Legal corporatism: Germany

undermine the basis for the organization of social interests. The best examples can be found when governments are committed to market liberalism, such as in the United Kingdom under Margaret Thatcher in the 1980s.

For present purposes, the most important of the core functions shared by all states are accumulation and legitimation, to use the language of post-Marxists such as O'Connor[3] and Offe,[4] though we prefer "economic imperative" to "accumulation."[5] States must encourage economic growth by providing a favorable climate for financial investment and business activity in general, so preventing disinvestment and capital flight. Insofar as political stability depends on public support, states must also secure the political economy's legitimacy.

Environmentalists, we argue, have a much better shot at achieving their goals when they can attach their agenda to the state's economic or legitimation imperatives. Two trends that could in principle apply to all contemporary developed societies suggest how environmentalists might go about doing so: the rise of ecological modernization and the politicization of risk, the details of which we discuss in due course. The fact that these trends apply differentially shows that imperatives do not fully *determine* the content of public policy; their application is discursively mediated. As we show, the discourse of ecological modernization allows attachment of some environmental values to the economic imperative in some states more than others. This discursive mediation does not dissolve the material reality of the imperative in question, which cannot be wished away.

In evaluating the results of and prospects for different strategies, we are interested in more than the content of public policies. Success can also come in terms of environmental outcomes to which policy may or may not contribute, such as changes in business practices or even cultural change. Ultimately we also care about the structural transformation of the political economy in a more sustainable direction.

The first state to accept environmentalism into its core actually did so without the benefit of either ecological modernization or the politicization of risk, so we begin with this pioneer.

When Statism Made the Most Sense: The United States in the 1970s

It made perfect sense for environmentalists to seek and accept the embrace of the state in the United States in the 1970s. The antiwar and civil rights movements had radicalized vocal and significant segments of the population. Politically motivated violence—from race riots to assassinations—exacerbated the sense of crisis. Confronted by a plethora of radical demands, the Nixon administration identified the environmental movement as the least threatening element of the counterculture and environmental degradation as perhaps the least intractable of all the major problems on offer at the time. The movement for its part could move smoothly and immediately into policymaking because the United States is the best example of a *passively inclusive* polity (see Table 4.1). Its relatively open and fragmented character induces activists to organize as interest groups in order to influence public policy through lobbying, fundraising, participating in public hearings, litigation, and the like. The pluralist ethos of U.S. politics promises that government "respond[s] to actions taken by well-organized, politically knowledgeable, and effectively mobilized groups."[6]

Environmentalism in the early 1970s directly challenged the economic imperative by claiming that economic growth was inconsistent with the idea of ecological limits. Thus its embrace by the state is on the face of it puzzling. The movement's neo-Malthusian warning that exponential human economic and population growth would eventually violate the fixed quantity of the world's resources or the capacity of the biosphere to accommodate stress challenged basic economic policy presuppositions. Especially as economic growth showed signs of slowing, the limits discourse failed to make any impression at all on the content of public policy, anywhere.

However, the environmentalism of this era undeniably spawned widespread policy innovation in the United States. At the beginning of the 1970s, the United States created a federal Environmental Protection Agency to control pollution, enacted a National Environmental Policy

Act requiring all government agencies to consider the effects of their plans via the new device of environmental impact assessment, set up a Council on Environmental Quality to advise the president, and passed a host of significant laws such as the Clean Air Act and the Water Pollution Control Act.

The federal government's acceptance of environmentalism indicates not just that environmentalists were welcomed into the state—in a passively inclusive state, that is never a problem. They immediately reached the state's core; economic concerns were no obstacles to adoption of environmental policies. The reason for this success is that environmentalism could be attached to the state's legitimation imperative. For a few years the interests of environmentalists (notably cleaner air and water and wilderness preservation) matched a core need of the state (legitimacy). By embracing what looked like the least radical and least threatening aspect of the counterculture, the Nixon administration, with strong congressional support, sought to rebuild the political economy's legitimacy without acceding to any more radical countercultural demands. Environmentalism did not undermine legitimacy, but other radical movements did threaten the state and liberal democracy.[7] The defining interests of the environmental movement were not the same as any state imperative. However, the fact that legitimation was being undermined by the antiwar, civil rights, and New Left movements meant that a movement that could bolster legitimacy in a different direction could be included to profound and lasting effect. Nixon's 1970 State of the Union address cast the environment as an issue of "common cause" that would move the country "beyond factions." Nixon gained legitimacy in the face of pressure from antiwar and other activists, and split the environmental movement from the New Left.

When Economics Dominates, Statism Makes Little Sense

The conditions that enabled the integration of environmentalist concerns into the core of U.S. public policy vanished with the waning of the legitimation crisis associated with the counterculture and the onset of the energy crisis with the OPEC oil embargo in late 1973. The economic imperative and its associated need for security of energy supply now greatly weakened the bargaining position of environmental interest groups. A foretaste came with the immediate exemption of the

Trans-Alaska Pipeline from environmental impact assessment requirements by a vote of Congress. George W. Bush's 2001 withdrawal from the
Kyoto Protocol on greenhouse gas emissions is simply the latest in a long
line of energy-related occasions when environmentalists encountered the
economic imperative and lost. This record leads us—but not the major
included groups—to question the wisdom of following a statist strategy
when the deck is stacked against effective results due to unremitting conflict with the state's core economic imperative. Eventually radical wilderness defense groups such as Earth First! and the environmental justice
movement that arose in the late 1980s and 1990s did question the wisdom of an insider strategy. In a passively inclusive polity, these movements arose largely in response to a kind of passive *exclusion* practiced by
the established major groups in association with government; local
activists *felt* excluded and so engaged in alternative forms of action. It
takes great determination to retain this critical distance in the face of the
pull of passive inclusion, and indeed aspects of the environmental justice
movement were absorbed into government in the 1990s.[8]

While we cannot prove that economics dominates environmentalism
by examining every conflict over three decades, we can take a brief look
at the high point of inclusion and access in the early Clinton years to illustrate our case, for if an insider strategy fails at this time, it surely fails
at any time.[9] The first two Clinton years are instructive because the
Democrats also controlled Congress. These years featured more high-
level access for environmentalists in the executive branch than ever
before. But the result was a catalog of disappointments on every major
environmental issue, from fuel economy standards and energy taxes to
the failure to reform public lands management.

The United States was exceptional in the speed and extent of its embrace
of environmentalism in the early 1970s because it alone faced a truly profound legitimation crisis. After the energy crisis in late 1973 the United
States ceased to be exceptional; in common with other states, it gave priority to economics over environment, emphasizing nuclear power and exploration for new sources of oil and gas. The Carter administration's brief
flirtation with conservation soon gave way to an emphasis on synthetic
fuels and other expensive and heavily polluting energy supply technologies.

In Norway the dominance of economics amid energy insecurity
confirmed the position of the "hydropower complex" at the heart of

policymaking, despite the incorporation of environmental organizations into the Norwegian state in the early 1970s. Norway briefly toyed with a nuclear program, but a country with such wealth in hydropower and oil did not need it. Large-scale protests combined with legal and lobbying action and the opposition of the Environment Ministry failed to prevent the construction of a large dam at Alta authorized in 1980; the Environment Ministry was simply excluded from the state's core. Later, energy in Norway meant offshore oil, and environmentalists were unsuccessful in keeping oil exploration out of fragile Northern waters.

In Germany energy insecurity led to an "environmental moratorium" and wholesale commitment to nuclear power, despite a social movement mobilized against it. Set on this course, the German state in the 1970s and early 1980s refused any point of access to the environmental movement.

Organized environmentalism had made few inroads in Britain in the 1970s, and a weakly incorporated movement was powerless to prevent the expansion of nuclear power. Energy crisis was just one more reason to exclude environmentalists from the core of the state. Legalistic public inquiries into proposed nuclear developments were a more subtle governmental response than Germany's exclusions, but these inquiries were a sham designed to head off opposition, their pronuclear recommendations a foregone conclusion.[10] Economic concerns are of course broader than energy supply, and all four countries saw other ways in which economics overrode environmental concerns.[11]

Economics dominates the political agenda of all countries most of the time, so when does it ever make sense for environmentalists to seek to gain access to the core of the state? And why would the state let them in? With the passing of the groundbreaking U.S. role in environmental policy enabled by a link between legitimation and environmentalism that temporarily overrode economics, more promising developments have begun in states with very different sorts of orientations to social movements. We turn now to the character of these developments, which while seemingly of universal validity are in practice available on very different terms in different kinds of states.

Norway: Actively Inclusive Statism and Weak Ecological Modernization

The widespread impression that Norway's environmental policy record is one of the best in Europe and the world is in many ways justified.[12] The failure of the U.S. President's Commission on Sustainable Development to have any impact at all on policy can be contrasted with Norway's systematic embrace of sustainable development since the mid-1980s. The basic idea of sustainable development is that economic growth can be redesigned to respect ecological parameters (as well as principles of intergenerational justice). Perhaps it is not surprising that the idea should flourish in the home of former Prime Minister Brundtland. However, this begs the question of why economics was no obstacle in Norway while it has proven insurmountable in the United States.

Norway has since 1991 pioneered a regime of green taxes upon environmentally damaging activities, including a carbon tax on fossil fuel combustion (business opposition to green taxes remains and has managed to secure some exemptions,[13] but this resistance has largely been overcome). The "hydropower complex" no longer defines part of the core of the state that is off limits to environmentalists, and no controversial large dams have been built since Alta in the early 1980s. Norway protects wild areas, and pollution is comparatively low (though a small population in a large land area helps). Environmentalists now sit on key policymaking committees in many government agencies, not just via the Environment Ministry (to which their German counterparts are restricted). It is these committees that really make public policy in this "country of a thousand committees."[14] Thus interest group engagement dominates environmental politics, but very differently and to more obvious and direct policy effect than in the United States.

With few exceptions, in Norway we see cooperative relationships between business, environmentalists, science, and government. Should we cast Norway as the poster child of environmental statism because all the key actors have embraced it and appear to be happy with its undeniable policy successes? Before rushing to universalize the Norwegian experience, we ought to step back and examine the reasons for its success. There are essentially two reasons: the character of the Norwegian state, and its embrace of a discourse of ecological modernization. The second can be universalized, the first cannot.

Norway is an *actively inclusive* state (see table 4.1). It is corporatist in the way it organizes interests into the state, but unlike other corporatist countries welcomes and indeed fosters many interests beyond business and labor. Groups receive funding (operating and project grants) and organizational support from the Ministry of Environment and other departments, as well as seats on key policymaking committees. In return, groups agree to help implement government policy. This "organizational society"[15] therefore involves tight integration of interest groups into the state, which is very different from the looser and more competitive arrangements of the United States.

Active inclusion by itself does not, however, overcome the problem of conflict between economic and environmental concerns, which requires in addition acceptance of ecological modernization by government and key interests. Ecological modernization puts economics and environment in a positive sum relationship—"pollution prevention pays" is a popular slogan. The idea is that environmental criteria such as sustainability and the precautionary principle can make capitalist production more efficient and consequently profitable. Lower pollution indicates more efficient materials use. It is cheaper to redesign technologies to produce less pollution than to clean up pollution after the fact. Moreover, a clean and healthy environment means happy and productive workers. In this basic or "weak" form[16] ecological modernization leaves the structure of the liberal capitalist political economy intact. Aside from Norway, ecological modernization has found a voice in several other West European countries. It attracts many environmentalists because it requires environmental conservation to be taken seriously even while economics remains the first concern of governments. Environmentalists in actively inclusive Norway are particularly well positioned to join ecological modernization, helping to initiate and control programs in tight association with industry and government. In so doing, they have attached their interests to the state's core—via the economic imperative—more securely than at any time and place since the United States around 1970.

There is, however, a downside to this success. Norway's policy committees operate mostly in secret. There is little interchange between group representatives and ordinary members, the latter having even less influence in Norway than in the United States. Secure in their government funding, environmental groups do not need a large membership. The Norwegian Society for the Conservation of Nature is the largest and most important group, with 28,000 members. Its counterparts in Sweden (which has about double the population) and Denmark (with about the same population) exceed 200,000 members.[17] This lack of grassroots influence on policy is exacerbated by the persistent absence of radical activism outside the mainstream groups, in stark contrast to the other three countries we are considering. Such activism has been dormant since (unsuccessful) antidam protests at Mardøla (1970) and Alta (1980).

The 1990s saw surges of activism in the UK antiroads movement and the U.S. environmental justice movement. In contrast, Norway in the 1990s saw the establishment of the Environmental Home Guard, which has no members, only "participants" who pledge to behave in ways that support sustainable development. The only hint of unorthodoxy exists with the Bellona Foundation, which has staged Greenpeace-style actions. But Bellona is a kind of "protest business," with no grassroots, that also does consultancy for businesses. A small and marginal green party (despite proportional representation, which elsewhere allows green parties to flourish) reflects perhaps the unimportance ascribed by environmentalists to parliament.

Does it matter that Norway's environmental movement is lacking in numbers, radicalism, activism, and autonomy? This lack, secured by the actively inclusive state structure, guarantees that ecological modernization remains moderate and centrally coordinated, with no room for critique of the underlying makeup of the (heavily oil-dependent) political economy. But if a truly green state requires more than the thin sort of democracy that exists in Norway, then the insubstantial green public sphere and the lack of grassroots influence on policymaking (indeed, the lack of grassroots) look more troubling.

Radicalizing Ecological Modernization in the Risk Society

Ecological modernization in a stronger form would involve more fundamental transformation of the political economy.[18] Structural change would be on the agenda, rather than reliance on the technological fix. So, for example, rather than promoting lower-polluting and more efficient car engines, public policy would address the issue of why private cars are such a large part of the transportation mix, and why cities are constructed with such large distances between homes and workplaces. This strong form has so far had little influence in policymaking anywhere, although it has made some progress in Germany. We argue that its prospects are minimal in the absence (as in Norway) of a critical green public sphere raising fundamental questions and prompting more discursive and democratic negotiation of the transition to an ecological modernity. This line of reasoning suggests that if one wants a more truly green state, one needs a lively and oppositional green public sphere.

Such a critical oppositional sphere is in turn facilitated by the degree to which a polity experiences a risk-related legitimation crisis. In Ulrich Beck's "risk society" scenario, politics becomes increasingly dominated by conflicts over the generation, distribution, and amelioration of risks concerning nuclear power, genetically modified organisms, food safety, toxic chemicals, and the like. This new politics ushers in a "reflexive modernity" in which postindustrial society faces the unintended consequences of its industrial legacy. Reflexive modernization involves "subpolitics" where nongovernmental actors (including social movements) solve social problems in innovative ways without relying on the administrative state. Subpolitics occurs when environmentalists organize boycotts and protests against corporations and when they negotiate with corporations to make corporate activities or products less destructive. In the terms we have established, risk society heralds crisis in the state's legitimation of the political economy. Just as in the very different sort of legitimation crisis that the United States faced in the early 1970s, an opportunity opens for environmentalists to connect their interests to the state's legitimation imperative. Of course, this connection now applies only to those aspects of their interest that involve risks, especially the risks of pollution and poisoning. This scenario does not play out equally everywhere; notably, the risk society thesis seems to be irrelevant to Norway. However, it does resonate with political developments in the other three countries we are considering.

Does this legitimation crisis therefore enable more effective environmentalist action within the state? Beck himself is hard to pin down in these terms. On the one hand, he speaks approvingly of the Greens' entry into government and their subsequent ability to help make public policy.[19] On the other hand, Beck resists the idea that subpolitics is to be taken seriously only if and when disparate risk issues being articulated in the public sphere can be bundled into a cohesive policy package by the state.[20] Despite its lack of cohesion and authoritativeness, subpolitics possesses a rationality of its own. For Beck, therefore, ecological democracy requires a public sphere as well as state institutions, although the critique of expert reasoning always starts to unfold in the public sphere. Beck casts the theory of the risk society in universalist terms: "How does modern society deal with self-generated manufactured uncertainties?"[21] Yet he also recognizes that different societies construct risks differently and thus calls for comparative analysis to develop the implications[22] without actually doing any himself.

Weak ecological modernization can do quite well with conventional state-based politics and more moderate interest group action, as we have seen for Norway. Strong ecological modernization entails a more radical and discursive subpolitics of the sort Beck postulates. We now examine Germany with such prospects in mind.

Germany: Antistatism, Stronger Ecological Modernization, and Subpolitics

Germany has a different kind of state than Norway. Though it is corporatist like Norway,[23] its orientation toward new social movements has been *passively exclusive* (see table 4.1). In what might be termed Hegel's victory over Kant, the German state has favored abstract legal norms over liberal rights and has provided few opportunities for public participation along the lines in Norway. In this system of legal corporatism certain long-standing interest groups (business, labor, health, social services) are effectively public bodies and cooperate closely with government in making and implementing policy. But any new groups seeking that status faced a secretive bureaucracy suspicious of outsiders. This was clearly true of the new social movements of the 1970s, including environmentalism. Even organizations that predate the protest era have received only restricted access, when they could offer expertise useful to government agencies. Access to the bureaucracy expanded with the establishment of the federal Environment Ministry in 1986. However, given its marginal involvement in core policymaking,[24] this ministry has performed a cooptive function.

The antistatism of Germany's new social movements arose against this backdrop of passive exclusion. Their lack of access to the state forced movement groups to become and remain *movement* groups much more than was true for their U.S. and Norwegian counterparts. The groups and parties formed in the 1970s—Federation of Citizens' Initiatives for

Environmental Protection (BBU), *Die Grünen*, German Federation of Environmental and Nature Protection (BUND)—coalesced around resistance to nuclear power, though this was not the only issue of the day. The peace movement was just as significant, with overlapping membership in environmental and peace organizations being the rule rather than the exception. At the zenith of social movement activity, in 1983, environmental, peace, and women's groups logged some 9,200 separate protests nationwide.[25] The state was closed; neither parliament nor the executive was eager to engage in a nuclear debate, and all the major political parties supported nuclear power.[26]

Though environmentalists had no direct access to policymakers, they were not without influence. Following the cancellation of several high-profile nuclear energy projects in the late 1970s and early 1980s, the main parties gradually embraced green policies, including antipollution programs, both to limit the electoral prospects of the Greens and to curtail protest. This response indicates a risk-related legitimation crisis of the political economy. On the economic front, ecological modernization started to influence policy in the 1980s, when environmentalists remained excluded from government.

Tougher regulations have since significantly ameliorated the worst forms of pollution.[27] And nuclear energy—once the cause célèbre of environmental mobilization—is due to be phased out, albeit less quickly than many activists have demanded.[28] This decision would have been unthinkable without the antinuclear movement's influence on social values. It is as true of Germany as anywhere that inclusion means moderation,[29] and so deradicalization of the Greens. The former "anti" party has both changed parliament and been changed by its norms and values, disappointing Fundis[30] and satisfying Realos.[31] The difference is that gradual inclusion in the wake of passive exclusion has only partially pulled the rug out from under the more radical wings of the movement.

Passive exclusion in Germany diminished as environmental groups embracing ecological modernization gradually made their way into the state. However, radicals such as the BBU still shun the state, and passive exclusion remains the norm in some areas. Thus the antinuclear movement could still mobilize large numbers of activists in a separate public sphere in the late 1990s. Well-organized protests against shipments of reprocessed nuclear wastes headed for "temporary" storage in Germany took place even after the negotiated nuclear power phaseout. In that bargain, the Green party consented to future shipments. However, moderate as well as radical environmental groups rejected the Green party's compromise, joining nonviolent protests against the shipments in 2001.[32]

The German antinuclear movement is less comprehensive than the oppositional green public sphere of the 1970s and 1980s[33] but remains more significant than in the United States, Norway, and Britain. Less unremittingly confrontational than before, it has developed a range of strategies. One legacy of passive exclusion is the existence of independent policy institutes. For example, the Institute for Applied Ecology, founded in 1977, carries out research in support of court cases. Thus subpolitics now involves research institutes (including those without movement origins) as well as movement groups, joined by a growing number of for-profit consultancies from which government departments and firms can seek information and advice.

Oppositional public spheres flourish most easily in the presence of a passively exclusive state whose imperatives bear no similarity to movement interests. When imperatives and interests move into accommodation, as with ecological modernization and the rising importance of risk issues, and as passive exclusion eases, then the oppositional sphere can wither. Activists can pursue insider strategies without necessarily being coopted and frustrated. However, entrenched legal corporatism in Germany means that exclusion has only been lifted partially and unevenly. Thus, especially in the antinuclear area, we find a persistent oppositional public sphere. Skeptics might still argue that contemporary trends in Germany show only that activists have to wait a bit longer before being included than in more inclusive states. But even if the skeptics are right, the terms of that inclusion are significantly different.

Statism in Perspective

We have argued that ecological modernization means that for the first time environmental interests can be attached to the core economic imperative of states, while risk issues enable renewal of the association with the legitimation imperative previously seen in the United State around 1970. Conceivably, these two connections might eventually render conservation an additional imperative, creating a green state with the environment as part of its core business. However, ecological modernization and risk-associated legitimation crises are not present in all states equally. And different kinds of states convert these two developments into quite different sorts of opportunities, to which green political theorists ought to be sensitive.

There really is an important difference here between Germany, on the one hand, and the United State and Norway, on the other. Consider the historical point of departure of each of the movements we have analyzed. In the United State, the environmental movement did not have to wait long for the state's offer of inclusion on terms that promised—and delivered—some significant legislative achievements. But the movement's mixed record since the mid-1970s shows that it paid a price for not having had a chance to develop a large and lively oppositional public sphere within which to hone the arguments and critical skills of its members. However, it was very hard for environmentalists to resist the continued pull of passive inclusion, and it took great effort on the part of a new generation of activists in the late 1980s and 1990s to secure limited resistance to this pull.

Our analysis of Germany demonstrates that a passively exclusive state is, ironically, more hospitable to the emergence and maintenance of an autonomous green sphere than are its more inclusive counterparts. Comparative analysis reveals that the character of state-society relations changes the configuration of perils and promises associated with inclusion. Even if activists are headed ultimately for inclusion in the state, it makes a great deal of difference whether they are incorporated as reflexively aware former activists (Germany) or as professionals schooled in moderate bureaucratic organizations (Norway and the United States). Green politicians and activists in Germany remain conscious of the degree to which their successes rely on continued mobilization in civil society.[34] The situation is very different in the United States, where leaders of the major groups have a top-down perspective that disparages radical alternatives, as many environmental justice activists have pointed out.

Though we have said less about Britain here, the active exclusion experienced in the Thatcher era (see table 4.1) had more serious consequences for environmental movement strategy than the milder passive version practiced across the North Sea in Germany. In Britain after 1988, as active exclusion began to soften, relieved environmentalists readily agreed to rejoin consultations with government, around sustainable development in particular. However, mainstream groups were overwhelmed by this turn of events as, in the words of one interviewee, they were "barnacle-encrusted" rather than "muscle-bound" with these new obligations. This paralysis was partially relieved by the arrival of an antiroads movement in the early 1990s, interpreted by Doherty[35] as the belated arrival of new social movements in Britain, and later by the emergence of a green public sphere focused on issues of food safety. The experience of the United Kingdom suggests that the worst legacy of an era of active exclusion may be in just how easily the mainstream groups were then mollified. Germany is very different because the legacy of passive exclusion is strongly critical.

This sort of critical democratic legacy may turn out to be even more important in the long run. The significance of the state structure is likely to decline as the role of nation-states is undermined by regional movements demanding greater cultural and political autonomy, and by economic globalization and political integration. We can say little more about these trends here than to suggest that they are likely to require greater reflexivity and flexibility on the part of movement groups. As movements reevaluate their strategies vis-à-vis states whose power to shape policy appears to be in decline, subpolitics may come to rival classic processes of state-oriented policymaking. Movements rooted in vital green public spheres may well be better prepared to defend their defining interest in these new arenas beyond the state.

We can now summarize the lessons we have drawn from comparative analysis of the four countries for the possibility and desirability of environmental action in association with the state.

In the United States conventional interest group action within the state made perfect sense in the early 1970s. After that, the rewards of such action became meager. However, this did not lead the major groups to change their strategy; either they did not realize what had happened, or they could not resist the incentives of passive inclusion. For such an insider strategy to make sense once again, ecological modernization must get on the U.S. policy agenda. But ecological modernization has made no headway in U.S. policy discourse, still dominated by conflicts between economy and environment. This standoff has been confirmed by the policies of the George W. Bush administration and its supporters in Congress.

However, conceptualization of a fundamental conflict between economy and environment applies as much to leaders of environmental groups as it does to conservative antienvironmentalists.[36] Public land management is still seen as a fight between wilderness defenders and resource users (loggers, miners, and ranchers). The antitoxics movement has, as Lois Gibbs puts it, "plugged the toilet" by making it hard for new waste disposal sites to open. But this success has failed to induce industry to devise efficient ways to produce goods while generating less toxic waste. The contemporary U.S. environmental policy paradox is that the public sphere necessary to convert weak into strong ecological modernization did eventually come into existence in the environmental justice and antitoxics movements. What is missing is weak ecological modernization to begin with.[37]

Norway illustrates both the accomplishments and limits of a thoroughly statist environmentalism. Environmentalists have long been included in the core of the state, and weak ecological modernization is entrenched there more than anywhere else. However, what we currently see in Norway is probably as good as it gets. In the absence of any signs of a critical green public sphere, nothing stronger can be envisaged. To develop such a sphere of the sort required for stronger ecological modernization and associated subpolitics in Norway would require truly heroic efforts by activists.

Germany is where the prospects for linking the environmental movement's defining interests to core state imperatives are now strongest. The legal corporatist state long shunned environmentalists and provided few points of access but otherwise left them free to organize in civil society as they saw fit. The vibrant green public sphere that resulted from the movement's exclusion, often quite successful in influencing public policy and collective outcomes, also provided environmentalists with the necessary backbone to push for a greener state once the state's passively exclusive stance began to soften in the late 1980s. (The comparative inability of environmentalists to take advantage of a parallel erosion of active exclusion in Britain indirectly supports our claim concerning the unintended virtue of passive exclusion.) A dual insider/outsider strategy then came to make sense. Along with the decentralized subpolitics that accompanies risk issues, Germany features a stronger form of ecological modernization than other states. The implication is that an interesting range of strategies with, against, and aside from the state is now available.

The United Kingdom, a more complex case that we have treated briefly, long illustrated the futility of conventional interest group action in the context of an unresponsive and indeed hostile state that tried to undermine the ability of environmentalists and others to organize and articulate their demands. Unlike Germany, no oppositional sphere emerged until (paradoxically) that state became more responsive in the 1990s. As it slowly shakes off the legacies of active exclusion, a more interesting mix of strategic possibilities for environmentalism opens. Ecological modernization was long resisted in Britain, where government insisted on scientific proof of a hazard before acting, the opposite of the precautionary principle. But even in Britain, ecological modernization began to make inroads around 2000. The Department of Trade and Industry embraced photovoltaic energy. The Royal Commission on Environmental Pollution recommended discursive and democratic reconfiguration of pollution control (with little response to date from government). And in 2001 a climate change levy on fossil fuels used by industry and government was introduced (see chapter 3 in this volume).

Combining Political Theory and Comparative History

Environmentalism and environmental political theory are both quite youthful enterprises. Environmentalism only began under that name in the late 1960s. The relevant political theory that began to emerge in the 1970s was crude and Hobbesian, the main exception being Bookchin's ecoanarchism.[38] It took some time to go beyond these limited beginnings. Youth is actually a good excuse for inattention to history. For if environmental concerns provide an entirely novel challenge to industrial society and industrialism, and if government and politics have never previously tried to respond to that challenge, then the main task is clearly to think imaginatively about how the political world could be different.

But now we have a history of three-and-a-half decades of environmental concern and political response. Moreover, there is not just one history, there are many histories, as environmental challenges have been met (or ignored or scorned) in very different ways in different societies and polities. Here we include polities other than the state, covering regional political structures such as the European Union, local governments, international regimes and networks, and global institutions. Thus there is plenty of grist for assessment of how different sorts of theoretical positions might play out in different situations.

Of course, many green proposals have not received a trial anywhere, and this becomes increasingly true with the radicalism of the proposal. So again, radicals have more reason than moderates—statist moderates in particular—for insensitivity to contextual variation in their models. But often there are relevant experiences that can be drawn upon. For example, bioregionalism at one level proposes wholesale political reorganization and transformed consciousness—about as radical a green program as can be imagined. But at another level bioregional authorities already exist in the form of river basin commissions and the like, some of which consciously engage in ecosystem management.[39] Of course, such bodies have to coexist with more established forms of political authority, and generally they have not been able to benefit from much in the way of ecocentric consciousness on the part of the relevant human populations. Yet we can still draw lessons from their experiences. We might ask, for example, whether small doses of bioregionalism are actually counterproductive in the presence of (say) a conventional administrative state, or whether on the other hand they actually erode some of the ecologically questionable aspects of that state. We could also investigate whether the presence of bioregional authorities itself promotes or impedes the development of ecosystemic awareness on the part of key political actors and a broader public. In comparative terms, we might ask whether such innovations have prospered more or less when a state adopts ecological modernization as policy, or whether inclusive states are good or bad for bioregional development. For example, it might be the case that if a state is relatively exclusive in its orientation to social movements, those movements might instead focus their energies on novel alternative political structures such as river basin commissions, to the benefit of the latter.

The dynamics of history can also be instructive. In the United States at the federal level, a mostly unchanging structure of government is overlaid by substantial shifts in the way legitimation and economic concerns open up or close off opportunities. As we have seen, particular political circumstances in the United States can make environmental action of the conventional interest group variety sometimes very productive, sometimes futile. A very different dynamic is observable in Germany, where a political history of passive exclusion produces a dynamic green public sphere

that in turn enables a relatively strong version of ecological modernization to be pursued once the state becomes somewhat more inclusive,
beginning in the late 1980s. Again, this finding is historically contingent.
This relatively strong version of ecological modernization might wane if
and when the country's green public sphere becomes less of a force for
policymakers to contend with.

These sorts of experiences provide plenty of useful material for the the-
orist. Here we are not referring to just horror stories about particularly
disastrous governments or international organizations, or fables about
how green some particular innovation or place really is. Instead, what we
advocate is systematic comparative history, which can explode the stylized facts that political theorists of all sorts (not just greens) often trade
in. This is hard work: but as Max Weber once pointed out, politics is
often about the slow boring of hard boards.

This is not to say comparative history should replace political theory.
That would be both very constraining and very conservative, for how
then could anything different be imagined? What we recommend is a productive dialogue between comparative history and political theory, to the
benefit of both. In this dialogue, political theory provides the imagination
and inspiration, and guides us to the salient points in history, highlighting
negative and positive experiences. Comparative history for its part is
much more than a reality check on idealistic proposals: it is also a source
of ideas and insights about real possibilities for green change.

Notes

This chapter reproduces some material first published in Hunold and Dryzek,
"Green Political Theory and the State: Context Is Everything," *Global
Environmental Politics* 2 (August 2002): 17–39.

1. For a detailed account and critique of the universalistic tendency in green political theory, see Hunold and Dryzek (2002).

2. Developed at greater length in Dryzek, Downes et al. (2003).

3. O'Connor (1973).

4. Offe (1984).

5. These two imperatives do not exhaust the state's core. In addition, states must
secure domestic order, obtain security in the international system of states, and
raise revenues to finance these other imperatives.

6. Camacho, ed. (1998, 216).

7. Crozier, Huntington, and Watanuki (1975).

8. See Schlosberg (1999).

9. For more details, see Dryzek, Hunold et al. (2002).

10. Wynne (1982).

11. For examples, see Hunold and Dryzek (2002).

12. Sverdrup (1997).

13. See Kasa (2000).

14. Klausen and Opedal (1998).

15. Selle and Strømsnes (1998, 5).

16. Designated by Christoff (1996) and defended by Mol, (1996).

17. Selle and Strømsnes (1998).

18. Peter Christoff; see chapter 2 of this volume.

19. Beck, *World Risk Society* (Cambridge: Polity, 1999), 34, 42.

20. Beck (1999, 42).

21. Beck (1999, 31).

22. Beck (1999, 3).

23. Lehmbruch and Schmittter, eds. (1982); Offe (1980).

24. Pehle (1998); Weinzierl (1993).

25. Balistier, (1996).

26. Kitschelt (1986, 70).

27. Jänicke and Weidner (1997).

28. Hunold (2001).

29. Tarrow (1994).

30. Tiefenbach (1998).

31. Offe (1998); Raschke (1993).

32. For details, see Hunold (2001).

33. See Rucht and Roose (1999).

34. See Dryzek, Dounes et al. (2003, ch. 7).

35. Doherty (1999, 276).

36. For rare exceptions, see Gore (1992); Hawken, Lovins, and Lovius (1999).

37. Schlosberg and Dryzek (2002).

38. Bookchin (1982).

39. Kai N. Lee (1993).

5

Environmental and Ecological Justice: Theory and Practice in the United States

David Schlosberg

While much work has been done in the past few years on the definition of environmental justice, this work has focused exclusively on theories of distributional justice and on applying that framework of justice to nature, particularly with a goal of ecological sustainability in mind.[1] My concern, however, is that conceptions of justice can be understood much more broadly than they are in this environmental context. Recent discussions of social justice have pushed beyond the distributive paradigm into questions of recognition, difference, and political participation.[2] These conceptions have not yet made it into the discussions of justice within environmental political theory, nor have they been central to theorizing about democratic designs and the potential of greener states.

In examining the "justice" of the environmental justice movement in the United States, I have found claims for justice to be about more than just distribution of environmental goods and bads.[3] The issue of distribution is always present and always key, but issues of cultural recognition and political participation are crucial components of movements' definitions of environmental justice and are often tied to distributive issues. In particular, the environmental justice movement has been consistently pushing for state agencies, decision-making processes, and administrative procedures to be more open to the cultural recognition of excluded groups and expanded democratic participation more generally. A thorough notion of environmental justice would both reflect the theoretical discussions on expanding the definition of social justice and take note of a similar discourse in the movement. The argument for defining environmental justice in a tripartite manner—in both theory and practice—comes from a theoretical perspective but also from demands made by environmental social movements.

We can also apply this framework to ecological justice. The theoretical approach to environmental justice has really been dichotomous: justice in terms of the conditions and experiences of those communities exposed to environmental risks, and justice to nature (ecological justice). In the latter sense, it is not enough to talk of the distribution of environmental goods and bads now and in the future. The framework around maldistribution must be examined, and issues of the recognition and participation of future human generations as well as the natural world must be addressed as part of a larger definition and practice of ecological justice. One of my central claims is that the same language of social justice can be applied to both environmental arenas. The discursive shift in identifying issues of recognition and participation as issues of justice might be a way of bringing together the human-based and nature-focused emphases for environmental and ecological justice.

This shift in the understanding of justice complicates green movements' demands on the state. Justice is never only a theoretical enterprise. There are crucial institutional implications to expanding the notion of environmental justice, and this chapter explores specific democratic and institutional transformations (developed by both green movements and green theorists) necessary for implementing a broad notion of environmental justice. My key claim is that environmental justice can only be addressed with state attention to all three components of justice: the distribution of environmental goods and bads, cultural recognition of traditionally excluded groups (including nature itself), and democratic procedures that expand both the participation and the scope of environmental decision making. One important lesson, however, is that it takes an active and critical movement to examine, critique, and push the administrative state's response to environmental injustice in the United States.

The Recent History of Social Justice

Justice, in the realm of contemporary political theory, has been almost exclusively concerned with the question of the equity of the distribution of social rights and goods. Rawls's classic *A Theory of Justice*, for example, defines justice as "a standard whereby the distributive aspects of the basic structure of society are to be assessed." Brian Barry differentiates issues of justice from those of right and wrong along these lines—justice is referred to only in cases where some distributive consideration comes into play. Theories of justice focus on the schemes and processes of a just distribution, the structure and rules guiding just institutions (impartial vs. substantive, or procedural vs. consequentialist), what is to be distributed (goods, rights), and what the principles governing those proposed distributions should be (needs, desert, or entitlement, for example).[4]

But as Iris Young has argued, "While distributional issues are crucial to a satisfactory conclusion of justice, it is a mistake to reduce social justice to distribution."[5] In moving toward justice, issues of distribution are essential but incomplete. Young asks not only what distribution looks like but also—crucially—what *determines* poor distributions. Distributional injustice, she argues, comes directly out of social structures, cultural beliefs, and institutional contexts. The central question regarding distributional justice is not, in the first instance, What is the best model for distribution? but How is the current maldistribution produced? If distributional differences are constituted in part by social, cultural, economic, and political processes, any examination of justice needs to include discussions of the structures, practices, rules, norms, language, and symbols that mediate social relations.[6] This does not mean that we ignore distributional issues, but rather we include them in a broader understanding of justice. Similarly, Fraser's project in *Justice Interruptus* (1997) is to demonstrate that justice requires attention to *both* distribution and recognition.

Central to these authors is the root of unjust distributions: the elimination of institutionalized domination and oppression. Recognition, then, along with inclusion in the political process, becomes the key to relieving both social oppression and distributional inequity.[7] And as Young certainly explores, such an expansion of the understanding of justice requires more than simply revised distribution patterns.

Gould agrees that justice entails recognition and, like Young, links such recognition to political participation. She argues that "taking differences seriously in public life requires . . . a radical increase in opportunities for participation."[8] All these theorists note the direct link between a lack of respect and recognition and a decline in a person's membership and participation in the greater community, including the political and institutional order. In focusing on the elimination of institutionalized domination and oppression, Young argues that justice must focus on the political process as a way to address a variety of injustices. Democratic decision-making procedures are thus both an element of, and a condition for, social justice.[9]

A tripartite notion of justice, then, vastly expands the potential role of the state, or at least the use of participatory mechanisms. But oppression generally, and recognition more specifically, requires a broader focus. One of Young's criticisms of theories of distributive justice is that they take all goods as static rather than as the outcomes or functions of social relations and institutional processes. Distributive problems happen for a reason—some institutional, others cultural, social, or symbolic—and those reasons, practices, and norms must themselves be addressed. Additionally, recognition is not really a good; it is a relationship, a social norm, embedded in social practice. Distribution focuses on the state as a neutral arbiter, but a state cannot allocate or simply distribute recognition as it could other goods. This is not to say that states do not have a role in the politics of recognition; they can provide constitutional recognition of national minorities or legislative action—affirmative action laws, language rights, exemptions from certain laws for cultural or religious groups—aimed at redressing lack of recognition.[10] A state can also attempt to allocate participatory opportunities, which may assist in overcoming issues related to maldistribution. So, state institutions can become examples of the recognition of difference in the political realm and validate that difference in the social realm. But states cannot distribute recognition in the cultural and social arenas, where recognition is also demanded by social movements and actors.

Importantly, the development of concerns beyond distribution in justice theory has been heavily influenced by the discourse and practice of social movements in the past few decades. Calls for the recognition of group differences have at times eclipsed claims for social and economic equity, yet the two demands more often exist simultaneously in the same movement. U.S. civil rights activists in the 1960s often marched while holding a sign proclaiming "I Am a Man"—certainly a call for more than education or voting rights. Recognition was seen as an underlying and central demand of justice (and beyond a focus just on the state, into the social realm). It may seem to some theorists improper to shift the focus away from the traditional territory of distributive justice toward the post-material demands of new social movements around race, gender, and sexuality, as young and others do. But this shift arises not only from the limits of the theoretical focus on the distributional paradigm but also simply in response to the empirical reality of the demands of these movements.[11] Environmental justice, in practice, exemplifies this shift.

For a movement that has the term *justice* in its name, it is rather odd that there has not been a thorough exploration of the term in the literature of the movement. Still, in a variety of collections on the topic, mentions of equity (in the distribution of environmental ills), recognition (with a focus on cultural and racial recognition), and participation (particularly authentic, as opposed to inauthentic or token, inclusion) are numerous and ever-present.[12]

Obviously, the environmental justice movement in the United States focuses on justice as an issue of distributional inequity. Studies that demonstrated such inequity spurred the movement.[13] But also central to environmental justice struggles is an engagement of issues of individual and cultural meaning and identity. Individuals and communities insist on recognition as an integral part of their political demands. Struggles for environmental justice "are embedded in the larger struggle against oppression and dehumanization that exists in the larger society."[14] Environmental justice activists often see their identities devalued and make a direct connection between the defense of their communities and the demand for respect. The response to this is not solely a focus on redistribution, or even on the demands for recognition; it is empowerment and voice, which brings us directly to the procedures of the state.

Environmental justice activists call for policymaking procedures that encourage active community participation, institutionalize public participation, recognize community knowledge, and utilize cross-cultural formats and exchanges to enable the participation of as much diversity as exists in a community. Obviously, through these principles and policy suggestions, a shared and respected role in the decision-making process is a key demand of the movement. Coming to voice and to participation is central to environmental and social justice as it breaches a range of structural and cultural obstacles, including cultural degradation, oppression, and lack of political access. Environmental justice groups consistently demand a "place at the table" and the right to "speak for ourselves." The Principles of Environmental Justice include calls for procedural equity.[15]

The common objection raised to this expansion of the environmental justice discourse is usually articulated like this: "Members of environmental justice organizations desire recognition and demand participation, to be sure, but they would trade them in a heartbeat for distributional equity." The problem with this response is that it assumes that (re)distributional equity can occur within existing social, economic, and institutional conditions. The point of including issues of recognition and participation in a larger theory of justice is that distributional equity simply *cannot* come about otherwise. Environmental justice groups *will never have the opportunity* to trade recognition for a better distribution of environmental bads; such a distribution will not come about without satisfaction of the broader elements of justice: recognition and participation in environmental decision making.

Recognition and Ecological Justice

I would like to move into the more difficult question of applying such a broad notion of justice first to nature and then to the state. The first part, the extension of justice in terms of recognition and participation to nature, is somewhat more challenging because advocates of ecological justice do not explicitly use these terms. Theories of ecological justice stick closely to the distributional paradigm; in addition, advocates for the recognition of nature and ecological democracy articulate their position outside the language of justice. Yet the argument beyond the distributive paradigm fits here as well.

As with environmental justice, there are *reasons* for the poor distribution of ecological goods and bads, and *reasons* for our lack of attention of extending distributive justice to nature and future generations. As with social justice generally, we need to examine structures, mores, norms, language, and symbols that mediate our relation with nature. Much of this has been done in the vast literature of green theory—certainly a large number of green theorists have argued that there is an institutionalized and culturally embodied malrecognition of nature. But this has not been done from within a framework of justice.

There are a couple of hurdles to jump before extending notions of either justice or recognition to nature. First is the rather obvious question of whether justice is something that even can be extended to nature. Most theorists of justice, from Rawls to Barry, dismiss the notion that justice can be extended beyond the human community. The common argument is that justice and injustice are only applicable to relations among creatures considered moral equals. Sustainability can be addressed using the language of distributive justice, however, because the issue is our treatment of future generations of humans, our moral equals. Dobson notes that the preference for leaving nature and animals out of traditional theories of justice (including those of Rawls, Nozick, and Walzer) seems to come out of a desire to exclude nature, not from sound theoretical reasoning, and that this desire arises from a fear of giving nature an equal moral footing.[16] But crediting the recognition of nature in exploring the extension of social justice to nature does not necessitate putting animals or nature itself on an equal moral footing with human beings. Leopold, one of the key founders of contemporary environmental thought, viewed nature as an extension of our own moral community, to which we have obligations; but, as Sagoff argues, Leopold held this view without advocating an equal right for flora or fauna, or an egalitarian moral system within nature.[17] Instead, this form of recognition simply extends a concern for, and a recognition of, a nature, which is our community, context, and home.

Another hurdle is the attempt to find grounds for extending recognition to nature. Taylor and Honneth, key proponents of extending recognition into a conception of justice, both focus on the individual *psychological* aspects of the need for recognition. All misrecogition, then, even systemic social and cultural domination, is about a psychological loss to individuals —disrespect.[18] Extending such a concern to nature would obviously impute a subjectivity to nature that many wish to avoid.

Fortunately, Fraser dismisses this focus on the individual psyche and offers a framework applicable to nature. Her structural argument is that misrecognition is "a *status injury* whose locus is social relations, not individual psychology." Fraser offers three different forms of misrecognition not necessarily tied to the psychological status of the victim: cultural domination, nonrecognition (being rendered invisible), and disrespect (being routinely maligned or disparaged in stereotypic public and cultural representations).[19] None of these demand a focus on the psychological effects of the victim, but rather force attention on the institutional, cultural, and symbolic norms and practices that spawn such misrecognition.

Certainly, we can see nature being subject to all three of these forms of misrecognition. Here the key to justice is misrecognition on the part of social and political norms and institutions, not the psychological affects on the affected subjects.

Fraser's focus is on gender, but the language used to legitimate recognition concerns works as well for nature. Just as redressing gender injustice requires attention to both distribution and "the status order" of contemporary society, so does redressing environmental and ecological justice. The remedy for the injustice of misrecognition in the realm of gender, argues Fraser, is cultural or symbolic change: the revaluing of disrespected identities. Fraser admits that this may involve a wholesale transformation of societal patterns of representation and communication. "Overcoming misrecognition, accordingly, requires changing institutions and social practices."[20] The point here is to make the same argument with regard to nature.

One common tactic in constructing a recognition of nature addressed by green theorists is a focus on the physical integrity of nature and the recognition of nature's own processes of unfolding potential, evolution, and growth. The recognition of the physical integrity of nature can be based on a respect for nature's "bodily integrity," the recognition of the potential in nature to develop, a respect for autopoiesis, and a respect for agency in nature (though not subjectivity or rationality). This is certainly the more ecocentric and bioregional argument, in particular the respect for autopoietic, or self-organizing and self-correcting, systems.[21]

Honneth makes the claim in his discussion of recognition that physical abuse is one key form of disrespect. Clearly, we can expand this notion of the recognition of physical integrity to nature, so that an abuse of that integrity, or a harm to the "body" of nature, is an element of disrespect and malrecognition. The language of a right to physical integrity is brought in for the same basic reason for both human and natural physical integrity: the respect of agency and a respect for the development of potential. In essence, this is all embodied in Low and Gleeson's first principle of ecological justice: "Every natural entity is entitled to enjoy the fullness of its own form of life."[22] We can see recognition, then, as necessary for the unfolding or realization of the potential of nature, both human and nonhuman. This form of recognition of nature requires a move away from a solely individualistic notion of recognition to a broader, ecological one applicable to habitats and ecosystems: the recognition of the potential of a landscape or an ecological community to flourish.

But this type of recognition of nature can come from a human-centered perspective. Hayward makes a much more direct argument that respect for nature comes directly out of a respect for ourselves and each other.[23] Hayward argues that human beings have an interest in self-respect and integrity, which provides reasons to respect nonhuman beings and their environments. If we have an interest in respecting ourselves and others, we do not have a reason to withhold that respect from the rest of nature. Basically, Hayward argues for a concern for nature based on rational, enlightened, and expanded self-interest rather than a belief in the intrinsic value of nature.[24]

Environmental Justice, Reflexive Modernization, and Ecological Democracy

An expanded language of social justice moves the discussion from the theoretical realm of ideal distributional models to the relationship between the oppressed and the state. In opening issues of cultural recognition and political participation, the state's approach and processes come under scrutiny, in addition to distribution. Here I turn to state responses, both actual and potential, to a broad notion of environmental and ecological justice.

Not surprisingly, responses to calls for environmental justice on the part of the state in the United States have been primarily distributional in tone. The first major legislative proposal on environmental justice, sponsored by then-Senator Al Gore and Representative John Lewis in 1992, was solely distributive in its analysis and proposed solutions (though it was never passed by the then-Democratic-controlled Congress). Similarly, the Environmental Protection Agency's first attempt to come to grips with the environmental justice issue focused exclusively on the distribution of environmental risks.[25] Both of these policy moves were criticized by many in the U.S. environmental justice community for not taking into account racial discrimination (the issue of cultural recognition and disparagement) and for not including the input of many academics and activists who had been working on the environmental justice issue for years (issues of both recognition and, more directly, participation). Even the high point of national policy on environmental justice, the Executive Order signed by President Clinton in 1994, was focused almost entirely on distributional issues; it required federal agencies to identify and address the disproportional impact on health or environment on people of color and low-income communities.

The few responses on the part of the state that did attempt to address recognition and participation as aspects of justice often fell short. Environmental justice activists have been less than satisfied with participation offered them by, for example, the Environmental Protection Agency (EPA) in its advisory committees on environmental justice. The National Environmental Justice Advisory Committee (NEJAC) began as the EPA named environmental justice a top priority early in the Clinton administration. Made of stakeholders, many of whom had traditionally been ignored by the EPA, the NEJAC listened to hundreds of community members around the country testify on local environmental issues. It passed numerous resolutions and gave the EPA much advice, but it was only an advisory body and could not make policy. While many local and individual problems have been addressed via the NEJAC, numerous members have questioned its influence. A "place at the table" will be welcomed, but will be seriously questioned if that participation does not result in a real change in the level and quality of community recognition in the development of environmental policy. Just because people are given some sort of voice does not mean that they will be satisfied with a process that continues to deny them real, equitable results. Many environmental justice activists have criticized inauthentic participation: access without influence is a type of false inclusion, or attempted co-optation, and results in disempowerment and increased cynicism regarding government generally.

Policymakers and agencies need to understand that simply providing one element of justice—some studies of distributional inequity, some recognition of activists and communities by validating their issues, some limited notion of participation by including stakeholders in policy discussions—will ultimately be unsatisfactory. Arguments arise that the policymakers or agencies are merely engaging in inauthentic strategies to buy time and distract the movement; a more strongly worded critique would be that these political entities are bestowing a certain level of (ultimately inauthentic) recognition or inclusion in order to defuse the movement and ultimately deny it distributional equity, real recognition, and real participation.

States are also structurally constrained, not least the United States. Environmental initiatives usually run head-on into the imperative of states to support economic growth.[26] In the United States, for example, every time major environmental initiatives are perceived to harm economic growth, they are defeated or dismissed. The concept of ecological modernization can be used to overcome this impasse by arguing that good environmental policy can both protect communities and nature and add to the economic bottom line. But this argument has gone nowhere in the United States; the George W. Bush administration, as exemplified by its energy policy, only thinks of the environment/economy interface in zero-sum terms.

A stronger form of ecological modernization, however, has taken root in the environmental justice community in the United States. Here the focus is on the legitimation imperative of states rather than the economic. It certainly makes sense for environmental justice activists to focus on demanding that a legitimate and just state address the distribution of environmental bads, the malrecognition of communities subject to those bads, and the participation of the public in environmental decision making. These demands for environmental justice open institutional opportunities for the state to rectify the growing problem of environmental legitimacy.[27]

The notion of reflexive modernization is helpful here and offers the beginnings of a structural response to the inability of the state to address environmental issues generally and environmental injustices specifically. Reflexive modernization can be defined quite simply, though its repercussions are immense. Ulrich Beck[28] notes that *reflexive* can refer to the fact that modernity has unintended consequences—reflexes—that are now threatening to undermine the legitimacy of state and economic structures. But perhaps more directly, *reflexive* means reflective, as in a populations coming to terms with both these effects and a more critical response to them. Beck argues that

reflexive modernization is the attempt to regain a voice and thus the ability to act, the attempt to regain reality in view of developments that are the consequences of the successes of modernization. These developments call the concepts and formulas of classical industrial society fundamentally into question from the inside, not from crisis, disintegration, revolution or conspiracy, but from the repercussions of the very ordinary "progress" on its own foundations.[29]

And, importantly, the repercussions of modernity are also called into question by the responses of social movements like the environmental justice movement.

The very legitimacy of a state, based on both public safety and democratic inclusion, is threatened in a realm where states are perceived to be collaborating with, condoning, or otherwise enabling such insecurities and risks. The progress of modernity itself, with help from the state, has put the legitimacy of the state at risk. In this case, a more reflexive modernization, in particular, reflection focused specifically on *ecological reflexivity*, is a way to tie together environmental concerns for both human and natural communities and institutional mechanisms that address recognition along with substantive and procedural justice. Environmental legitimacy can be gained through an institutionalization of reflexive concerns and procedural justice.

I return later to this discussion of the relationship between environmental justice and the possible reconstructive institutional responses in light of reflexive modernization. But the unintended effects of modernity have been felt by more than just the populations represented by the environmental justice movement; nature itself is at risk, and ecological justice broadens the inquiry. And this has even further repercussions for the response of the state.

Certainly, we can read the exclusion of nature, in terms of its invisibility in policymaking, as an institutional impediment to doing justice to nature. The parallels between the exclusion of disrespected human communities and nature are quite clear here. As Fraser argues, when "patterns of disrespect and disesteem are institutionalized, for example, in . . . social practices and group mores that structure everyday interaction, they impede parity of participation, just as surely as do distributive inequities . . . A society whose institutionalized norms impede parity of participation is morally indefensible, *whether or not it distorts the subjectivity of the oppressed*" [italics in original].[30]

Again, the criticism of such an exclusion does not depend on psychological harm. In this case, a harm to the physical integrity of nature or a violation of nature's agency as a result of exclusion is enough to warrant reflection on the institutional structures that lead to these violations. As Young argues in the case of social justice, the exclusion from the process of decision making and governance is itself an injustice, not only because it is a result of the lack of recognition and cultural dismissal of the party involved but also because it is that exclusion that brings about distributional inequity: "Put this way, the connection between democracy and justice appears circular. Ideal processes of deliberative democracy lead to substantively just outcomes because the deliberation begins from a starting-point of justice."[31]

Two issues need to be brought into political discussions in order to do justice to nature. First, how are we to bring the recognition of the variety of institutional and cultural biases against nature—those that lead to distributional problems (including sustainability) and those regarding nonrecognition that lead us to make nature invisible—into environmental decision making? And second, how are we to bring nature itself into democratic discourse?

Clearly, more open and participatory structures of environmental decision making are key. Much has been written on the topic,[32] and I see no need to restate basic arguments. The only addition I make here is a conceptual one: such models of environmental democracy are key aspects not only of expanded democratization but of expanded notions of environmental justice as well. It is crucial that movements for environmental justice insist on participatory and procedural mechanisms to address injustice. The right to participate is central to the principles of environmental justice developed by the movement in 1991, and critiques of undemocratic procedures and the demand for meaningful participation are standard in community demands. Activists complain about the "step up to the microphone and have your say in less than fifteen minutes" approach to public participation; they demand more meaningful deliberation as part of a more legitimate process.[33] In the academic realm, procedural justice is also central. Williams and Matheny's "dialogic model" of social regulation, for example, includes access to usable information, a broad pattern of opportunities for citizen participation, and policymaking institutions that can adjust to the ambiguity and difference in communities.[34] Such recognition and participation are not only arguments for expanded ecological democracy but also integral elements in achieving justice.

The point is not only the basic democratic one of involvement in decisions that affect the participants but also the larger one of expanding discourse in both political and civil society so that different understandings and experiences of the environment, and in this case nature as well, are heard and intersubjectively recognized in a democratic context. Participation is aimed not only at strategic, instrumental ends such as policy decisions but also at getting diverse understandings recognized by others and shifting preferences that are left unchallenged in an aggregative process. In recent attempts at "collaborative" environmental decision making, even policy "failures" (where there is no decision or implementation) are intersubjectively successful. Participants often leave saying they do not *agree* with others but understand their positions and the reasons for those positions much better and more sympathetically than before.[35] Such political engagement encourages the recognition of difference and ideally the crafting of policy with such difference in mind. This is the essence of an ecological reflexivity.

Beck argues that democracy in general is becoming increasingly reflexive in theory and practice. Various issues and areas that until now have been excluded from the sphere of political oversight, protected by the state, or removed from schemes of public participation are becoming increasingly subject to public inquiry. Within this transformation, the "claims of different expert groups collide with one another, as well as with the claims of ordinary knowledge and of the knowledge of social movements. . . . The knowledge of side-effects thus opens up a *battleground of pluralistic rationality claims.*"[36] The unintended consequences of modernization and industrialization are being brought to public attention by affected and subjugated groups or their proxies. Uncertainty, tied to the increased distrust of the state and scientific experts, has led to a demand for more voices, different interpretations, and nontechnobureaucratic language especially in discussing environmental issues. This is the avenue through which both recognition and participation may increase, both for communities suffering from environmental injustice and for nature.

Experiments in broader discursive environmental decision making have been increasing in the United States, in part resulting from the demands of the environmental and the environmental justice movements. Collaborative decision making is one main focus, especially in natural resource decisions. Central to these deliberative processes is a connection to community and place. Recognition of communities and the land itself is the basis of the process. As the editors of one of the few academic overviews of the practice put it, collaboration "emphasizes the importance of local participation, sustainable natural and human communities, [and] inclusion of disempowered voices."[37] Numerous collaborative processes, especially in the western United States, have brought together various perspectives from the community and put them in a room with representatives from government agencies, industry, and the scientific community. The idea is to get beyond the adversarial model that has left so many disenchanted with the standard process of environmental decision making in the United States.

In more urban settings, the environmental justice movement often focuses on the institutionalization of public oversight of particularly controversial facilities. Many states require a local advisory committee when a facility is initially licensed or when it comes up for renewal of a permit, and environmental justice activists have insisted on thorough and authentic public participation in these processes. These committees "offer the opportunity for a qualitatively deliberative process, one that creates an opportunity for lay and technical people to work together, have a dialogue, and reach consensus."[38] Some communities have gone a step further and brought permanent status to such advisory committees. In Eugene, Oregon, for example, a local toxics board was established to oversee the handling and reporting of toxic substances in larger production facilities. The board has representatives from the environmental community and industry, and is central to both the oversight of toxics management and the distribution of information to the public. Such institutions provide an ongoing center for participation, discourse across difference, and importantly, the information necessary to make environmental decisions in the community.

These experiments in community collaboration and advisory groups are few and far between, however. The broadest and most promising arena for diverse recognition and public participation is the development of electronic participation in the rule making of government agencies. Numerous federal agencies have implemented Internet-based public participation as a way of meeting the required public comment process in regulatory rule making. The E-Government Act of 2002 brought about a uniform protocol for electronic rule making on a single Web site with links to all agency rule-making efforts.[39] On this site, the public can offer comments on proposed rules and on others' comments on those rules. The result is often an interesting discourse far more broad and open than the current public comment process, which is dominated by industry. There are dangers, of course; agencies may insist on one-way submission of comments rather than discourse. They may also limit what counts as acceptable discourse by paying attention only to legal and scientific commentary. But the potential is still there: the best example is that of 50,000-plus public comments in an open forum leading to the development of rules on organic food. The online pressure helped defeat the U.S. Department of Agriculture's attempt to include things like irradiation, sewage sludge fertilizers, and genetic engineering in the official definition of organic food in the late 1990s.

In all these processes, however, we should remember that diverse *human* participation is not necessarily the only end of environmental democracy. Institutional participation could, in a sense, be extended to nature that is experiencing an infringement of physical integrity or potential. This is where Dryzek's notion of ecological communication becomes not just an element of ecological democracy but of ecological justice as well. In the last decade Dryzek has argued for the recognition of agency in nature; he suggests extending communication to entities that can act as agents even though they lack subjectivity. If we accept nature as an agent, one whose physical integrity and "bodily" processes are respected, we should also listen to its speech. Dryzek argues that we should listen to the signals emanating from nature and treat these signals from the natural world with the same respect as we do signals coming from human subjects.[40] Disruptions to the physical integrity of nature, especially, should catch our attention, things such as global warming, species extinction, droughts, and mad-cow disease.[41] Just as Young[42] wants to expand such discourse to include forms of communication other than the blatantly purposive and argumentative, Dryzek accepts something as nonrational as signals from nature. He, of course, is not suggesting the actual presence of nature in democratic conversations; the call is for an expansion of the politics of ideas, brought about by institutional openness rather than a politics of presence.

Such discourse allows for the presentation and intersubjective recognition of different points of view, including interpretations of nature's signals. Let me give an example. In a public hearing regarding the fill of wetlands for the construction of a semiconductor manufacturing plant, a woman gave her testimony dressed as an endangered Fenders Blue butterfly, which lived in the wetland. The testimony was poetic and described the effect of the construction and the everyday work of the plant on the life of the butterfly. The audience—quite large and rowdy given the controversy over the construction—gave rapt attention, and a strong point was made. Unfortunately, the testimony was being given to a colonel in the Army Corps of Engineers, who was visibly uncomfortable and who had no way of incorporating the testimony into his decision-making process, which was based entirely on whether the plan violated the Clean Water Act. The point is that processes that are more amenable to the inclusion of such testimony—participatory mechanisms open to signals from butterflies—can bring recognition of both nature's signals and various human interpretations of them.[43]

It is crucial that both environmental justice and ecological justice have an integral element of the inclusion of affected communities—human and natural—in democratic discourse and decision making. In this case, however, nature is included by proxy. Proxies are already commonly used in liberal decision making, such as those that act on behalf of children's or prisoner's rights. Even existing generations—the young, but not yet "communicatively competent"—are taken into consideration by the proxy of interest groups. Future generations, which cannot even send signals as nature can, may participate by having proxies take their concerns into present discourse; we can make the same argument for nature. Key, however, is a broad representation of interpretations of the effects on nature; just as children have numerous proxies in the form of interest groups, so should nature be represented with multiple voices.[44]

The first step in the development of environmental and ecological justice is more reflective and critical individuals, communities, and movements; that much we have seen growing, in particular in environmental justice movements in the United States. But the more reconstructive moment of a reflexive modernization requires that such diverse and critical knowledge regarding nature and the environment be brought into more ecologically reflexive institutions. Beck argues that modernization demands this step; ecological democrats argue that democracy demands it. I argue that a broad understanding of environmental and ecological justice requires it as well. Elements of this transformation are apparent most thoroughly in the demands of the environmental justice movement in the United States and in some nascent institutional innovations on the part of the state. The ecological state, in order to address environmental and ecological justice, must continue to reflexively evolve the crucial role of participatory and discursive institutional structures in achieving just ends. At this point, the environmental justice movement makes those demands; it is still to be seen whether those more interested in ecological justice will as well.

Notes

I want to thank all the participants in the ECPR workshop on Environmentalism and the State for their input on an earlier version of this chapter; editors John Barry and Robyn Eckersley; and Bill Chaloupka, Tim Luke, and John Meyer. For financial support I thank Max Oelschlaeger and the Program on Community, Culture, and Environment, and the Organized Research Program, both at Northern Arizona University; the Social and Political Theory Program, Research School of Social Sciences, Australian National University; and the Australian-American Fulbright Commission.

1. See especially Dobson (1998); Low and Gleeson (1998).

2. Iris Young (1990); Fraser (1997); and Fraser (1998).

3. Schlosberg (1999); Schlosberg (2003).

4. Rawls (1971, 9–10); Brian Barry (1999); and David Miller (1976).

5. Iris Young (1990, 1).

6. Iris Young (1990, 22).

7. Young is not the only one who insists on recognition as an integral part of justice. See Charles Taylor (1994) and Honneth (1992; 1995), both of whom argue that a lack of recognition is as much an injustice as a lack of goods.

8. Gould (1996, 181).

9. Iris Young, (1990, 23). None of this, she argues, crosses the liberal no-fly zone into particular conceptions of the good. "The liberal commitment to individual freedom, and the consequent plurality of definitions of the good, must be preserved in any reenlarged conception of justice" (36). Social justice, for Young, refers to institutional conditions and the social norms that lead to exclusion from the community of justice. Theories of justice may strive to take place behind a veil of ignorance or impartiality, but actual injustices do not—hence the need to address the cultural and institutional aspects of justice in dealing with real policy issues.

10. The literature on state-sponsored recognition is extensive, including Kymlicka (1996); Kymlicka (2001); Kymlicka and Norman, eds. (2000); and Iris Young (2000).

11. Unfortunately, advocates and practitioners of green theory and philosophy (with few exceptions) have not picked up on the calls to extend analyses of justice beyond the distributive realm. In Dobson's (1998) otherwise thorough and comprehensive study, he makes clear his position that "all justice is distributive." Similarly, Low and Gleeson, in *Justice, Society and Nature* (1998, 133), insist that the "distribution of environmental quality is the core of 'environmental justice'—with the emphasis on *distribution*." This is especially odd given that their two central principles of environmental justice—"every natural entity is entitled to enjoy the fullness of its own form of life" and "all life forms are mutually dependent and dependent on non-life forms"—are not about distribution at all. Rather, they focus on recognizing and respecting the potential of nature and the dependence of humankind on the realization of this potential in nature. These principles get more at the underlying social and cultural *conditions* of environmental maldistribution.

12. Bunyan Bryant and Paul Mohai, eds. (1992); Bunyan Bryant (1996); Bullard, ed. (1993); Camacho, ed. (1998); Faber, ed. (1998); and Hofrichter, ed. (1993).

13. United States General Accounting Office (1983); United Church of Christ Commission for Racial Justice (1987).

14. Pulido (1996, 25).

15. The Principles of Environmental Justice have been published in numerous places. See, for example, Charles Lee, ed. (1992); Dryzek and Schlosberg, eds. (1998).

16. Dobson (1998, 172).

17. Leopold (1949); Sagoff (1993, 86–87).

18. Honneth (1992, 190–191).

19. Fraser (1998, 25, 27).

20. Fraser (1998, 26).

21. See, in particular, Eckersley (1992); McGinnis (1999).

22. Low and Gleeson (1998, 156).

23. Hayward, (1998).

24. The basic idea of the "preservation" of nature can be seen as a good and so, as a litmus test of justice, could be labeled illiberal. But including the natural world in the community of justice, and in the deliberation of justice, remains procedural. Justice flows from recognition and discourse, in particular recognition and discourse that attempts to undermine past institutionalized dominations. Those address the procedural conditions for justice, not particular pictures of the good. Still, and admittedly, the range of available and acceptable pictures of the good life would certainly be narrowed, just as it was for some when recognition and the franchise were expanded to blacks, women, the colonized, and indigenous peoples. But there is a key difference between reducing available notions of

the good life in order to protect the possibility of justice for all, and insisting on particular notions of the good. Justice extended to nature may do the former, but certainly not the latter. See also Dobson's discussion of this point in *Justice and the Environment* (1998, 202).

25. United States Environmental Protection Agency (1992).

26. See chapter 4 in this volume. Also see Dryzek, Downes et al. (2003).

27. See Schlosberg and Dryzek (2002).

28. Beck (1998, 84).

29. Beck (1997, 15).

30. Fraser (1998, 26).

31. Iris Young (2000, 34).

32. Starting with Dryzek (2000); Plumwood (1998); Mason (1999); Williams and Matheny (1995); and the collections by Doherty and de Gues, eds. (1996), Lafferty and Meadowcraft, eds. (1996), and Mathews, ed. (1996).

33. Charles Lee, ed. (1992); Cole and Foster (2001, 111–112).

34. Williams and Matheny (1995); Hunold and Young (1998); and Robert Lake (1996).

35. Brick, Snow, and Van De Wetering, eds. (2001); Robar (1999).

36. Beck (1998, 91).

37. Brick, Snow, and Van De Wetering, eds. (2001, 2).

38. Cole and Foster (2001, 112).

39. <http://www.regulations.gov/>.

40. Dryzek (1995, 20, 21).

41. Global warming, for example, is demonstrated not just in atmospheric studies but also by a slew of individual signals coming from nature—songbirds returning earlier, butterfly species moving north, insect eggs hatching earlier, and weather-related issues such as increased rainfall in certain areas and generally the earlier arrival of spring. All these individual global warnings adds up to global warming.

42. Iris Young (1996).

43. Similarly, the presence of sea turtles at the Seattle World Trade Organization protests in 1999 demonstrated the exclusion of nature from the deliberations.

44. With apologies to Dr. Seuss, there is never a single Lorax speaking for the trees.

6

Penitent Destroyer? The Philippine State in Pursuit of Environmental Justice

Raymond Bryant and Karen Lawrence

The Philippines might not appear to be the best place in the developing world to assess positive aspects of environmental governance by the state. After all, the Philippine state has long been intimately associated with political corruption and environmental devastation. It has been, to borrow a phrase from the title of one work on the subject, a prime force in "plundering paradise," that is, the country's rich stock of biological diversity and natural resources.[1]

The systematic environmental degradation that was the flip side of the "crony capitalism" that enriched the few at the expense of the many reflected a turbulent history of resource overexploitation. The nadir was reached during the regime of plunder presided over by Ferdinand Marcos and his political associates beginning in the 1960s and ending with his downfall during the People Power Revolution of 1986.[2] Natural resources were a license to print money as the "legal slaughter of the forests" and other resources intensified.[3]

It was not always this way. Colonial governance, first under Spain and then under the United States, contributed to natural resource extraction and associated environmental degradation.[4] But, at the same time, the Philippines benefited from the establishment of a fairly robust management regime centered on the forestry bureau. The latter was able during the first half of the twentieth century to enforce a measure of regulation predicated on the principles of scientific forestry. For all its flaws (and there were many), this regulatory regime did manage to maintain some order in the nation's forests.

All that changed in the early 1950s as the opportunity to seize resource rents proved too tempting for successive generations of Philippine politicians. In a political system in which political patronage was closely allied to control over logging and mining leases, there was little scope for scientific forestry or any other system that restricted extraction in aid of long-time management or conservation goals. Environmental degradation was deeply embedded in the political economy of Philippine society. Thus, citizens traded votes for gifts, politicians traded leases for political support and personal enrichment, and companies traded money for the right to do business.

If the bedrock of this political and economic merry-go-round was rent-seizing behavior, the impact of this process was devastating on both the nation's natural resources and the institutions (such as the forestry bureau) set up to manage those resources. During the period 1951–1986 the Philippines lost 55 percent of its forest cover in a process that led to the extinction of an estimated 40 percent of the country's endemic flora.[5] The forestry bureau itself was widely seen to be in the pocket of the logging industry. Foreign aid agencies thus sought to bypass the bureau as much as possible, turning to a nascent environmental nongovernmental organization (NGO) sector as the only viable alternative.

And yet, by the mid-1990s the Philippine state had already earned a reputation for "born-again environmentalism," with many observers pointing to it as an emerging world leader in community-based resource management. How can this change be explained? Indeed, to what extent is high-minded official rhetoric actually reflected in positive change on the ground? What are the elements of this seeming conversion from environmental bad boy to sustainable resource management guru? In this chapter we explore these questions to assess the prospects for sound environmental governance and the greening of the state in one country of the developing world. We do not claim that the Philippine experience is representative of that of the countries of the developing world at large. Nor do we claim that the findings from our regional case study, Palawan, are necessarily typical of those that would be found in other regions of this diverse archipelago nation. What we do hope to show is how general arguments about either the resource depravity or environmental beneficence of the state require serious qualification in a context shaped by myriad political, economic, cultural, and ecological factors.

People's Power Revolution as Environmental Opportunity

The much-celebrated People Power Revolution of 1986 provided a unique window of opportunity for environmental reformers to seek to effect basic change in the resource management orientation of the Philippine state. Following the downfall of Marcos and the installation of Corazon Aquino as the new president, reformers based in the NGO sector saw their chance. Assorted NGO leaders were appointed to senior posts in the Aquino government. Thus, the human rights activist Fulgencio Factoran Jr. became secretary of the newly reorganized Department of Environment and Natural Resources (DENR) in 1987. He and his successors to that post relied on the advice of a series of influential NGO leaders—Delfin Ganapin Jr., Celso Roque, Tony La Vina—who served in various undersecretary roles during the late 1980s and 1990s. The role of the NGO sector in assisting the Philippine state in, among other things, environmental matters was enshrined in the national constitution in 1987.

There was certainly a "foreign hand" in this change. As the Aquino government took charge of the Philippine state, Western lending agencies led by the U.S. Agency for International Development (USAID) sought to use aid money under their control to reinforce the momentum behind a reformist agenda. In the case of the DENR, for example, money was provided for a community reforestation program in the late 1980s on the condition that local and national NGOs would be the primary vehicle through which money would be disbursed. Similarly, the debt-for-nature swap that provided the starting point for the national integrated protected areas program of the 1990s was led by NGOs—the international World Wide Fund for Nature (WWF) and the leading Philippine environmental NGO, the Haribon Foundation.[6]

The changing temper of the times was also implicated in these changes. Following publication of the report of the World Commission on Environment and Development in 1987, political leaders around the world fell over each other in the rush to promote themselves and their states as supporters of the new buzz phrase "sustainable development."[7] By the early 1990s, and in a process sanctified by the convening of an Earth Summit in Rio de Janeiro, Brazil, in June 1992, it was politically obligatory to be seen to favor sustainable development and environmental conservation.

Under President Aquino (1986–1992) and her successor, Fidel Ramos (1992–1998), the Philippines sought to position itself as a leader in the developing world on the integration of environmental and developmental issues. Building on an international reputation associated with the People Power Revolution of 1986, the Ramos government swiftly created the Philippine Council for Sustainable Development (PCSD) in September 1992 soon after assuming office. The PCSD was designed to be the main national forum in which state agencies and other interested stakeholders such as NGOs could collectively map the country's sustainable development future. A key outcome of the PCSD was Philippine Agenda 21, the national blueprint for sustainable development in the twenty-first century, produced after much discussion and debate in late 1996. For President Ramos, this document embodied "a spirit of unity, solidarity and convergence" and reflected "a truly participatory decision-making process."[8]

The NGO sector was somewhat less celebratory about the PCSD and the PA21 process. Some, such as Cristi Nozawa of the Haribon Foundation, believed that despite its limitations the process was a means by which NGOs and others in civil society could prod agencies such as the DENR further along the path of reform. PA21 indicators of social and environmental progress could be used to bolster reformers within the state. Membership in the PCSD itself was also a means of "getting ammunition" about state practices that could be used to strengthen criticism of deficient policies and practices.[9] Others, such as Philippine Rural Reconstruction Movement leader Horacio Morales, pointed to the absence of time-bound plans in the PA21 document, meaning that it was difficult if not impossible to say what the indicators would mean in terms of specific programs. According to Morales, "translation was the problem" in what seemed fated to be an exemplar of "cosmetic environmentalism."[10]

Worries about "cosmetic environmentalism" grew during the 1990s as many environmental activists began to suspect that the Philippine state was long on development and short on sustainability. At least three factors were behind this growing skepticism about the greening of the Philippine state in the 1990s. First, the country was formally and officially committed to rapid modernization. In the 1990s this was mainly associated with the commitment of the Ramos government to turn the country into a Newly Industrialized Country (NIC) by the year 2000. This national goal, ambitious in the extreme, intensified the pressure on the already beleaguered natural environment. Thus, in sector after sector, from mining to manufacturing, the Philippines was declared "open for business," often with devastating consequences.[11]

Second, the onset of the Asian financial crisis in 1997 only added to the development difficulties and dilemmas of the Philippine state. Not only did it dash all hope of attaining NIC status in the short to medium term, it also meant that there was greater pressure than ever to fall back on the country's natural resources as a means to finance development projects and to service the country's large debt. Thus, mining initiatives were intensified, ecotourism ventures were launched, and there were even plans at the DENR to lift the ban on lumber exports.[12] The country was now open *and* desperate for business.

Finally, and perhaps most important, the skepticism of environmental reformers was occasioned by the persisting political and economic influence of elite families or clans in spite of the People Power Revolution of 1986. That these powerful individuals and clans often owed a good proportion of their wealth to unsustainable natural resource exploitation practices was cause for concern in weighing up the fashionable environmental rhetoric that many of them bandied around Congress.[13]

So, is the putative greening of the Philippine state since 1986 nothing more than an elaborate front to generate domestic and international political support and prestige? Not quite, it would seem. In fact, the record of the Philippine state is more complicated then either critics or reformers allow and reflects myriad political, economic, and cultural processes and battles. In what follows, we provide a detailed case study of one set of community-based resource management initiatives in the Palawan region, the country's so-called final forest frontier and the site of much of the Philippine's residual biological diversity. In the process, we hope to illuminate just some of the political negotiations and struggles that have informed environmental management in the country since the late 1990s, which give us some purchase on the question of the possible greening of the Philippine state.

Community-Based Natural Resource Management in Palawan

Situated in Northern Palawan, the 34 km body of water known as the Malampaya Sound is one of the most productive in Palawan and one of the most economically significant in the Philippines. The Sound is also recognized as a valuable biodiversity site; it is, for example, the only known habitat in the Philippines of the Irrawaddy Dolphin. The water draining into the Sound incorporates half of the Municipality of Taytay, about 90,000 hectares of watershed. The most significant subcatchments are the Ipil and Abongan rivers, which drain into an extensive wetland and mangrove forest. Within the watershed, habitat diversity is very high. Thus, Mt. Capaos contains remnant montane forest that adjoins valuable lowland rainforest, while on the coast old-growth mangroves link to beach forests, and offshore, seagrass beds and corals.

This diversity has long provided livelihood opportunities for over one hundred settlements living around the shores of the Sound. However, efforts in 2000 to promote community-based natural resource management in the context of the creation of an official protected area for Malampaya Sound were situated in the context of a local political economy of long natural resource exploitation and conflict. They were affected by the uneven articulation of a green agenda within the Philippine state at the local, regional, and national scales.

State and Plural Environmental Claims in Northern Palawan

To appreciate the role of the state in environmental matters in Malampaya Sound, it is important to understand that role in terms of a historical process of layering by which various official agencies and levels of government asserted jurisdiction in the area.

During the Spanish occupation from 1662 until 1873, Taytay was the capital of Calamianes region, Northern Palawan.[14] Taytay was key in the colonization process of this part of Palawan, and under its direction the modern municipalities of El Nido, San Vicente, and Dumaran were all formed. If this historical process was itself conflict-prone, in modern times the passage of the Local Government Code of 1991 led to enhanced intermunicipal squabbling over boundaries because the share of provincial taxes that a municipality would get was based on size and population. Thus, for example, Taytay, or more accurately, the powerful coterie of families that dominate its politics, has sought to enhance its urban status through efforts ensuring its territory is not given away to its smaller neighbor and rival El Nido.

Territorial conflicts also arise at the national government level in terms of the environment, again with implications for the Malampaya Sound area. Thus, in 1992 the Strategic Environmental Plan for Palawan was made law, which created the Palawan Council for Sustainable Development. This regional agency was given the mandate to manage Palawan's resources in a sustainable fashion. However, it was not made clear how this new agency was supposed to work with the Department of Environment and Natural Resources (DENR), which has a national mandate to manage the environment. After years of arguing about who had the authority of environmental projects and policies in Palawan, an agreement was reached in 1994 whereby the Palawan Council was empowered to approve projects prior to subsequent confirmation by the DENR.

This agreement was fine on paper, but in practice there were severe limitations on the ability of this regional agency to act. Based in the capital of Palawan, Puerto Princessa, the council was not provided with sufficient funds or personnel to function effectively and in keeping with its mandate. Much of that mandate came down to ensuring that local governments and DENR officials in the province implemented local development projects in a sustainable manner. As a result, monitoring and enforcement has been patchy, as every government environmental project has involved discrete rounds of negotiation regarding official authority and participation. This has had a serious knock-on effect in terms of local environmental practices. For example, businesses have suffered disruption in their work because they need an environmental compliance certificate sanctioned by both the council and the DENR.

If territorial and political tensions between state agencies render difficult the articulation of a unified official vision on local environmental management, entrenched rival economic interests in Malampaya Sound constitute an added complication to the achievement of a green state in the Philippines. The aquatic resources of the Sound itself have been severely disrupted over the years by such rivalry. Indeed, periodic collapses in fish and other stocks have necessitated draconian measures to restrict extraction until supplies were revived.

A central factor in the ecological and political tensions here is the fact that the rates of extraction and volumes of catch are very different for users of the Sound, reflecting uneven technological and capital opportunities. There is, above all, a large gap between commercial large-scale and small-scale operators, with the political climate usually favoring the former over the latter. However, in-migration to Malampaya Sound has meant that the number of small-scale fishers has increased, with the result that the demand has grown for greater access to dwindling resources for this group. That many of these fishers are indebted to traders who buy their produce even as they proffer loans of goods and fuel, locking them into a perpetual debt relationship, only adds to the sense of desperation surrounding local fishing struggles.[15]

That desperation has had severe environmental implications in the area. In the scramble to make a living, fishers have sometimes resorted to destructive fishing techniques such as the use of dynamite or sodium cyanide. These techniques are more "efficient" than traditional means at extracting resources and were introduced by migrants or transient fishers from other regions in the Philippines. And yet, while boosting catches temporarily for the individuals concerned, and when combined with the large volumes of fish caught by the small trawlers still allowed to operate in the Sound, the overall impact has been catastrophic. Small-scale fishers have seen their daily catch reduced from 30 kg to 2–3 kg, with those using the traditional dugout canoes and hook and line being the hardest hit. Widespread ecological damage has also occurred as coral reefs have been destroyed and with them essential fish breeding grounds and nurseries.

Where were the various agencies of the state in all of this? According to community residents, the representatives of the various agencies, especially those in local government, were thoroughly implicated in this process of social conflict and environmental degradation. A few communities along the Sound were without land title even as large commercial fishing vessels were overexploiting their traditional fishing areas—in both cases, conditions linked to the actions of powerful members in local government. Key members of that government were seen to be protecting those behind the sodium cyanide and live fish trade, the collusion with dynamite fishers, and the giving of permits to large trawler vessels to operate in the area. Community cynicism about various state agencies was rife. For example, the coast guard was known as the "cash guard" and the maritime police as the "money-time police"—in short, state agencies were synonymous with corruption.

As a result, resource degradation, social conflict, and intrastate divisions over environmental authority constituted a complex and difficult setting for the greening of state policies and practices. There is nothing unusual, though, in this particular configuration of political, economic, cultural, and ecological circumstances in a country long characterized by resource "plunder." And yet, because of residual environmental attraction in terms of rare and scientifically valued biological diversity, Malampaya Sound has been one among a number of biodiversity hot spots nationwide that have been sites of acute state interest. As such, the site provides evidence by which it is possible to gain some purchase on arguments surrounding the putative greening of the state.

Two events in 1998 served as an ecological wake-up call for both residents and state agencies. The first disaster was a toxic red tide in the area that infected local marine produce and resulted in the death of a young child. The second disaster was an unexpected typhoon that hit northern Palawan, destroying fish cages and ponds, and many houses, and causing extensive damage in general to property and crops.

Paradoxically, the disasters of 1998 provided a window of opportunity for a national conservation program to garner local support for the idea of declaring Malampaya Sound a protected area. The program was the European Union–funded National Integrated Areas Program (NIPAP) which had been initiated in 1995 and sought to work with the DENR, local government, NGOs, and local residents to establish a series of protected areas in sites of national biological importance.[16] This program had received a mixed reaction in other places where it was essayed around the country but nonetheless was firmly supported by senior political leaders in Manila. Indeed, in association with key legislation (the National Integrated Protected Areas System Act of 1992), NIPAP was widely seen to be a leading example of how the Philippine state was adhering to its commitments in the aftermath of the Rio Earth Summit. In brief, NIPAP has been an integral part of the wider effort to green the Philippine state.

The disasters of 1998 meant that many community members in Malampaya Sound were, in principle at least, willing to listen to the NIPAP case. However, local government members were firmly against the creation of a protected area in their bailiwick. This situation, combined with other protection opportunities elsewhere in the country, meant that at NIPAP Malampaya was considered a no-hope situation. By December 1998, NIPAP staff had recommended that the area should only receive enough funding to support minimal activities that would scarcely reverse decades of environmental degradation or protect residual biological diversity.

The intervention of a Manila-based NGO, Environmental Science for Social Change (ESSC), at this time, however, was critical in a process that reinvigorated the NIPAP option of environmental conservation at Malampaya Sound. There were various overlapping strands to this effort—an effort that required luck as much as skill in weaving together a coalition that would be amenable to this environmental initiative.

One lucky break was a change of leadership at the Palawan Council for Sustainable Development. Thus, Attorney Antonio Aliswag, a former activist with the Haribon Foundation, was appointed head by incoming President Joseph Estrada. The new national administration was keen to reallocate political appointments (and hence patronage) to its campaign supporters. As it happened, Aliswag had been a friend of the Mayor of Taytay's late husband such that his appointment ushered in a new and decidedly less antagonistic approach between the Palawan Council and local government in the area. Indeed, compromise and dialogue became the norm.

These personal connections enabled Aliswag to talk with the Taytay mayor about the merits of NIPAP in a new context shaped by reciprocal trust and friendship. At the same time, Aliswag worked with his DENR counterparts to resolve long-standing turf considerations that had emerged in the context of the NIPAP and related environmental initiatives. Thus, for example, the two sides clarified through a memorandum of agreement that the council, not the DENR, would chair the Protected Area Management Board, the multiactor local board that actually would run the conservation work.

Personal politics also loomed large in the subsequent appointment of local staff for the NIPAP scheme. Thus, the protected areas superintendent (appointed by the NIPAP leadership based in Manila) appointed the brother of a municipal councillor, the husband of another councillor, the son of a local powerful DENR officer, and the brother of the vice mayor. This sort of personal politics was a standard part of Philippine politics and was an indispensable element in any greening of the state locally. It was also, though, a matter of sharing ideas and building trust between political players in the context of developing a political-cum-environmental discourse that could serve as the basis for NIPAP's introduction in the area.

A case in point was the experience of the Philippine Working Group (PWG), an informal national policy dialogue group invited by the ESSC to the Malampaya Sound in February 1999. This group, comprising senior NGO and state representatives (e.g., the DENR), was interested to understand watershed management and biological diversity regeneration potential in the area if protected areas status were to be accorded through NIPAP. This group visited Malampaya after having visited a comparable site in Northern Palawan (El Nido), where protected area status had already been accorded. At Malampaya Sound its members consulted with a variety of individuals and groups: local communities, the protected areas superintendent, local DENR staff, municipal councilors, and the Mayor of Taytay. Although the group was small, it represented key institutions that the mayor recognized and respected. Questions and concerns that the council and the mayor had regarding the NIPAP scheme (and the associated NIPAS Act of 1992), notably concerning the allocation of power and the effect on local government control (for instance, over taxation), were explained through a constructive dialogue.

Much of the work of PWG at Malampaya Sound involved communicating the viewpoints of the various parties to one another and dispelling local political insecurities. It was explained, for example, that the Protected Area Management Board (PAMB) was not a new government but a coordinating body to develop environmental policies for sustainable management of the area. The mayor as part of the local government had a role to play in this board. Equally important here was the professional tone in which these crucial discussions took place. The PWG and the ESSC was able to show the mayor a different process of advocacy, one involving reasoned dialogue between competent professionals. Meanwhile, the whole process strengthened the position of those councillors who already supported the NIPAP by giving their voice a new legitimacy locally.

The dialogue surrounding the visit of the PWG was no mere talking shop. Rather, it was crucial in dispelling misapprehensions and distrust and thus building bridges between local and regional actors whose support was vital if green thinking was to become green reality at Malampaya Sound. Thus, local government leaders began to trust ESSC (the NIPAP-linked NGO) and displayed a new openness to listening to the wishes and grievances of local communities. Specifically, they felt reassured that NGOs such as the ESSC were not manipulating communities to pursue nonlocal agendas, but rather that community concerns and requests for environmental protection were real enough. As a result of this change of attitude, subsequent dialogue between NIPAP staff and the local government was much easier. The protected area superintendent was finally able to establish relations with the mayor and to explore in more detail project aims and objectives. In light of these discussions, the mayor moved from opposing the scheme to according it her firm support.

A parallel form of "dialogue" involved in the constitution of a political-cum-environmental discourse for environmental conservation in Malampaya Sound was community mapping. This process, pioneered by NGOs such as ESSC in the 1990s and accorded growing respect in official circles, seeks to understand local conflicts and overlapping resource use concerns through the creation of visual indicators of current practices.[17] Initial mapping had already been done by ESSC but had been stymied by local government opposition. With the new attitude of the latter, the NGO felt confident to resume mapping so as to acquire a fuller understanding of resource use within the watershed of Malampaya Sound. The reinvigorated process that continued through 1999 and 2000 was also a means to gauge the true extent of community demand for a resource protection scheme, such as that offered under the NIPAP, for instance.[18]

A critical step at this time was the creation of the Protected Area Management Board as the main body to decide local policy for the protected area. The Palawan Council for Sustainable Development chaired the PAMB along with the DENR and local government staff. Other board members included barangay, or district, captains, local people's organizations, NGOs, and representatives of indigenous peoples living in the area. In total, the Malampaya PAMB consisted of forty-seven members. Once local government opposition ended, the body began to meet, and by July 1999, with the mayor in place as co-chairperson, the management unit had political momentum.

As the difficult political jockeying for position thus settled down, the actual process of following the legal steps needed to attain protected area status accelerated. This was no mere formality but rather a long and labor-intensive process of consultation and technical preparation. Consider, for example, the developments needed to prepare the Malampaya case under NIPAP and the NIPAS act. The NIPAP model used from 1999 onward focused on completing the required thirteen legal steps. These are the compilation of maps and technical data; initial screening and analysis of data; public notification of proposed boundaries; initial public consultation; a census and registration of local residents; biological resource profiling; the preparation of an initial protected area plan; public hearings; regional review and recommendations; national review and recommendations to the president; presidential proclamation; congressional action; and finally legal demarcation. The implementation of these steps involved hundreds of people and all of the official and voluntary agencies discussed previously.

The process began with formal notification—this was finished within a month in 1999. Then came a series of preliminary consultations that focused on distributing leaflets and giving education talks at schools on the merits of conservation and the NIPAP. Initially three community meetings were held, with sixty-five participants. Seventeen school seminars were given that reached 1,753 students, and three seminars for adults, with 141 participants.

Meanwhile, the data from community mapping were integrated and analyzed, forming the basis of the Initial Protected Area Plan (IPAP), which was completed in March 2000. By using community mapping as a process to develop the management plan, approximately 688 people were involved and another 404 people were involved in the verification process for the seascape zones. Over one thousand people from twenty-four barangays participated in the IPAP process. Initial screening and data analysis also began in October 1999 and was finished by March 2000. A team from the provincial DENR office conducted interviews with communities in eighteen barangays. In total, sixty-six people participated, seventeen of whom were women. The ensuing report confirmed the ESSC map-based evaluation but recommended that the marine boundary should be closer to the shore for ease of monitoring.

Resource profiling was conducted during six months by a team from the regional office of DENR and was completed after the Initial Protected Area Plan was submitted by ESSC. The data from this work also confirmed the community observations made by ESSC. The census of occupants in the proposed protected area proved the most difficult and time-consuming task of all. The population identified within the area ended up being 27,828 (or 5,369 households). The area in which these people lived was estimated at 11,475.5 hectares. However, interviewed residents tended to underestimate their own areas of land for fear of the data being used to monitor tax receipts or initiate land speculation.

Nine public hearings were subsequently held during April 2000 in a range of local communities. This tally reflected a compromise between the ESSC (which wanted more) and NIPAP staff (which wanted less) and reflected contrasting objectives of thoroughness versus time and cost effectiveness. The upshot was that public consultation was uneven—out of twenty-two barangays, four had no representation, and two Tagbanua groups (indigenous people) were also not represented at the public hearings. In total, four hundred people attended the public hearings. And yet, subsequent documentation of the meetings did not include all points raised in the meetings, raising further questions as to the quality of the feedback gained through this crucial step in the NIPAP process.

In May 2000 further public input was sought when a Malampaya 3-D model was made and put on display in Taytay town, thereby providing an opportunity for students, politicians, and local people to share local views about their area. They used the symbols given by NIPAP to show where rivers ran, landslides occurred, and crops were planted. In total there were eighty-six participants, and it proved to be a valuable activity in providing local government and local residents with a role in identifying resources as part of the planning exercise.

The next step was a strategic planning workshop for PAMB members where problems were identified and solutions proposed. There were shortcomings here. This workshop was nonetheless able to acknowledge some of the problems of the area in a collective fashion and decide upon a vision for the protected area.

The general management plan was completed in July 2000 and integrated the vision and assorted insights of the various parties (including residents) garnered during the public hearings and consultations. The plan also tried to integrate the proposals for the protected area with other pertinent policies and practices, notably the fisheries code. The plan also provided comprehensive guidelines to the Protected Area Management Board so that this agency could use it as the basis for detailed management activities. The general management plan for Malampaya Sound was then passed on to the DENR for detailed review. Thereafter, the plan went to President Estrada, who signed a presidential declaration in July 2000 proclaiming Malampaya Sound a protected area under the NIPAS Act. A bill was then put before the Philippine Congress. Assuming that Congress will pass the bill, the protected area for Malampaya Sound can then be finally, demarcated, and the full legal and financial basis for environmental conservation in the area will thereby be in place.

This summary of the process surrounding the creation of a protected area at Malampaya Sound serves to underscore the complex political choreography that must go into this sort of exercise. Not surprisingly, there is much that can and does go wrong in the pursuit of official environmental conservation initiatives. The case of Malampaya Sound is no exception.

For one thing, chronic underfunding plagued the NIPAP process at Malampaya Sound. This state of affairs was partly occasioned by the initial opposition of local government to the proposed protected area, opposition that led NIPAP's leaders to shift funds to other "less intractable" settings. Yet, as the process gained momentum subsequent to the new stance of local councilors and the Taytay mayor, funding restrictions continued to impede progress at Malampaya Sound. On the one hand, local protected area staff lacked resources—a permanent office, the means to patrol the planned protected area (such as fast motorboats), and even paychecks, as salaries were paid in an alarmingly erratic fashion because of budget constraints.

On the other hand, NIPAP staff sought to resolve this impossible situation by cutting back on "expensive" community consultations in a process that inevitably damaged the democratic pretensions of the entire conservation initiative. As noted, a number of communities were left out of the process; indeed, even in cases where communities were consulted through public hearings and the like, there was usually inadequate time to enable all to attend and have their say. Further, educational materials explaining the NIPAP scheme were often ill conceived. Thus, for example, money was wasted on expensive glossy brochures in English as well as Tagalog-language materials written at an advanced level not understood by many of the residents of the area, who were poor migrants from Visayan-speaking areas.

Such inattention to community needs and sensitivities reflected a broader limitation of the NIPAP process, that is, a worrying vagueness about community input in that process. Thus, framing legislation (the NIPAS Act) does not define how the communities should be involved in the declaration process, only that they should be so engaged. As a result, outside experts are left largely to their own devices in terms of ascertaining the level of community input in the process. This has led in similar settings around the Philippines to local community unrest and opposition to "externally imposed" conservation.[19]

Yet this sort of inattention to the local context flies not only in the face of official rhetoric on the greening of the Philippine state but also arguably of common sense. After all, the support of local communities for conservation is critical, since without it protected area declarations are meaningless. Conservation rarely stands on its own for long. Livelihood strategies, health improvement, or tenure security are necessary ways of linking community life to conservation. These could have been used within the NIPAS legal framework, but the NIPAP initiative either dropped them or gave these activities little time or money.

The NIPAP process was never able to resolve all intrastate tensions and divisions. If local government was brought on board with promises of local political influence and the prospect of outside money (project and economic spin-offs such as ecotourism), basic institutional differences between the NIPAP organization and the DENR persisted. In many respects, the NIPAP was rather like a Band-Aid sticking on the much larger and better-established DENR—few of its activities were integrated into existing DENR structures and procedures, making long-term sustainability of the projects questionable. Instead, DENR staff tended to absorb NIPAP-destined resources into its own set of practices at the local and regional levels even where this might contravene the spirit if not the letter of the memorandum of agreement between the two sides. Thus, local staff assigned to work through NIPAP tended to persist in reporting to DENR superiors, and a fast boat intended for NIPAP staff at Malampaya was commandeered by the DENR.

From Plunder to Penitence

In a sense, intrastate squabbling over who should control conservation personnel and equipment is a decided improvement over previous squabbles over who would be in charge of activities that degraded the environment. The greening of the Philippine state is thus bound to generate a measure of internal squabbling over the spoils of conservation. In this view, an excessive focus on official wrangling and turf struggles is liable to lose sight of the much bigger good-news story at stake here: the shift in state policies and practices from one broadly based on natural resource plunder to one increasingly focused on environmental conservation.

There is certainly evidence from the Malampaya case study to support this view. True, resource degradation has persisted in the area, notably linked to destructive fishing practices by small and large fishers alike. And yet, the injection of the NIPAP process into the area in the late 1990s has had the salutary effect of concentrating the minds of both residents and politicians on issues of local sustainability. The disasters of 1998 added a sense of urgency to this process. To some extent at least, the complex and painstaking political negotiations that have underpinned the proposed protected area at Malampaya have brought on board a range and number of actors that bodes well for the long-term prospects of local conservation.

And yet, as this chapter has highlighted, all is not completely well with the NIPAP process at Malampaya Sound. Persistent intrastate tensions aside, there is the glaring weakness of the process in terms of local community input. The latter has been all too often formulaic and partial in nature, reflecting the relatively low priority accorded to community concerns and interests in the conservation initiative. This is surely a counterproductive stance in a context in which local support is widely acknowledged to be vital to successful conservation. Indeed, as expectations of local communities continue to rise (not the least because of pervasive official rhetoric) that conservation will be linked to community livelihoods and concerns, there is a growing danger that social conflict will be the inevitable result if initiatives such as the NIPAP "get it wrong."

It is too early to tell whether the uneven articulation of a green state in the Philippines will translate on the ground into a coherent strategy integrating conservation with livelihoods. Much depends certainly on the persistence of pressure from outside the state. As we have discussed, a variety of forces have come together since the mid-1980s to prompt a process of greening. Thus, there was the political revolution associated with the People Power Revolution and the concomitant downfall of the autocratic Marcos. Shifts in donor concerns linked to the upsurge of interest in sustainable development both provided a financial incentive for the greening of the state and nurtured a Philippine NGO sector keen to chivy successive state leaders down this path. This particular combination of political, economic, and social factors has been linked to the promotion of a series of conservation initiatives around the country, including Malampaya Sound in Palawan. Thus, fundamentally, continued progress in terms of the greening of the state is predicated on sustained outside pressure from donors, scholars, and the NGO sector.

Yet even this is insufficient. Our case study scarcely highlighted best practice. To maintain the momentum for change, then, requires more than the well-intentioned intervention of sympathetic outsiders. Indeed, there is a clear and pressing need for a much more effective and systematic effort to embed local residents in would-be protected areas at the heart of the decision-making process. This case is particularly relevant to current resource management changes sought in Indonesia (and elsewhere in the region). It has an equally strong history of plunder under twenty years of dictatorship under the Suharto administration. It remains to be seen whether similar attempts to green the state under "reformasi" can be achieved. Although by no means best practice, our case does highlight alternative conservation approaches that emphasize inclusive dialogue processes with local people. If the recent history of conservation in the Philippines (as elsewhere in the developing world) can be summed up as the move from coercion to consultation, the latter is still an inadequately implemented strategy, both for gaining the support of local communities and as a basis for a green state.

In the end, official penitence is not enough but must be accompanied by a genuine commitment to promoting the welfare of local residents, many of whom have been the principal victims of a long and sordid history of state-sanctioned plunder in the country.

Notes

1. Broad and Cavanagh (1993).
2. Thompson (1995).
3. Ross (2001, 54).
4. Kummer (1992); Tucker (2000).
5. Kummer (1992); Ross (2001).
6. Korten (1994); Ross (1996).
7. Redclift (1987).

8. Philippine Council for Sustainable Development (PCSD) (1987, iii).

9. Nozawa (1996).

10. Morales (1997).

11. Serrano (1994); Kalaw (1997); and Environmental Science for Social Change (ESSC) (1999).

12. Beja (1999).

13. Gutierrez (1994); Coronel, ed. (1996); and Sidel (1999).

14. Jacinto (1995).

15. Rebecca Rivera (1997).

16. National Integrated Protected Areas Program (1997).

17. See Walpole et al. (1994).

18. For details, see Lawrence (2002).

19. Rood, (1998); Raymond L. Bryant (2000).

II

The State and Transnational Environmental Governance

7

Greening the Constitutional State: Environmental Rights in the European Union

Tim Hayward

The most fundamental commitments and obligations of states are generally enshrined in their constitutions. When considering what states can do to promote environmental protection, therefore, it is appropriate to look to the constitution as a significant potential source of laws and policies that can serve that end. In this chapter, the specific focus is on the potential role in greening the state of according constitutional force to a provision that guarantees, in the words of the Brundtland Report, a fundamental right of all individuals to an environment adequate for their health and well-being.[1]

The basic question is, Would a state be greener with a constitutional environmental right than without? I examine the prima facie reasons for both affirmative and negative answers. I note that because the effectiveness of constitutional environmental rights depends crucially on how a state implements and enforces its constitutional commitments, which no two states do in an identical manner, this presents a problem for any attempt to attain an answer to the question with any significant degree of generalizability. It is with regard to this problem that there are distinct advantages in considering the question in the context of states that are members of the European Union (EU). As states bound by law to fundamental norms that are not necessarily of their own making, the specificities of the individual states' constitutional culture, environmental policies, rights enforcement mechanisms, and so on, can to a certain degree be bracketed out in order to focus on the question whether provision of a substantive environmental right with constitutional force has the potential to add anything to the environmental and human rights provisions that already bind them.

Accordingly, I seek to identify the main environmental rights currently enjoyed by citizens of states within the EU and to assess whether these could be significantly enhanced by the provision of a fundamental substantive right to an adequate environment, entrenched or binding at the constitutional level of the EU. The environmental provisions of foundational treaties and European Community law relating to the environment are considered. The European Union has a commitment of a fundamental kind to high standards of environmental protection, and although in treaties it is not expressed in terms of a fundamental right, this commitment, which can be said to have the equivalent of constitutional force, informs policy principles and directives, some of which may in practice, under certain circumstances, issue in environmental rights for citizens. It is shown that the protections they offer, while significant, fall short of what might be expected of a substantive environmental right with constitutional force. The environmental protections afforded by human rights law are then considered. This examines the scope of substantive and procedural environmental rights as currently available in Europe. The focus is particularly on the European Convention on Human Rights (ECHR) and the Aarhus Convention, both of which have authoritative status at EU and member state level. Again, though, while some scope for invoking nonenvironmental human rights for environmental ends is noted, and the potential for citizens to exercise procedural rights to these ends is acknowledged, it is shown nevertheless that a substantive environmental right with constitutional force would not be inconsequential.

Although this chapter focuses on the specific context of states within the EU, this context also captures significant aspects of broader global trends. It is increasingly the case that the continued preeminence of the nation-state as sole authorized administrative agency for a territory is not equally matched by its having sole sovereignty with regard to the norms it has to administer. Pressures for constitutional environmental rights, or greening the state more generally, thus come not only from within states, in particular from agents of civil society, but also from without, from the influence and precedents of international agreements and treaties. To be sure, the situation of European states is not directly comparable with that of all states throughout the world, especially poorer ones, not only because of the sui generis nature of the Union but also because its member states have already attained a certain level of development, rights protection, and environmental protection, which are not equally matched by all states. Nevertheless, as indicated at appropriate points in the course of

EU-specific arguments, and highlighted in the conclusion, aspects of the argument are generalizable to non-European democratic states to the extent that they have comparable development, rights, and environmental records.

Rationale and Approach

That states can and should make some form of constitutional provision for environmental protection is now hardly a matter of dispute. Globally, more than seventy states include provision for environmental protection in their constitutions, and in at least thirty cases this takes the form of environmental rights.[2] No recently promulgated constitution has omitted reference to environmental principles, and many older constitutions are being amended to include them.

The advantages for environmental protection of constitutional-level provision are that it enshrines a recognition of its importance at the highest political and legal levels; it offers the possibility of unifying principles for legislation and regulation; and it secures these principles against the vicissitudes of routine politics while at the same time potentially enhancing possibilities of democratic participation in environmental decision-making processes.[3]

Whether the provision should have the form of an environmental *right*, however, is a distinct question.[4] Certainly, the advantages of constitutional provision for environmental protection are potentially the greater if it does have this form. Rights can mark the seriousness, the "trumping" status in relation to lesser obligations of the state, of environmental concern, and they articulate this concern in an institutionalized discourse with some established mechanisms of enforcement, thus providing means for citizens and their associations to challenge the state when it fails to meet its obligations. Giving constitutional force to rights of environmental protection can give this a due weight in the balance with other social values that already have the status of rights, particularly those associated with economic development, rather than being seen as a partisan cause.

Whether these advantages would necessarily be realized in actuality, however, is another matter. At this stage I consider three reasons why they might not. One is that rights may not be the most appropriate means of providing environmental protection. Another is that existing environmental and rights provisions might already achieve what an express environmental right aims at. A third reason is that states do not necessarily fully live up to their constitutional commitments. Considering the first two reasons will help, respectively, delimit and focus the question; considering the third will require us to reflect on appropriate methods for answering it.

Regarding the point that the aims of environmental protection are not necessarily most appropriately pursued by means of constitutional environmental rights (for humans), it has to be acknowledged that in considering the environment only under the aspect of its contribution to human health and well-being, this right does not capture all aspects of environmental concern.[5] It is therefore not expected that a constitutional environmental right would be sufficient to make a state as green as might be desirable according to a more comprehensive set of environmental aims. It does not follow, however, that constitutional environmental rights may not fulfill a necessary part of those aims, so that, taking a suitably circumscribed criterion of greenness, a state would be greener with than without them.[6]

The second possible reason for a negative answer, though, is that express environmental rights may not be necessary to achieve the aims even as circumscribed. The possibility of greening a state by means of constitutional environmental rights can reasonably be expected to presuppose on the part of the state an existing commitment, with constitutional status or its equivalent, both to a high standard of environmental protection and to human rights. These commitments are, after all, its constituent elements. But if a state is already committed to environmental principles and human rights, this leaves scope to doubt whether an additional commitment to a specific environmental right would necessarily make it any greener. It is possible under certain circumstances for constitutional or legal environmental provisions to have rights-like effects without the need for an express constitutional right to underpin them. It is also possible for nonenvironmental rights to have environmental applications. The question for this chapter is whether these possibilities hold.

Now clearly this is a question that can only meaningfully be asked in specific contexts about actual states, not of states in general or in the abstract, for it requires an investigation of actual provisions and how they are operationalized. Once attention is drawn to empirical characteristics of states we are brought to consider the third reason for a possible negative answer.

States do not in practice always give full effect to their principled constitutional commitments. Just because an environmental right is formally declared in a constitution does not necessarily mean the right will be implemented or enforced in a manner adequate to fulfill the aims apparent in its wording. In some states the political culture is such that constitutional provisions in general, and rights in particular, are treated as expressions of aspiration as much as or more than legally binding commitments. Even in states that do generally treat constitutional rights as binding commitments, though, the rights provided, or some of them, can be hedged in with various qualifications so that their actual implementation does not match the normative intention apparent on the face of the constitutional statement.

From this it follows that in order to answer the question it is not a satisfactory approach merely to look for what additional commitments may in principle be implied by a state's constitutional declaration of an environmental right, for this will not tell us whether in consequence of that declaration the state will be greener in practice. The need for the inquiry to have an empirical element is clear, but what sort of evidence would be useful, and how would it be attained?

One possible approach would be to draw empirical comparisons between states that have constitutional environmental rights and states that do not in order to determine which are greener. Empirical evidence can be adduced to suggest that there is not necessarily any positive correlation between the constitutional provision of environmental rights by a state and its actual protection of the environment or associated rights. Those states with the most extensive environmental rights on constitutional paper often compare unfavorably with other states with regard to their actual record in enforcing those and other rights. But we need to be cautious about the inferences that might be drawn from such comparisons, for the same reason that was flagged in relation to the first approach, namely, that in no two states are the relations between rights declarations, their implementation, and their enforcement identical.

An alternative approach, one that could be adopted for a state that already has constitutionalized environmental rights, would be to undertake longitudinal studies of the state's greenness before and after constitutionalization of the right to seek evidence of its effects. If such studies can control reliably so as to ascertain that the pressures that led to the constitutionalizing of environmental rights would not have led to an equivalent change in the degree of its greenness even without that formal commitment, they could provide an answer for that state. It has to be said, though, that there is still relatively little experience to go on for such states, and the evidence may therefore not be clear and conclusive. Furthermore, because this approach cannot be used directly to study states that do not already have constitutional environmental rights, the generalizability of its results will still be subject to the problems that I noted affect the other approaches.

Suppose, though, that these problems, stemming from the diversity of states' constitutional arrangements and cultures, are not so great as to preclude the possibility of a suitably subtle comparative method controlling for that diversity and thus yielding the answer I have suggested may be somewhat elusive.[7] There nevertheless remains one sort of variable to control for which presents difficulties of a qualitatively different kind. I am thinking about the significance of political will formation. This can be a key determinant of the declaration of a right, of its mode of implementation, and of the assiduousness of its enforcement. The question of what political will would be formed in what circumstances depends on numerous factors, but one of the factors it depends on, in states where constitutional environmental rights are a proposition for consideration rather than an accomplished fact, is the persuasiveness of the arguments in favor of the proposition. The outcome of actual deliberations about the question at the heart of this chapter can play a part in determining the answer to it in any particular context. We cannot expect the content and outcome of deliberations to be reliably predicted in advance. This represents a limiting factor on any purely empirical approach to the question: political will can have a bearing, in particular, on how seriously a state takes its own constitutional commitments, and so, since political will can always be in the process of formation, this matter cannot be adjudged purely on the basis of the state's historical track record.

From the standpoint of participants in the deliberative processes of political will formation, therefore, there is heuristic value and validity in pursuing the original normative question, in this hypothetical form: Would the state be greener with a constitutional environmental right than without *if* the assumption is made that the state takes its constitutional commitments seriously, in the sense of implementing and enforcing the constitutional rights as on the face of their declaration?

The heuristic value of the question is greater, though, in proportion as that further assumption can in fact be warranted. But how or when would it ever be? One sort of circumstance where the assumption might be warranted is one in which the state has to live up to its principled commitments, even in the face of countervailing pressures. The EU context provides a case of how transnationally recognized norms, such as those relating to the environment and human rights, can acquire the equivalent of constitutional force in states, even in the face of countervailing political traditions, and with relatively little regard for specific sociocultural or political contexts that could affect the manner of their implementation. The specificities of different states' constitutional culture play a less decisive role in determining how fundamental norms are implemented than would be the case if the states remained fully sovereign. This allows issues of implementation to be considered from the point of view of principled imperatives and conflicts rather than relatively contingent technical obstacles arising out of particular national circumstances.

So, of the three possible sources of a negative answer to the question, the first has been allowed for and the third is, as far as possible, to be controlled for. The main focus for this chapter, therefore, is on the second: Do the existing environmental and human rights provisions that are binding on member states of the EU already provide the protections that a formally declared right to an adequate environment would aim for?

Environmental Rights in European Community Law

European Community law does not provide substantive environmental rights, but it does comprise a considerable amount of legislation that may serve some of the ends such rights would be intended to achieve. Its policy principles and directives have underpinned developments in case law that suggests that environmental deterioration can lead to violations of rights.

EC Policy Principles

The Treaty on European Union, signed at Maastricht on February 7, 1992, provides that Community policy "shall be based on the precautionary principle and on the principles that preventive action should be taken, that environmental damage should as a priority be rectified at source and that the polluter should pay."[8] This is an unequivocal statement, with constitutional force, of principles of environmental protection; and no other program or policy is given this importance in the treaty. To be sure, policy principles do not directly confer environmental rights on individuals, but their implementation may nevertheless have significant rights implications. In particular, the potential of the "polluter pays" principle and the precautionary principle merit consideration.

"Polluter Pays" Principle   The basic idea of the "polluter pays" principle is that the polluter should bear the expenses of preventing and controlling pollution to ensure that the environment is in an acceptable state. As usually interpreted, the principle applies so as to attach liability for clean up to the original agent who contaminates or pollutes: it does not require the polluter to pay to an individual rights bearer; rather, it provides an allocative mechanism to internalize negative externalities. It is not obvious, then, that the principle generates rights.

Nevertheless, in order to enforce the principle, a legal regime of environmental liability has to be in place; and rights might at least indirectly be enhanced by tightening the liability regime. This suggestion is of particular relevance in a European context given that a White Paper on Environmental Liability was adopted in April 2004 whose text lays out the main features of a liability regime for damages to the environment.[9] The environmental liability regime could help enhance citizens' environmental rights in a number of ways, in particular by applying the principle of strict liability and by reversing the burden of proof in cases of environmental damage.

The principle of strict liability is of indirect benefit for citizens' environmental rights in that it undercuts a significant obstacle to success in civil suits, namely, the burden of proving fault or negligence on the part of the polluter. However, the principle does not of itself give rise to rights and is likely in practice to be restricted in application to activities classed as dangerous rather than to any activity at all. This restriction flows from a concern to balance interests in environmental protection against the interests of industry in not stifling innovation.

Regarding the burden of proof, legal actions against alleged polluters often fail because of the notorious difficulties in establishing causal links with regard to environmental harms. Environmental groups have long argued that the burden of proof should be on the defendant, so that after an initial evidentiary hurdle has been surmounted by the plaintiff, there would be a presumption that the defendant's activity caused the damage in cases where the substances or activities undertaken by the defendant are in principle capable of resulting in the type of damage that has occurred. Such a reversal would significantly enhance the effectiveness of citizens' and campaigners' procedural rights. However, because of pressure from industry, the White Paper proposals stop short of reversing the burden of proof, turning it into an alleviation of the burden of proof for the plaintiff. They have been able to invoke arguments in favor of a presumption of innocence.

It thus appears that measures necessary for successful implementation of the "polluter pays" principle would be measures that also enhance (procedural) rights of concerned citizens and campaigners to hold polluters to account. The principle itself, though, does not directly generate environmental rights. The logic of a commitment to the effective implementation of the principle actually implies the need for a fundamental environmental right.

Precautionary Principle   The precautionary principle may be a more promising basis for generating rights.[10] According to this principle, when an activity raises threats of harm to human health or the environment, precautionary measures should be taken even if cause-and-effect relationships are not fully established scientifically. This means that the burden of proof of the harmlessness of a new technology, process, activity, or chemical is the responsibility of its proponents, not the public.

However, does (or could) the principle provide a basis for rights citizens can actually rely on? The interpretation of the principle is subject to considerable contestation, and issues of interpretation arise at each stage of the specification and operationalization of the principle. To begin with, the prima facie case for precaution—the existence of threats of serious or irreversible environmental damage—has to be established. However, the principle itself does not supply clear guidance as to the degree of proof required before the principle becomes operational. Even when the genuine possibility of the threat is established, this does not mean that the proposed activity is necessarily prohibited. Rather, it is treated as a factor to be taken into account in a cost-benefit analysis. A problem in trying to identify cost-effective measures in environmental cases is that the effects are not established. Hence there are scientific uncertainties, but the uncertainties also have a political dimension because any comparison of costs and benefits involves contestable assumptions about where, when, how, and on whom each should fall. Thus, even with regard to a threat of serious or irreversible environmental harm, there is no guidance inherent in the principle as to the weight to be given to such a factor in reaching a final decision in conflicts between environmental and economic values.

So, although the status of the precautionary principle within the EU and more generally seems well established, and despite its undeniable importance in imparting substantive meaning to environmental rights, the inherent uncertainties involved in applying it mean the principle cannot in itself be considered a source of rights and cannot make fundamental environmental rights redundant; on the contrary, in its operation there are situations where independent appeal to such rights can be necessary.

Directives

Most EU environmental laws are directives, a form of law designed to impose obligations on member states while being flexible enough to take into account differing legal and administrative traditions. Directives are binding on all member states, but the choice and method of aligning each national legal and administrative system is left to the discretion of the member state. Because directives specify general goals, they are not necessarily or primarily intended to confer rights on individuals. Nevertheless, legal scholars have adduced reasons to think that some directives are capable of generating rights. Some argue this on the grounds that directives are capable of direct effect, and that a necessary condition for the direct effect of a directive is that it does bestow rights on individuals. Alternatively, where direct effect is not possible, rights may be generated from directives via the principle of state liability, as established in cases such as *Francovich*.[11] I consider these two lines of argument in turn.

Direct Effect   The doctrine of direct effect has been formulated, in a case where an environmental directive was at issue, in the following way:

Wherever the provisions of a directive appear, as far as their subject matter is concerned, to be unconditional and sufficiently precise, those provisions may be relied upon by an individual against the State where the State fails to implement the directive in national law by the period prescribed or where it fails to implement the directive correctly.[12]

There are parallels between this doctrine and that of the self-execution of constitutional or treaty provisions, with the requirements of unconditionality and precision applying to each. In practice, the requisite conditions for self-execution are more likely to be found to obtain for negative mandates than for positive ones,[13] that is, for mandates that put some constraint on the state as opposed to those yielding a positive obligation on it, and this informal requirement seems to be broadly borne out for directives of EC law, too. Perhaps the most significant point, though, is that not all, or even the majority, of environmental directives have direct effect.

State Liability and Environmental Rights: The Significance of *Francovich*
Some commentators argue that environmental rights can and do flow from directives without direct effect via the principle of state liability, as developed by the International Court of Justice in *Francovich* and subsequent landmark cases.[14] The Court of Justice listed three necessary and jointly sufficient conditions of state liability for not correctly implementing a directive: first, the rule infringed must be one established for the protection of individual rights; second, the scope of such rights must be ascertainable in the light of the directive in question; third, there must be a causal link between the damage suffered by the plaintiff and the violation imputed to the member state.

The significance of *Francovich* with regard to environmental rights is, however, a matter of some debate. There are differences of opinion, particularly, on the question of when an environmental directive entails the grant of rights to individuals. In Miller's view, and especially because of the essentially programmatic nature of directives, the "rights" they give rise to are in effect a legitimate expectation that state obligations be honored, but a legitimate expectation is not a right. Somsen, though, maintains that even on a restrictive interpretation of a "right," there are a number of environmental rights that could be protected by the *Francovich* remedy.[15] These include directives that are primarily concerned with the protection of human health against the adverse effects of certain types of pollution.

Nevertheless, environmental cases, as Miller has observed, are not typically the sort to which *Francovich* rulings might be applied.[16] Because many environmental directives, if not directly effective, allow states a margin of appreciation, they do not fit the *Francovich* criteria for state liability. Rather, they would be judged in accordance with the Court's doctrine on state liability for breaches of European Community law, as further elaborated in subsequent judgments, most notably in *Brasserie* and *Factortame*,[17] to cover cases in which, unlike *Francovich*, a directive leaves a wide margin of discretion in taking legislative decisions. In such cases, the conditions for *Francovich* liability are modified so that instead of the requirement that the contents of the individual's right be established on the basis of the directive, it is required that the breach must be "sufficiently serious, a manifest and grave disregard of the limits on the exercise of power."[18] Clearly, this criterion of seriousness involves matters of political judgment. A substantive constitutional environmental right could help provide criteria of seriousness. More generally, to succeed in holding a state liable for a breach of rights would seem normally and minimally to require a prior authoritative statement of those rights.

The main conclusion I draw from this brief consideration of European Community environmental law is that whatever rights may be inferred from directives and even policy statements, it makes a significant difference, particularly in view of how much debate turns on the clarity of statements of the rights to be protected, if the rights are themselves clearly stated with the equivalent of constitutional authority. A genuine commitment to the principles underpinning the policies and directives does, I suggest, strongly imply a commitment to the principle of a constitutional environmental right; the limits on the application of them suggest the need for implementation of such a right.

Using Human Rights for Environmental Protection

It remains to ask, however, whether the commitments of an environmental right can be fulfilled by existing human rights that are recognized within the European Union.[19]

The Environmental Potential of Existing Substantive Rights in the European Convention and EU Social Charter

Article 2 of the European Convention provides a right to life, which Stefan Weber argues is the European legal provision most appropriate to protect the environment, invoking the suggestion that its rationale is the protection of life from all possible threats, including those presented by environmental deterioration.[20] Nevertheless, this is probably a minority view, and while the right to life may have some potential application in the environmental field, it has not yet been successfully invoked.[21] Moreover, it would only seem to apply in relation to drastic and present harms, or at least to direct threats to life, and thus not cover other serious environmental concerns.

Some of the concerns not covered by the right to life might appear to be covered, though, by the right to health, provided in Article 11 of the European Social Charter, Part I, which is a right of everyone to benefit from any measures enabling them to enjoy the highest possible standard of health attainable. The Social Charter does not provide for an individual complaint procedure, its application being supervised through the submission by states of reports that are examined by the Committee of Experts. That committee has taken the view that Article 11 requires states to take measures to prevent certain forms of environmental pollution; however, the requirement is very general, with an undefined threshold of protection, so that states are generally found to be in compliance with it. Moreover, even if the committee were to be more critical, its opinions would not be binding. Hence this right is not a very promising candidate for fulfilling the aims of a fundamental right to an adequate environment.[22] Similar points apply to Article 3 of the Social Charter, which provides a right to safe and healthy working conditions.[23]

Interestingly, a right that has been used to set potentially important precedents for environmental protection is provided by Article 8 of the European Convention, a right to respect for one's private and family life and one's home. A particularly significant precedent was the 1994 case of *Lopez-Ostra v. Spain*.[24] The applicant had suffered serious health problems from fumes from a tannery waste treatment plant, and her attempt to obtain compensation from the Spanish courts had been completely unsuccessful. The European Court of Human Rights held that there had been a breach of Article 8, and this was the first time the organs of the European Convention found a breach of the Convention as a consequence of environmental harm. This judgment may be claimed to have enhanced the legal protection of the environmental victim by opening the door to applying Article 8 to nearly all sources of pollution, and not only to noise emissions, as in previous cases. Nevertheless, this right is still ultimately tied to the concerns its words state—private and family life—rather than to the environmental well-being of individuals, whoever and wherever they are, in public or private spaces.[25] So while the expansive interpretations of this right illustrate the possibilities for stronger environmental rights—and these have been further illustrated in the subsequent landmark case of *Guerra and Others v. Italy*[26]—it remains likely that such possibilities can only be fully realized through the instantiation of more specifically environmental rights.

Procedural Rights and the Aarhus Convention

Perhaps the most significant area of development of environmental rights in Europe as elsewhere is that of procedural rights relevant to the civil, political, and legal possibilities for environmental protection. Their development was given a further impetus by The Convention on Access to Information, Public Participation in Decision Making and Access to Justice in Environmental Matters, generally known as the Aarhus Convention (1998).[27] This agreement, to which both the EU and its member states are signatories, represents probably the most important step yet taken toward environmental rights protection: it establishes rights—to information, to participation in decision making, and to access to justice in environmental matters—which it expressly affirms are aimed at securing the right to a healthy environment.

It is beyond doubt that these procedural rights have a necessary and important role to play; a question, though, is whether they will also, as some commentators believe, be sufficient to that end.[28]

Right to Environmental Information   Access to adequate information in the environmental field is a sine qua non for the successful exercise and enforcement of environmental rights. Even prior to Aarhus, some significant elements of such a right were already in place, and to pave the way for ratification of the Convention, with its more stringent requirements, the EU has had to prepare a new directive on access to environmental information.

Yet while an adequately enforced right of access to environmental information is an indispensable prerequisite for effective and democratic measures to protect the environment, it is equally clearly not sufficient on its own because there has also to be scope for putting the information to effective use. This, though, is what the other two procedural rights are intended to enhance.

Rights of Participation   The practical significance of rights of participation in environmental policymaking, in decision-making processes
regarding environmental developments, and in the determination of
environmental standards has also long been recognized. The Aarhus
Convention acknowledged that greater clarification is needed in defining
which environmental issues must include public participation, and that
the concept of the interested or affected party should include NGOs as
representatives of legitimate collective interests.

Nevertheless, the public participation provisions relating to decision
making on policies, plans, programs, and legislation have been criticized
for being so weak as to be more like recommendations, even though these
are some of the most important forms of environmental decision making.
Provision of a substantive environmental right, by contrast, could be
expected to carry some weight in deliberations at the higher levels of decision making as well as to enhance prospects of securing environmental
outcomes against competing interests through public influence at other
levels.

Access to Justice   Another necessary but insufficient condition for effective realization of substantive environmental rights is procedural rights
to seek legal redress in the environmental arena. These include "rights
to object to ministerial and agency environmental decisions; and rights to
bring action against departments, agencies, firms, and individuals that
fail to carry out their duties according to law."[29]

With regard to the availability and effectiveness of these rights prior to
the Aarhus Convention, three particular problem areas were identified.
One was the general slowness of many administrative and judicial appeal
procedures. In principle, the demands embodied in the Aarhus Convention would do something to ameliorate this problem. Another,
though, is the high fees and costs: the prohibitive expenses include bonds
that often are set too high for parties with limited means who are acting
to protect the environment. The Aarhus Convention does not appear to
offer much to overcome this obstacle, which is left to individual states
to deal with. A third obstacle concerns restrictions on legal standing to
take action. The Aarhus Convention has gone some way to ease these
restrictions, reflecting the growing consensus that public interest groups
whose activities show that they have a genuine interest in protecting the

environment should have standing without having to wait for the relevant public authority to take action. Ultimately, though, whether actions admitted actually succeed on their merits depends on the basic principles courts are to apply, and a substantive environmental right could give guidance that may otherwise be lacking.

In all, the Aarhus Convention has certainly set in train real advances for environmental rights, but environmentalist citizens' organizations have been critical of extensive weaknesses, loopholes, and ambiguities in the text, and have described the compliance mechanism for the Convention as the weakest of any in international environmental law. The Aarhus Convention can thus be criticized for not going far enough to meet its own ends. Its preamble states that "adequate protection of the environment is essential to human well-being and the enjoyment of basic human rights, including the right to life itself," and it includes express recognition "that every person has the right to live in an environment adequate to his or her health and well-being." It stops short, however, of providing means for citizens directly to invoke this right.

It is this last point, rather than specific weaknesses of the Aarhus Convention itself, that I think most significant. It remains the case for the moment, as when Dinah Shelton wrote in 1993, that "there is no right to a clean environment to be balanced with other rights or with Community policies."[30] Procedural rights alone do too little to counterbalance the prevailing presumptions in favor of development and economic interests. Indeed, procedural rights can cut both ways: they enable parties to both challenge proposed action by the state and to resist such challenges. Such considerations can reasonably be argued to point to the need for a substantive environmental right that stands above political contestation.

It seems, then, on the basis of the considerations advanced here, that a substantive environmental right in Europe would not be inconsequential.

Conclusion

We have seen that environmental rights derivable from existing environmental and human rights law can achieve a good deal but fall short of what could be expected from a substantive environmental right with constitutional force. This could underpin changes in legal presumptions so as to strengthen principles of liability—civil and state—for environmental harms, and ease the burden of proof on citizens and associations that seek to challenge environmentally harmful practices. It could also enhance prospects for challenges to inadequate laws and regulations. Part of the reason it could achieve these ends is that it would allow rights of environmental protection to have a determinate status in relation to other social goals that are already protected as rights instead of being seen, as at present they sometimes are, as the values of a partisan cause. Thus, they have a role in firming up the protections that could be achieved through the exercise of procedural environmental rights.

Nevertheless, two limitations on the practical purchase of these arguments need to be noted. One is that it is doubtful whether there is an imminent prospect of a Europe-wide environmental right. An obviously appropriate place for one would be the EU's Charter of Fundamental Rights and Freedoms, which would be the document of fundamental rights in any European constitution; but although an article about environmental protection is included, its wording and placement make it considerably weaker than a substantive right to an adequate environment.[31] In this regard it is worth noting that the development of EU norms can be influenced by precedents from member states. Furthermore, the European Court of Human Rights, which has already demonstrated a readiness to recognize the nexus between environment and human rights, "may note the existence of human rights–enhancing practices and policies taken by Contracting States and 'raise the standard of rights-protection to which all states must adhere.'"[32]

The second limitation on the scope of the arguments presented here concerns their generalizability to states beyond Europe. Among developed states with constitutional democratic governments, formal disparities are not great: EU directives stand in a relation to state laws, which is comparable to constitutional provisions within states; its human rights jurisprudence corresponds to international norms; and as I have sought to indicate, the issues of justifying and applying the relevant legal principles are generalizable enough to admit of useful comparisons. Where the arguments may have less purchase, however, is in poorer states, which have more serious problems living up to their formal commitments. There are clearly limits to the usefulness of seeking to hold states to obligations that it is materially beyond their capacity to fulfill. The source of a potentially damaging criticism of the argument of this chapter is that it has focused on affluent states and disregarded their relations to poorer states. The critical question that might be asked is whether enhancing citizens' environmental rights in rich industrialized countries could have the net effect of further displacing environmental problems onto poorer countries, meaning that effective rights in the latter are diminished. My response to this is that the existence of global injustice does require us to address moral questions about the obligations of the rich with regard to the environmental rights of the poor, but there is reason to think that an international regime of environmental rights would be more robust if those rights are constitutionally recognized as fundamental by those state powers that are most influential in formulating and developing international law.

Notes

The author wishes to thank Lynn Dobson, Russell Keat, and the editors of this volume for suggestions of improvements to earlier versions of this chapter. Initial research on this topic was funded by ESRC research grant (R000222269), which is gratefully acknowledged.

1. World Commission on Environment and Development (1987, 348).

2. See Ksentini (1994, 178, n.2); Hayward (1998, 178, n. 2).

3. See Hayward (2002).

4. For an overview of the issues, see Brandl and Bungert (1992).

5. A central general objection is that they are anthropocentric. See, for instance, Redgwell (1996). For a critical discussion of objections to anthropocentrism, see, for instance, Hayward (1997).

6. Thus I would claim that a constitutional environmental right would support, more strongly than would a nonrights constitutional provision, several of the criteria of a green state as proposed by Peter Christoff in chapter 2 of this volume. For instance, giving rights to environmental welfare a more comparable status to rights of economic development would serve to promote integration of policies in these areas. It would also underpin a stronger budgetary commitment to human welfare environmental issues. Furthermore, it would support higher levels of ecocitizenship by making the exercise of procedural environmental rights more likely to have effective environmental outcomes, and thus also support the motivation to enhance stronger cultural and political institutionalization of ecological values.

7. According to Brandl and Bungert (1992, 81), in modern democracies of the Western world, at least, which are highly industrialized and hence polluted but also with substantially developed technical and legal means to cope with environmental pollution, "the basic constitutional issues are the same, even if the relevant provisions reflect difference in terminology, degree of abstraction, or the pattern of current preferences in each country."

8. Article 130r(2) of Treaty on European Union, as amended by Treaty of Union 1993.

9. European Commission (2000).

10. On whether the precautionary principle generates rights, see Miller (1995, 389); on controversies concerning the meaning of the precautionary principle, see, for example, Hughes (1995) and Fisher (2001).

11. International Court of Justice, case C-6/90, *Francovich v. Italian Republic* (1991), ECR I-5357.

12. International Court of Justice, case C-236/92, *Difesa della Cava*.

13. Fernandez (1994). For a critical discussion on this point, see also Scheinin (1994).

14. On the *Francovich* ruling and the conditions for the taking of direct effect, see Christopher Miller (1995, 382ff.) and Shelton (1993, 569ff.) On the implications of the ruling, see also Caranta (1993) and Somsen (1996).

15. Somsen (1996).

16. Christopher Miller (1995, 385).

17. Joined Cases C-46/93 and C-48/93, *Brasserie du Pêcheur* and *Factortame III* (1996) 1 CMLR 889.

18. See Somsen (1996, 140).

19. On the status of ECHR rights in EU, and the question of deriving environmental rights from them, see, for instance, Shelton (1993); DeMerieux (2001); Desgagné (1995); and Acevedo (2000).

20. Weber (1991).

21. Churchill (1996, 90). For more promising precedents outside Europe, though, see, for instance, Michael R. Anderson (1996).

22. Desgagné (1995, 271); Churchill (1996, 103).

23. Churchill (1996, 102).

24. For background on the case, see Alfred Rest (1997).

25. Thornton and Tromans (1999, 41) summarize the limits to the extent to which Article 8 can protect the environment. See also Desgagné (1995, 273, 283).

26. Acevedo (2000).

27. The Aarhus Convention, developed under the auspices of the UN Economic Commission for Europe (ECE), was signed in June 1998 by thirty-five countries from this region, which covers the whole of Europe as well as parts of Central Asia, United States, Canada, and Israel, although the North American countries opted out of the process. The Convention has also been signed by the European Community.

28. See, for example, Douglas-Scott (1992) and Handl (1992). Alan Boyle (1996) leans to this view as regards international law, but he allows that within a constitution there may be a better case for substantive rights (64).

29. Eckersley (1996, 230).

30. Shelton (1993, 582).

31. For the text, current status, and other information about the Charter, see its Web site, <http://www.europarl.eu.int/home/default_en.htm>.

32. Acevedo (2000, 446).

8

Greening the Nation-State: From Exclusive to Inclusive Sovereignty

Robyn Eckersley

If a green posture toward the nation-state can be discerned from the diverse writings of green political theorists and fellow environmentalists, it is that the nation-state plays, at best, a contradictory role in environmental management, facilitating both environmental destruction and environmental protection. At worst, it is fundamentally ecocidal.[1] Indeed, there are very few radical political ecologists and green political theorists who are prepared to defend the nation-state as an institution that is able to play a positive role in securing sustainable livelihoods and ecosystem integrity. Moreover, those interested in global political ecology are increasingly rejecting the "statist frame" through which international relations and world politics have been traditionally understood, preferring to understand states as but one set of actors or institutions among a myriad of actors and institutions on the global scene that are implicated in ecological destruction.[2] In all, the radical green analysis seems to point toward the need for alternative forms of political identity, authority, and governance that break with the traditional statist model of exclusive territorial rule.

In this chapter, I take the position that this green antipathy toward the nation-state and state-centric analyses of global ecological degradation should not be taken as a reason for avoiding an inquiry into the emancipatory potential of the nation-state as a significant node in any future network of ecological governance. This is especially true given that we can expect states to persist as major sites and channels of social and political power for at least the foreseeable future and that any green institutional transformations of the present political order will, short of revolution, necessarily be path-dependent. In any event, if it is indeed the case that states are so deeply implicated in ecological destruction, then an inquiry into the potential for their transformation or even their modest reform into something greener would seem to be compelling. To the extent that those who reject a statist analysis still concede that the state has an important role to play, the question arises as to what that role ought to be, given its present limitations and trajectory. After all, implicit in the day-to-day policy demands made of the state (both domestically and internationally) by environmentalists is a notion of what the state ought to be doing (or not doing)—in short, a green ideal or vision of what a "good state" might look like. Actively defending and cultivating such an ideal would seem to be politically and strategically necessary if the green movement is to avoid unwitting, ad hoc reinforcement of the destructive or oppressive tendencies of states in the course of pursuing its green public policy goals.

I am concerned to encourage a debate among green theorists and activists as to how we might rethink the nation-state and the state system from a critical green perspective (which I call critical political ecology). I acknowledge the contradictory role of the nation-state in managing ecological problems but suggest we search for ways of amplifying the state's role as an environmental protector while dampening its ecologically destructive potential over time. These complementary, paths point toward less exclusionary ideals of sovereignty, democracy, and citizenship yet retain the nation-state as a container of social processes (albeit with some potentially radical reworking of the meaning of "nation" and "national sovereignty"). I suggest that while in the long run such an approach provides a fundamental challenge to the link between territorially based structures of democratic rule and particular peoples, in the short to medium term it sees the state as a crucial facilitator in the transition toward more ecologically responsive governance.

By way of theoretical preliminaries, my critical political ecology framework approaches the state from a structurationist, or critical constructivist, perspective, which emphasizes the mutual constitution of agents and social structures.[3] Whereas mainstream rationalist approaches to international relations (namely, neorealism and neoliberal institutionalism) regard the principle of state sovereignty as an immutable ordering principle of world politics that is accepted as a given, critical constructivists understand state sovereignty as a protean concept, the meaning of which is determined by a web of constitutive discourses that are constantly contested and evolving (such as the norms of nonintervention, self-determination, and their subsidiary discourses, such as the rules of war, the so-called right to develop, the principle of permanent sovereignty over national resources, and so forth). The lesson for the green movement is that by playing a more informed and self-conscious role in the debates over the meaning and application of these norms, the movement might help to redefine sovereignty as an ally in its broader global project.

Three Standard Green Critiques of the State

Green theorists (and many environmentalists) have been highly skeptical of the nation-state and the state system. The three most significant (and recurring) of these critiques concern

- The anarchic character of the system of sovereign states, which is understood as structuring a dynamic that leads to the "tragedy of the commons."
- The parasitical dependence of states on private capital accumulation; that is, the state is inextricably bound up with, and fundamentally compromised by, the promotion of capital accumulation, which is a key driver of ecological destruction, and states are now actively promoting economic globalization in ways that further undermine their own political autonomy and steering capacity.
- The highly centralized and hierarchical character of states as institutions, with imperatives that are fundamentally at odds with the green vision of a more participatory democracy and human-scale, decentralized forms of governance.

In support of these three propositions, there is no shortage of detailed historical accounts of the various ways in which particular states (whether communist or capitalist, developed or undeveloped) have acted as resource plunderers and active prosecutors of environmentally destructive and sometimes violent agendas, most graphically during times of war but also during times of peace.[4] Moreover, if one of the defining features of states is that they hold the monopoly of legitimized violence, with democracy featuring as a contingent rather than defining characteristic of states, then they would seem by their very nature to represent institutions that run contrary to the basic green principle of nonviolence.

Taken together, these three general objections would appear to provide a powerful green indictment of states per se (rather than just particular "ecocidal" governments), with the implication that the prospects for the development of more ecologically responsive states are bleak. This reading also has significant short-term tactical and longer-term strategic implications for environmental movements and green parties struggling with limited resources, both of which, without further analysis, would seem to be best advised looking for alternative sites of political action.

Yet we should not be too hasty to assume that the structures and social dynamics referred to in these three analyses are necessarily always anti-ecological and always mutually reinforcing (although they often can be) or that they provide a complete green analysis and evaluation of the emancipatory potential of states as governance structures. Moreover, on their face, none of these arguments addresses the crucial question of state legitimacy or places any store on the possibilities of deepening the democratic accountability of states to the citizens of particular states, to transnational civil society, or to the society of states in general. It is as if the democratic form of the state were dismissed being not merely as contingent but also as illusory in the sense that it is typically overridden by the structural imperatives of international anarchy, global capitalism, and administrative hierarchy. These are, to be sure, deeply problematic structural dynamics for those concerned to secure global environmental integrity. However, they are not "iron laws" but rather constantly evolving practices that can change in character and influence depending on the movement of social forces and the prevailing social and cultural conditions and understandings. Indeed, one does not have to search very far to find historical examples of how each of these dynamics can be qualified, restrained, or otherwise moderated by state and nonstate agents acting back upon states, which in turn have acted back upon economic and social structures. Here, we might single out three, mutually informing developments that have served to moderate, and in some exceptional cases work synergistically to transform, the respective "logics" of anarchy, capitalism, and administrative hierarchy:

- The rise of environmental multilateralism, including environmental treaties and declarations and international environmental standards
- The emergence of sustainable development as an alternative development strategy and of ecological modernization as a new "competitive strategy" of corporations and states
- The emergence of domestic environmental legislation, including new democratic discursive designs within the administrative state (such as

community right-to-know legislation, community environmental monitoring and reporting, third-party litigation rights, environmental and
technology impact assessment, statutory policy advisory committees,
citizens' juries, consensus conferences, and public inquiries

It is beyond the scope of this chapter to conduct a detailed and systematic
evaluation of these developments and the degree to which they may or
may not have qualified international anarchy, global capitalism, and
bureaucratic domination, not to mention other, less overarching political
dynamics.[5] In any event, we would expect the story to vary significantly
from state to state and region to region. Nonetheless, it is possible to
track some broad trends and to suggest a framework for how greens
might understand and selectively accentuate some of these positive trends
in relation to where and how they may be situated as political actors.
Here I concentrate only on the first two structural constraints, namely,
global anarchy and the compromised capitalist state. My critical political
ecology framework will be defended as an alternative to the deep pessimism of ecorealists, eco-Marxists, and radical political ecologists about
the possibilities of more ecologically enlightened state governance. Along
the way, I also seek to highlight the dangers of the green movement's turning its back on the state.

International Anarchy: Ecorealism versus Critical Political Ecology

In a recent critical assessment of the prospects for a green democratic
state, Michael Saward has pointedly asked, "Could it be that the contemporary state is simply not the type of entity which is capable of *systematically* prioritizing the achievement of sustainability?"[6] Historically, the
defense of state territory, military success, and the exploitation of natural
resources and the environment for the purposes of national economic
development have been widely understood as overriding state imperatives
that are common to all states and constitutive of the state's very form.[7]
Indeed, the exploitation of natural resources within the territory has
sometimes been justified as a "nation-building exercise" or intimately
linked with national security.

Saward's analysis essentially follows the neorealist analysis of the state
system. The hallmark of this perspective is that the rivalrous strategic
behavior of states is required by the anarchic structure of the state system,

despite the putative "higher rationality" of alternative arrangements and arguments, green or otherwise. The basic imperatives and interests of states, and their location in an anarchic world order, are such as to condemn environmental problems "to the periphery of international relations", including the discipline of international relations.[8] Since the parameters of domestic politics are constrained by systemic pressures, we can also expect that environmental protection will be relegated to the periphery of states' domestic politics as well. Put bluntly, it is simply not in the "interests" of states to take any concerted action to protect the global commons, the biosphere, or indeed their own territorial ecological integrity ahead of more "fundamental" security and economic goals that are dictated by the system.

One significant exception to this neorealist tendency to dismiss ecological problems is when they emerge as a source of conflict between states. This most typically occurs in cases of resource scarcity (particularly over basic resources such as oil and water) and is usually analyzed as a "geopolitical" problem. That is, to the extent to which neorealists have entertained the concept of "ecological security," they have done so within the framework of traditional notions of national security and territorial defense.[9]

The central problem with this neorealist understanding of the international order is that it fails to explain the fact that many states do routinely cooperate on environmental matters and occasionally even take unilateral measures to protect their environment despite the short-term competitive costs this might impose. We can certainly argue about how effective these measures have been, but we cannot sweep aside the record of environmental multilateralism and domestic environmental legislation as simply an inconvenient or irrelevant fact. The rapid proliferation of new international environmental organizations and multilateral environmental treaties, declarations, and strategies in recent decades therefore needs to be explained rather than reduced to strategic power play or summarily dismissed as mere exceptions that prove the neorealist rule.

Part of the blindness of ecorealism arises from its a priori assumptions about the anarchical structure of international society (and the rationality of states operating within this structure) rather than from a close examination of what states actually do. That is, the interests of states are simply regarded as givens and the social structures that construct them as immutable and overdetermining (making all states "unit-like," to borrow Kenneth Waltz's term), and a parsimonious explanation of state behavior is then deduced from these systemic constraints and the distribution of material capabilities among rivalrous states.[10] While social structures certainly impose pressures and constraints upon agents (this is the very character of social structures), critical political ecology is always open to the possibility that they can also be transformed by agents. In this respect, the neorealist analysis is not so much wrong as lopsided. In short, "it denies the role of practice in the making and possible transgression of social order."[11] Whereas neo-realism privileges structure over agency, critical theorists and constructivists seek to comprehend historical change as the result of the changing reciprocal relationship between structures and agents. As Linklater explains, "Whereas neorealism aims to account for the reproduction of the system of states, critical theory endeavors to highlight the existence of counterhegemonic or countervailing tendencies which are invariably present within all social and political structures."[12] Moreover, the conflicts between dominant and counterhegemonic tendencies are not necessarily a simple contest between states and social movements. More typically, the conflict is between shifting alliances of state and nonstate actors. That is, particular agencies or functionaries within states themselves can sometimes be part of counterhegemonic movements by acting in alliance with nonstate actors against other agencies within the state or against other states. To the extent to which green democratic states begin to emerge in the new century, we would expect and want them to play this kind of role on the world stage.

Ironically, it has been the further development of rational choice theory, particularly more sophisticated approaches to game theory, that has gone some way toward explaining why cooperation between states often turns out to be more likely than defection in situations of complex interdependence, and why the prospect of absolute gains, rather than merely relative gains, can be sufficient to secure cooperation between states.[13] Here, neoliberal institutionalists have made a major contribution to our understanding of environmental multilateralism in directing attention to the ways in which different institutional settings can affect the motivations of states to cooperate. Indeed, the bulk of academic work on environmental multilateralism is now conducted within a neoliberal institutionalist framework.[14] These heirs of Locke explain environmental multilateralism as an effective means for managing complex interdependence by removing uncertainty and improving the prospects for cooperation in a world of sovereign states lacking a central authority. Cooperation thus regularly takes place because it is often in the "enlightened self-interest" of states, notwithstanding disparities in material capabilities. However, neoliberal institutionalists still take states, their "interests," and the anarchic structure of the state system as fixed and given, and tend not to inquire into how changing intersubjective understandings between state and nonstate actors work to constitute and reconstitute some interests as more legitimate than others. In contrast, for constructivists, environmental multilateralism does not merely regulate the conduct of states with a given set of interests, it actually serves to constitute their identities, roles, and interests.

Critical political ecology is also able to acknowledge different logics or cultures of anarchy that may apply in different settings to explain why states do not always behave in mistrustful or rivalrous ways. International society may be anarchical, but this does not mean there is only one logic or culture of anarchy, as Alexander Wendt has shown.[15] Just as different social structures can produce different social roles and identities and different modes of relating, so can different cultures of anarchy produce different state roles and relationships. For example, Wendt shows how states may relate to other states as enemy, rival, or friend, and these roles correspond to three different cultures of international politics, Hobbesian, Lockean, and Kantian (these are identified by Wendt as "salient" logics and are therefore not meant to be exhaustive). Moreover, these different cultures of anarchy explain why states, when they inhabit certain roles, conform to certain behaviors and norms. That is, when they relate to other states as enemies, they are only likely to cooperate when implicitly or explicitly coerced; when they relate as rivals, they might also comply out of self-interest; and when they relate as friends, they comply principally because of shared understandings.

None of this is to deny the force of the ecorealist analysis in those domains where a Hobbesian culture prevails. My point is simply that such a culture does not always prevail—indeed, it is arguably no longer dominant. Here I would agree with Wendt's reading that the international behavior of states is mostly Lockean (rather than Hobbesian) but with increasing Kantian dimensions.[16] Irrespective of whether one agrees with this particular reading, for ecorealists to the deny or dismiss the possibility of something like a Kantian culture of responsibility taking a stronger hold on international society is to make the politically conservative move of sanctifying the Hobbesian culture as natural and immutable. A critical political ecology perspective, in contrast, would search for ways to transform that Hobbesian culture into a greener Kantian culture. This might mean, for example, taking environmental problems not simply as a traditional security threat to the state and to national interests but rather as an opportunity to expand the security reference point and the notion of interest to include regional and planetary biophysical integrity.[17] Such rethinking necessarily loosens the concept of territorial defense and calls for bolder forms of environmental multilateralism rather than a traditional buildup of defense capabilities.

Such rethinking also entails moving beyond the paradigmatically liberal notion of democracy, which still rests on the premise of a tight, territorially defined relationship between the rule makers and the ruled, and the liberal model of regulating state territorial rights, which is based on a presumption of noninterference with the freedom of the property holder or sovereign state. While neoliberals recognize the problems generated by complex interdependence, their solutions challenge neither state exclusive territorial rights nor the idea of states as individuated units that are merely externally related. Yet the insight that the self or individuated unit (whether understood as individual, community, state, or bioregion) can no longer rule or exercise autonomy effectively without some accommodation of interdependence and a broader set of transboundary/common concerns and responsibilities becomes an ontological and epistemological breakthrough at the point at which the basic units of the system are understood as internally rather than externally related. This recognition also enables a move away from a classical liberal understanding of freedom or self-rule toward a model that is closer to the civic republican understanding, with its associated ideas of civic virtue and responsibility for the common good. According to the republican understanding, freedom is something that is *constituted* by mutually negotiated and mutually recognized norms or common rules, whereas for the classic liberal, the social contract merely sets up a limited legal framework that authorizes a justified but limited *interference* with preexisting "natural" rights. An ecological understanding of autonomy or self-rule (whether of individuals, local communities, or abstract communities such as nations) would similarly be one that is constituted by communal norms, rules, and identities. The daring idea that such common norms and rules might one day constitute nation-states as "agents of the common good," custodians of the biosphere, public trustees, or planetary stewards may appear fanciful to neorealists and neoliberals, but the intimations of such a posture are already present in many multilateral environmental declarations, strategies, and treaties. This does not necessarily entail any relinquishment of the institution of sovereignty. Rather, it may merely involve a redefinition and broadening of the identities—indeed the very raison d'être—of states so that they are understood as custodians/caretakers of their own territories (not to mention the global commons) rather than simply as private controllers/exploiters.

Unlike neorealism and interdependence theory, a critical constructivist understanding of international society is able to acknowledge and comprehend the significant rise in environmental multilateralism and domestic environmental legislation over the past four decades (particularly in OECD countries, but also increasingly beyond) as a sign of potentially deeper change to the international order, not merely continuity. Moreover, it offers a means of understanding change not just at the level of policy but also in terms of the function and rationale of state governance. Indeed, over the last four decades environmental organizations, movements, and citizens' initiatives, along with progressive states and certain international organizations, have played a key role in helping to transform the mutually informing international and national discourses of legitimate state conduct in a greener direction, while also introducing a new layer of domestic state functions and practices. These achievements ought not to be overstated, but they have helped to nudge the constitutive discourses of sovereignty (most notably, the right to develop but also the security and rights discourses) and the domestic identities, interests, and regulatory practices of states in a greener direction.[18] Many of these achievements are merely rhetorical in the sense that the new discourse of sustainable development outstrips the shift in actual practices, but the environmental and broader green movements have nonetheless changed public expectations and provided new standards by which state behavior is to be judged and called to account.

Nonetheless, any further or deeper greening of states is likely to be postponed until such time as the systemic pressures on states arising from the ongoing development of global capitalism are alleviated. While critical ecologists would be foolish to ignore the ways in which the state system exerts pressure on states to accord priority to economic concerns ahead of environmental ones, they are also alive to contrary tendencies that have been made possible by domestic and transnational civil society acting back on states. Indeed, the possibilities for deeper structural transformations would seem to depend on further democratization of this kind. What is so special about democratization, as Beetham explains, is that it holds the key to breaking the self-confirming character of unequal power arrangements.[19] At a minimum, democracy must become a defining rather than a contingent feature of states in order that all citizens in all nations be empowered with the necessary civil and political rights to engage in transformative politics at all levels of governance. At a maximum, liberal democracy must give way to a more ecologically responsive democracy better able to account for and minimize the production and distribution of ecological risks and therefore less constrained by traditional understandings of sovereign rule. This would not necessarily require the end of states, but it would certainly require something more than the liberal democratic understanding of self-determination.

Global Capitalism and the Declining State?

This analysis of the state offered by radical political ecologists has much in common with the analysis of the competition state in the international political economy literature, which focuses on the decline of the nation-state, as a self-determining entity.[20] However, for most radical political ecologists, the question is not how we might retrieve traditional state-based democracy as we once knew it or imagined it. Rather, it is how we might extend democracy and engage in political mobilization *beyond* the state. While important, such a stance is far too dismissive of the state and forecloses the possibility of developing more ecologically responsive states.

Most radical political ecologists single out global capital accumulation rather than state sovereignty as the primary driver of global ecological degradation and environmental injustice. Accordingly, they tend to designate the state as a secondary, irrelevant, or deeply compromised power structure and therefore not a promising site of political struggle.[21]

Moreover, radical political ecologists have been in the vanguard of rejecting a statist analysis of global ecological degradation along with the assumptions and habits of thought of the mainstream traditions of international relations theory. According to Saurin, we must start by "drawing up accounts of the global structures of power, articulations of capitalism and distributions of consumption, and not the a priori privileging of the 'high' politics of the state."[22] More recently, Ken Conca has argued that we should not reify the state as the sole site of political authority because it is neither the primary nor only cause of unsustainable practices, nor the primary or only agent of global sustainability.[23] So far, all of this is consistent with critical political ecology. However, Conca miscalculates the problem when he goes on to argue that to approach the problem of global environmental governance as a matter of "greening the state" and "greening relations between separate, sovereign states" is to distort our understanding of the causes of, and solutions to, unsustainable practices. Saurin is even more blunt in declaring that "a focus on interstate relations is largely irrelevant to the explanation of global environmental degradation, nor is an elaboration of interstate relations likely to lead to any reversal of such degradation."[24]

The primary reason radical political ecologists reject a statist framework of analysis is that it disaggregates global production and consumption in arbitrary ways and therefore misidentifies where social power and the capacity to adjust lie. Capitalism operates at a global level in ways that leave highly uneven impacts on different human communities and ecosystems within and between particular states, with some social classes and communities leaving much bigger "ecological footprints" or "ecological shadows" at the expense of others. Moreover, "As economic globalization deepens, some shadows grow longer and some footprints grow larger."[25] Merely punishing those countries that are, say, heavy aggregate polluters ignores the fact that many consumers and financial interests located elsewhere benefit from the pollution without taking any responsibility for the costs. Moreover, states themselves are not meaningful units of consumption, and aggregate figures of wealth or pollution tell us nothing about the vast disparities of wealth, income, and risks within particular states. Thus, Conca argues, instead of allocating blame and responsibility to particular states, we should be monitoring and allocating responsibility to transnational commodity chains, from investment, resource extraction, production through to marketing, advertising, retailing, consumption, and disposal.[26] Here Conca points to the fertile potential for alliances between labor and environmental movements against "the financial and consuming centers" that benefit from new commodity chains. According to Conca, a new architecture of global ecological governance would have, alongside states, a range of nonstate nodes of governance that would enforce or encourage ecological stewardship, including ecocertification schemes such as the Forest Stewardship Council.

While such nonstate nodes of governance are appealing from a green perspective and indeed quite likely to grow in importance over time, it is difficult to see how this might occur without at least the concurrence of states. This is certainly not denied by radical political ecologists, but it is mostly sidestepped rather than explored in their quest for a new architecture of global governance. In short, in looking beyond the state, radical political ecologists seem prone to underestimate the state's own independent role in ecological destruction (a role that may be pursued for statist or nationalist rather than capitalist ends, such as military warfare); downplay the ways in which states themselves are responsible for actively orchestrating the new global neoliberal economic order; and consequently overestimate the possibilities of successful nonstate environmental regulation and stewardship occurring without the support of at least a critical mass of states.

In support of the first proposition, we need only point to the ways in which military training, weapons production, storage, disposal and above all, armed conflict have proved to be major causes of the most serious ecological degradation of the last century (especially nuclear, chemical, and biological testing and warfare). It follows that disarmament is one of the most urgent and significant steps toward global ecological integrity.[27] To be sure, the global business of arms production is obviously heavily implicated in, and has benefited from, the ecological devastation wrought by the military (as the phrase "military-industrial complex" suggests). However, it is difficult to see how the processes of disarmament might continue other than through the painstaking processes of multilateral negotiations between states that radical political ecologists appear to dismiss so summarily.

Second, while it is true that states are becoming increasingly incapacitated in the face of flexible specialization and economic globalization, as

Weiss has pointed out, states are "the midwives" and "catalysts" of globalization rather than its victim.[28] When radical political ecologists argue that attempts to green the state or state system involve a misidentification of where social power and the capacity to adjust lie, they seem to assume that global capital has been able to reorganize itself without the assistance of states. Yet capitalist markets cannot exist without the national legal systems of states, which provide basic stability, contractual certainty, and the protection of private property rights, both nationally and internationally. Accordingly, it is difficult to envisage how global capitalism can be reformed behind the back, as it were, of states on any systematic basis. The move toward a more sustainable society demands the regulation and in some cases proscription of a wide range of environmentally and socially damaging activities. This requires the deployment of the regulatory and fiscal resources of the state to ensure that the economy and society respect the integrity of the ecosystems in which they are embedded in order to minimize the consumption of energy and resources, reduce pollution, and protect life support services and biodiversity. The state also has the capacity to redistribute resources and otherwise influence life opportunities to ensure that the move toward a more sustainable society is not a socially regressive one—a very real prospect if environmental goals are not properly integrated with social justice goals. This state capacity arises precisely because it enjoys a (virtual) monopoly of the means of legitimate coercion and is therefore the final adjudicator and guarantor of positive law. In short, the appeal of the state is that it stands as the most overarching source of authority within modern, plural societies.

None of these points are meant to deny or downplay the growing consensus that states have lost a significant measure of political autonomy, steering capacity, and legitimacy in the new neoliberal world order. While nation-states still arguably constitute the principal form of political rule throughout the world, the idea that they occupy the "commanding heights" of governance, effectively and legitimately regulating and insulating social and economic life within their borders, has fallen by the wayside. So, too, it seems has the social democratic ideal of the welfare state, which has been superseded or slimmed down and made residual to the primary tasks of the new "competition state."[29] Nonetheless, as Cerny has pointed out, "Whatever the strengths and weaknesses of the nation-state, then, it is the central, active, structuring feature of a rapidly changing global environment."[30] Yet if states have actively orchestrated this state of affairs, then they can, at least in principle, work to deorchestrate it. Similarly, Hirst has suggested,

The new national sovereignty is above all the power to confer legitimacy and governmental competence to other agencies, international and local, but then to continue to support and sustain those agencies as a cooperative partner in a new scheme of authority. The nation-state does not thereby become functionless; rather it becomes the key node (the main source of legitimacy that ties the whole together) in a complex web of governing powers.[31]

Third, the flourishing of nonstate modes of ecological regulation is likewise going to require a significant degree of state orchestration. To be sure, nonstate forms of environmental regulation and stewardship, such as local environmental initiatives and ecocertification schemes developed by transnational environmental nongovernmental organizations (NGOs) are undoubtedly welcome developments and should be encouraged at every opportunity. However, they are likely to be suboptimal without the support of states. For example, Vanessa Gray's detailed examination of the work of U.S.-based transnational environmental NGOs in Colombia has shown that well-meaning efforts to work with local people in areas of high biodiversity in the South can be, at best, marginal in those circumstances where state infrastructure is weak, governments are corrupt, and the rule of law does not prevail.[32] Indeed, Andrew Hurrell has concluded that "many of the most serious obstacles to sustainability have to do with the domestic weaknesses of particular states and state structures."[33] This suggests that the building of "state environmental capacity" is a condition for, rather than obstacle to, the development of ecologically sustainable societies. In any event, it is dangerous to assume that nonstate alternatives are necessarily always more ecologically responsible or more democratically accountable than traditional state forms of democratic governance. For example, voluntary corporate initiatives will remain nontransparent, unaccountable, and ad hoc in the absence of the more systematic regulatory framework that states can provide.

In the light of the foregoing, the newly emerging political challenge for those interested in more ecologically responsive and democratic governance is to think about how state and nonstate nodes of governance might be articulated and coordinated, and how they might be made properly representative of, and accountable to, communities potentially affected by ecological risks that may not necessarily map onto the territorial borders of states. If one accepts that the development of a new architecture of global governance is unlikely to emerge without the support and concurrence of states, then it follows that working with and through states and the existing state system, among other systems, becomes an indispensable strategy for the green movement. While this understanding does not represent unbridled optimism, it is certainly much less pessimistic and skeptical than ecorealism or post-Marxist political ecology.

From Exclusive to Inclusive Sovereignty

So much for my plea for radical political ecologists to bring the state back into discussions of the future of global governance. It now remains to explore briefly the more challenging question of how the nation-state and the state system might be made more ecologically responsive. Here I focus on the transboundary and global dimensions of this challenge to the current liberal normative order.

Radical political ecologists have made a major contribution in highlighting the sometimes glaring disjuncture between the state-based mechanisms of democratic accountability and control, and the transboundary character of ecological problems. They have shown how there is no necessary congruence between the structures and agents that generate ecological problems, the social classes that benefit from them, those who have the expertise to understand them, those who suffer their negative consequences (in space and time), and those who must take formal political responsibility for them. Variations on this theme can be found in the green critiques of the administrative state, of the "scientific establishment," of the risk society, and of global capitalism, and in the environmental justice literature, which often focuses on the socially inequitable distribution of ecological problems.[34] Common to these critiques is the idea that the lines of accountability and control between civil society, parliament, the executive, the bureaucracy, business, and science are at best feeble and at worst dysfunctional. These problems are magnified when we turn from particular state-society complexes to the responsibility of nation-states to the society of states and to the global community in general.

The global dimensions of this failure in democratic accountability and control suggest the need for a new architecture of global governance that is able to break, at least to some degree, with territorial governance in order to foster greater transboundary democratic accountability and responsibility for social and ecological harms. This requires reformulating not only the purpose of states as special nodes of governance that frame the constitutional ordering of other nodes but also their form and democratic procedures so that they can better facilitate jurisdictional overlap and transboundary rule rather than exclusive territorial rule. After all, any theory of democratic rule (green or otherwise) is only as good as the institutions and procedures that give it practical effect. As Offe reminds us, in liberal democratic states, "the 'will' of the people is an artifact of those institutional procedures which we ostensibly only use to measure precisely that will. The will of the people does not exist prior to these procedures and independent of them, but instead arises in them."[35] This applies to voting in elections, referenda, and opinion polls. What cultures, norms, and accompanying democratic procedures, then, might summon a more ecologically responsive will, and how might state democratic procedures be used to capture that will or otherwise represent and take into consideration all those who might be put at risk by proposed policies, new technologies, or investment decisions, irrespective of their territorial locations?

In its internal dimension, the notion of sovereignty has been applied in political theory to the investiture of political and legal authority in the modern state. This has encompassed both the ultimate *source* of authority and the *proper scope* of authority, both of which laid down the framework for the legitimate exercise of political power. While the source of authority has shifted from the absolute ruler to the people, the scope has remained delimited in territorial terms. Moreover, in both the internal and external understandings of sovereignty there remains a profound presumption in favor of territorial *use*, just as there is with the bourgeois property holder. These essentially liberal understandings of territory and property link self-determination or freedom with the rational (more efficient) mastery of nature. As Conca observes, the liberal constitutive discourses of sovereignty (including the accompanying leitmotif of the domination of nature) effectively serve to render the conventional understanding of state sovereignty unproblematic.[36] That is, they provide the meaning, context, and normative force to a particular regulative ideal of state sovereignty while also concealing significant tensions and contradictions contained within it.

Two cumulative steps need to be taken for those who are interested in questioning the territorially contained character of democratic states, along with the powerful presumption in favor of use or exploitation vis-à-vis protection. The first is to cultivate norms of nationhood and citizenship that are cosmopolitan, outward looking, and concerned not to "externalize" problems to present or future "strangers." Daniel Deudney, for example, has argued for the development of a "terrapolitan" (Earth-centerd) rather than Westphalian or cosmopolitan conception of sovereignty, communal identity, and legitimate political authority.[37]

The second is to build these norms into the practices and procedures of domestic and multilateral governance. This might take the form of symbolic/aspirational statements of obligations to humankind and the global environment in state constitutions backed up by a range of new democratic procedures, due processes, and decision rules that "open out" the moral and political community.[38]

Such domestic measures work best when shored up by multilateral agreements with other states that confer reciprocal rights of citizenship (and with that rights of political participation and legal standing) to people living outside the state territorial boundaries in those circumstances where they may be seriously affected by proposed developments taking place within a particular state.[39] Such developments would break, at least to some extent, the nexus between the nation and the state, while also redefining the more traditional understandings of nation such that the source of connectedness between those constituting any particular *demos* is no longer nationality, ethnicity, religion, or language but rather a common exposure to actual or potential ecological harm. As I have pointed out elsewhere, such a political community may not necessarily be geographically contiguous or precisely specifiable in space or time.[40] I have also suggested the constitutional entrenchment of the precautionary principle as one parsimonious means of ensuring the systematic representation of future generations and nonhuman species. This decision rule, which can be extended to include the consideration of serious or irreversible environmental and health risks for future generations and nonhuman species, also serves as an evidentiary rule in placing the onus of proof on the proponent of proposed developments to prove the absence of such risks for human and nonhuman communities, now and in the future. The reciprocal observance of this decision rule by all states (made possible by, say, a Convention on Precautionary Risk Assessment) would provide one powerful surrogate mechanism for institutionalizing ecological and social responsibility toward the relevant community-of-fate in those cases where that community transcends state jurisdictional boundaries.

In the foregoing institutional innovations, while the liberal/republican idea would be maintained that the fundamental *source* of political authority is "the people," the latter would no longer always be regarded qua members of particular nation-states. Rather, they would remain sovereign but would compose a more variable and fluid community made up of all those who happen to belong, or who are likely to belong, to the relevant community-at-risk. In short, these new structures of democratic governance are inclusive rather than exclusive of those outside the nation-state in those circumstances where they may be seriously affected by proposed decisions. These is no reason why these innovations cannot be grafted onto existing state structures—indeed, it is difficult to envisage how else they might be effectively and systematically institutionalized and legitimized, at least in the short term. Such states would become what Ulrich Beck has called "transnational states," that is, states that have developed their sovereignty and identity beyond the national level.[41]

The broadening of notions of citizenship, identity, and community are not confined to the green sphere. Andrew Linklater, for example, has pointed to a range of developments already providing an important challenge to exclusionary accounts of sovereignty and citizenship and reaching some way toward "post-Westphalian" communities made up of citizens who have multiple loyalties and diverse rights of political participation that are not confined to particular nation-states.[42] It is therefore possible that the composite term nation-state may one day come to mean something different from what it means today, just as what it means today is significantly different from what it meant at the time of the Peace of Westphalia. Indeed, I have already suggested that the ecological crisis invites a critical rethinking of the relationship of states to their territories in the same way that it invites a rethinking of the relationship of bourgeois individuals to their private property. Just as the common law principles regulating the use of private property rights (e.g., the torts of negligence and nuisance) have proved to be innately conservative and inadequate in the face of mounting regional and global ecological problems, so have the customary international law principles regulating transboundary pollution proved to be largely ineffectual and inadequate. In each case, bolder, more experimental, and more forward-looking initiatives (domestic legislation, international treaties) have been necessary—initiatives that in some cases invite a reconceptualization of the relationship between property holder and property from that of absolute owner to trustee, guardian, or steward. In short, the underlying liberal notion of individual or community self-realization through the ownership and exploitation of private property or territory needs to be reexamined, sublimated, and eventually transformed to the point where the twin liberal ideas of the autonomy of the individual and the self-determination of political communities become more or less detached from notions of exclusive proprietorship over land. Such a critical inquiry into territorial rule would strike at the state's "relationship to a territory, to a geographically distinct part of the globe, which constitutes the unique physical base and referent of the state's institutional mission, its very body, the ground of its being."[43]

Notes

1. See, for example, Colin Hay (1996); Raymond L. Bryant and Sinead Bailey, (1997); *Third World Political Ecology* (London: Routledge, 1997); Conca (2000a); Dryzek (1992); Laferriere (1996); Lipschutz and Conca eds. (1993); Paterson (1999a); Sachs, ed. (1993); and Saurin (1996).

2. Conca (2000a); Lipschutz and Conca, eds. (1993); Saurin (1996); and Zurn (1998).

3. Giddens (1985); Wendt (1999). See also Price and Reus-Smit (1998) for an analysis of the sympathies between constructivism and critical theory.

4. See, for example, Kakonen, ed. (1994) and Peluso (1993). For more general discussions, see Hurrell (1994).

5. This is the subject of a larger work of mine: *The Green State: Rethinking Democracy and Sovereignty* (2004).

6. Saward (1998, 345).

7. See, for example, Giddens (1985).

8. Smith (1993).

9. An example of such an analysis is provided by Frederick (1999).

10. Waltz (1979).

11. Ashley (1984, 237).

---

12. Linklater (1996a, 283).

13. See, for example, Michael Taylor (1987); Axelrod (1984); and Ostrom (1990).

14. See, for example, Haas, Keohane, and Levy, eds. (1993); Oran R. Young (1994); and Porter, Brown, and Chasek (2000).

15. Wendt (1999).

16. Wendt (1999, 43).

17. Daniel Deudney's influential critique of the concept of ecological security assumes that the security reference point will remain that of the nation-state. See Deudney (1990).

18. See, for example, Litfin, ed. (1998).

19. Beetham (1991, 113, 117).

20. See, for example, Cerny (1990); Strange (1996); and Sassen (1996).

21. See, in particular, Raymond L. Bryant and Sinead Bailey (1997); Conca (2000a); Dryzek (1992); Sachs, ed. (1993); and Saurin (1996).

22. Saurin (1996, 78).

23. Conca (2000a, 142).

24. Saurin (1996, 85).

25. Conca (2000a, 149).

26. Conca (2000a, 149).

27. Finger (1994, 177).

28. Linda Weiss (1998).

29. John Gray (1998, 6).

30. Cerny (1990, 246); see also Sassen (1996) and Linda Weiss (1998).

31. Hirst (1997, 230–231).

32. Vanessa Joan Gray (2000).

33. Hurrell (1994, 155).

34. See especially Beck (1992); Dryzek (1992); Eckersley (2000a); Jänicke (1990); Paehlke and Torgerson, eds. (1990); and Schlosberg (1999).

35. Offe (1996, 91).

36. Conca (1995).

37. Deudney (1998).

38. Many states contain aspirational statements about environmental protection in their constitutions, but I am not aware of any such aspirations that extend beyond the nation or the territorial boundaries of the state.

39. See, for example, the United Nations/Economic Commission for Europe (UN/ECE) Convention on Environmental Impact Assessment in a Transboundary Context (adopted 1991, entered into force on September 10, 1997) and the Aarhus Convention (the UN/ECE Convention on Access to Information, Public

Participation in Decision-Making and Access to Justice in Environmental Matters, adopted June 1998). The latter Convention has been described by UN Secretary General Kofi Annan as "the most ambitious venture in the area of 'environmental democracy' so far undertaken under the auspices of the United Nations." <http://www.unece.org/env/pp/>.

40. Eckersley (2000a).

41. Beck (2000, 133).

42. Linklater (1996b).

43. Poggi (1990, 177).

9

Old States in New Bottles?
The Hybridization of Authority in Global
Environmental Governance

Ken Conca

The question of how to adapt the state into a more reliable, effective agent of environmental governance applies at a global scale no less than within the domain of individual states. Canards about market environmentalism or hopefulness about global civic voluntarism notwithstanding, it is impossible to envision the adaptations necessary for long-term sustainability without far-reaching, effective international cooperation. States are surely not the only agents of global environmental governance, but it goes without saying that they must be one such agent.

Nevertheless, my thinking about the state and global environmental governance begins with two pessimistic observations. First, modern states have generally not been ecologically neutral institutions. The emergence of the centralizing, industrializing, national state, with its capacity to centralize decision making, concentrate capital, strip local communities of their historical property rights in nature, supply coercive power, and protect elite interests, has been a key social innovation along the road to planetary environmental peril. Creating states oriented toward environmental protection is surely not impossible, but it means unearthing some deeply entrenched political-economic foundations of the state itself.

A second challenge that must be acknowledged from the start is that a rapidly transnationalizing world economy deprives the state of at least some of its potential ability to protect the environment, both domestically and transnationally. We must be careful not to take this argument too far. Globalization per se is hardly new, and in its latest manifestations it has been driven in no small part by state policy choices (such as aggressive trade liberalization and the relaxation of short-term controls on capital mobility).[1] Moreover, until the costs facing firms of relocating reach zero, states will retain some influence over the global production chains that snake in and out of their borders. But even if the idea of an inexorable race to the bottom oversimplifies, environmental regulatory strategies are greatly complicated by the growth of capital mobility, the hyperliberalization of trade, and the deepening transnationalization of production.

But this pessimistic image of an often unwilling and increasingly unable state must be balanced against a more hopeful observation: states can and do engage in purposeful collective action in response to international environmental problems. According to the United Nations Environment Programme, there were at least 502 international treaties and other agreements related to the environment in place by March 2001. More than one-third of these accords extend beyond a single world region. The rate at which states have entered into these arrangements has accelerated, with nearly 60 percent adopted since the 1972 UN Conference on the Human Environment.[2] While questions abound about the effectiveness of international environmental law, at least some of these interstate political arrangements have been sufficiently norm-disseminating and behavior-modifying to qualify as "international regimes."[3]

Given these countervailing observations, perhaps it is no surprise that the debate on the state's governing power and authority in an ecologically interdependent world has pointed in seemingly contradictory directions. Most of the large body of scholarship on international regimes conjures a world in which national governments come to perceive collective environmental problems, work toward cooperative solutions, and engage in social learning about problems and solutions that renders environmental protection more effective over time. States do so by overcoming uncertainty, mistrust, short time horizons, bargaining coordination problems, and other significant but hardly insurmountable barriers to collective action.

When one turns to scholarship on transnational civil society, however, this image of the problem-solving state is replaced by one of states that are increasingly eclipsed as the locus of power, agency, and decision-making authority in global environmental governance. A range of increasingly powerful and newly authoritative agents, including nongovernmental organizations (NGOs), transnational advocacy networks, expert scientific communities, and transnationalized social movements, are said to have wrested substantial control of the global environmental agenda away from states and assumed at least some of the governing power and authority traditionally falling within the state's purview.[4]

This raises a critical question: Is this dichotomy the full extent of potential or imaginable institutional arrangements for transnational environmental governance? In this chapter I argue that for a wide range of environmental problems—including deforestation, watershed protection, biological conservation, toxification, coastal zone protection, and critical ecosystem functions—environmental governance is indeed growing increasingly transnationalized. It makes sense to think of the increasingly routinized, reconciled, and embedded practices surrounding these problems as the institutionalization of global environmental governance. Yet in terms of the roles that states actually play and the foundations of authority on which those roles are based, the resulting institutional forms often bear little resemblance either to a formal interstate treaty or to a world civic politics that transcends the state. Understanding what states can and cannot do in these more complex and increasingly common settings is crucial if we are to create effective, accountable forms of global environmental protection.

To develop this argument more fully, this chapter explores the very different conceptions of state authority that underpin scholarship on international regimes and transnational civil society. The discussion then turns to several trends and forces that are constituting more complex institutional forms, rooted in more complex authority relations, around a wide swathe of environmental problems. To illustrate these propositions, I present examples from two specific domains—watershed governance and protected areas—in which the emerging institutionalization of global environmental governance exhibits a particularly multihued institutionalization of authority and governance.

Interstate Regimes, Transnational Civil Society, and the Question of Authority in Global Environmental Governance

Unquestionably, the past few decades have seen the emergence of international regimes and transnational civil society networks as two important mechanisms of global environmental governance. These developments led scholars to examine the forces driving the creation of these mechanisms, the conditions under which they were likely to emerge, the factors accounting for their staying power or adaptation, and their consequences for ecological outcomes.[5]

These two approaches present a strikingly dichotomous image of the state, its motives, its capabilities, and the foundation of authority on which it rests. Much of the literature on transnational civil society networks begins with the premise that environmental problems raise potential challenges to every component of the classic definition of a state as the sovereign union of a territory, a people, and a government. Environmental processes ignore borders and link places previously thought of as separate, raising profound questions about the exclusive character of territorial rule. Governments lack a convincing formula for reconciling environmental protection with growth-oriented modern society, producing what Thom Kuehls has described as a crisis of governmentality.[6] The transnational character of so many environmental problems and the power of planetary imagery pave the way for new, inherently transnational identity constructs.[7] The emergence of global environmental norms challenges the very distinction between what is domestic and what is international, a distinction that has been central to the conception of state sovereignty on which the modern interstate system is premised. The scope of these challenges to the organizing principles of both the state and the interstate system has led many scholars to suggest that transnational environmental networks constitute not merely functional responses to environmental problems but one aspect of a larger process of post-Westphalian, postsovereign transformation in world politics.[8]

In contrast, when one surveys the literature on international regimes, one finds not this turbulent image of an interstate system in crisis but rather a much gentler notion of gradual adaptation through global governance. This message might be stated as follows: States remain the authoritative actors in world politics. But they also recognize their interdependence, in this case, ecological interdependence rooted in the transboundary character of so many environmental problems. States therefore band together as collective problem solvers, gradually deepening the institutions of global governance by creating international regimes. Such regimes can and do cause states to lose some operational sovereignty (in the sense of the autonomy to act unilaterally). But in the process states also gain both a renewed endorsement of their formal sovereignty (because it is they, after all, who have the standing to participate in the regime) and a strengthened functional sovereignty (in the form of more effective problem-solving capabilities).[9] Thus, if there is a process of system transformation under way, it is not a rush toward postsovereign world politics so much as the softening and maturation of anarchy through the institutionalization of principles of behavior and shared governance. The implicit optimism of this perspective becomes explicit when married to state-embraced narratives about the possibilities of ecological modernization and sustainable development.[10]

Given these fundamentally different views of the state, one is often left with the impression that interstate regimes and global civil society constitute stark alternatives for global environmental governance. Few would argue that they are mutually exclusive, and many scholars examine their interactive effects, for example, how civil society networks shape regime content, or how regimes create space for nonstate actors to operate internationally. Moreover, at least some of the difference lies not in the mechanisms themselves but rather in the observer's scholarly orientation, given the sociological roots of much of the civil society literature and the international relations roots of most regime scholarship. Yet regardless of whether they are convergent or contradictory mechanisms, and irrespective of whether their differences lie in the eye of the beholder, our efforts to understand the extent to which states can play a constructive role in global environmental governance is based overwhelmingly on analysis of these two mechanisms.

But there is a great danger in drawing lessons from the relatively small set of cases at the heart of each of these two literatures or in presuming that they constitute the full array of existing or potential mechanisms. What if international regimes and global civil society constitute not stark alternatives but merely endpoints along a continuum of institutional possibilities? Might we be failing to see other forms of institutionalized governance that fall somewhere along this continuum, and might we be drawing premature, skewed, or cartoonish conclusions about the real or possible role of the state in international context?

One way to see the highly stylized, even extreme character of both interstate regimes and civil society networks as mechanisms of global governance is to focus on the critical question of authority. As David Lake has pointed out, "Despite the volumes written about it, authority is one of those terms—like power—that political scientists, and especially those in international relations, define only with difficulty."[11] Lake suggests that the paradigmatic definition of authority is that of Scheppele and Soltan: "A (a person or occupant of an office) wills B to follow A and B voluntarily complies."[12] Lake further identifies a few important connotations of the concept of authority defined thusly: it is never absolute, it is not synonymous with coercion (even though coercion sometimes "lurks in the background"), and while the basis of an agent's authority may require justification, the authoritativeness of resulting commands do not.[13]

This understanding of authority is useful because it rests upon the marriage of power and legitimacy, both of which appear to be in flux for a wide range of ecological problems across a wide range of states. Yet this definition is also limited in a few important ways. First, its emphasis on explicit, willful agency risks missing the structural and discursive dimensions of authority in much the same vein as Steven Lukes's classic critique of the scholarly failure to see the hidden faces of power.[14] Moreover, while authority is understood to be inherently relational, the relationship here is drawn as bilateral and immediate: A brings a measure of power to the table and B by its response accepts the legitimacy of that power. This free-floating, relational understanding of authority deemphasizes the important process of *role definition* in the relations between A and B, a process that exists prior to and extends well beyond the relational moment of this definition. In other words, most of the important politics has taken place prior to the command-and-compliance on which the definition is centered, and has involved a much wider array of agents. It is this larger process by which A's authoritative role is constructed and institutionalized that provides a useful entry point for thinking about the state and environmental governance, precisely because that process appears to be changing in ways that neither regime scholarship nor civil society scholarship has captured fully.

Those who emphasize states-in-charge and the adaptive maturation of sovereignty usually draw their accounts from the specific realm of interstate collective bargaining, which highlights the enduring capacity of states to build and legitimize, or to resist, formal cooperative arrangements. Observers who see a vibrant civil society usurping the authority of obsolete, dysfunctional states have focused instead on the transnationalization of entrenched popular struggles, where contestations against state authority are a central part of the political dynamic and where states therefore appear less authoritative by definition. What follows is a quick sketch of what each approach has to say about the nature and foundations of state authority. The discussion then turns to an array of global environmental problems in which authority relations tend to be configured in a more complex, hybrid fashion than allowed for by either of these conceptual poles.

Authority in Interstate Regimes

The most frequently cited definition of an international regime is still probably Krasner's: "Principles, norms, rules and decision-making procedures around which actor expectations converge in a given issue-area."[15] Over time, most scholars studying international regimes have both narrowed and emboldened this definition, positing that norms legitimize and delegitimize specific forms of behavior as opposed to merely altering mutual expectations. As a result, Rittberger's definition of regimes— "rules of the game agreed upon by actors in the international arena (usually nation-states) and delimiting, for these actors, the range of legitimate or admissible behavior in a specified context of activity"—is a more precise rendering of what the term has come to mean in scholarly practice.[16]

In theory, regimes define not only rules but also roles.[17] Regimes are institutions, which Young defines as "systems of rules, decision-making procedures, and programs that give rise to social practices, *assign roles to the participants in these practices*, and guide interactions among the occupants of the relevant roles."[18] This process of role definition is one of the important pathways by which international regimes, and institutions more generally, affect behavior.[19] The nuclear family is a good example of an institution that establishes not only the rules of the game but also the roles of the players, with widespread consequences for behavior both inside and outside the family unit. The parameters of these roles are sometimes flexible or subject to multiple interpretations, but renegotiation of those parameters is often difficult, and they give powerful shape to social relations through processes of identity formation and the generation of expectations. Another example is the practice by which governments accord sovereign standing to one another through practices of recognition and diplomatic exchange. Sovereignty is a set of behavioral rules *and* a construction of roles, in that states' rights and responsibilities are sharply differentiated from those of other well-established actors in world affairs.

Although many international environmental regimes have developed complex sets of rules, most have done so in a context where *roles* are taken as relatively fixed. For most states in most regimes, role differentiation exists in only a limited way and along only a few key parameters: donors versus recipients, members versus nonmembers, leaders versus laggards, sources versus sinks. These distinctions can be important; clearly, not all states are created equal within these institutions. Nevertheless, as institutions go, this handful of dualisms constitutes a highly limited, indeed quite primitive, form of role differentiation. Moreover, available roles are not only sharply limited but also defined, framed, and understood functionally rather than constitutively. By this I mean that regimes may specify various *functional* roles *for* governments but also assume their *constitutive* roles *as* governments. The rules may deal with tasks, opportunities, capabilities, and obligations, but they take questions of standing and legitimacy as essentially fixed and given. As a result, the state is both the subject and the object of most environmental regimes. National governments as agents of states are taken as the authoritative subjects of regimes: their bargaining, concurrence, and ratification determine whether a legitimate regime exists, and they assume responsibility for compliance. States are also the primary objects of regimes: governmental compliance is the presumed key to regime effectiveness, and governmental implementation is the regime's primary task as a means to that end.[20] This explains the emphasis in the literature on regimes as mechanisms for the dissemination of knowledge and the building of "state capacity."

Taking states as both the subjects and objects of regimes yields an emphasis on how rules legitimize or delegitimize state behavior. But it also crowds out the crucial question of how authoritative roles are constructed and allocated. Instead, the flip side of the presumption of state authority is simply to presume the absence of nonstate authority. Here it is important to draw a distinction between nonstate *influence*, which many international regimes recognize explicitly or implicitly, and nonstate *authority*, which most do not recognize. Nonstate influence in the design and conduct of environmental regimes is widely acknowledged; indeed, environmental regimes have been crucial cases at the forefront of scholarly inquiry into the role of nongovernmental organizations, advocacy networks, scientists' groups, professional associations, corporations, and other nonstate actors. As this body of research illustrates, there are multiple foundations for the expanding influence of the nonstate. One important source of influence is the ability to wield technical expertise; another is the capacity to press normative claims, such as those embedded in notions of environmental justice or intergenerational equity.[21] As Chayes and Chayes explain it, "A treaty regime in operation is a hugely complex interactive process that engages not only states and their official representatives but also, increasingly, international organizations and their staffs, nongovernmental organizations, scientists, business managers, academics, and other nonstate actors."[22] Acknowledging this complexity, many interstate regimes create explicit space for nonstate actors. Some make extensive use of ad hoc or formalized working groups that incorporate nonstate sources of technical, legal, or administrative expertise; many also include provisions for the participation of nonstate actors in conferences of the parties.

But we must be careful not to overstate the nonstate in these institutions. Elite individuals participating in working groups owe their positions to credentialing procedures that are determined by state members. The most reliable path to influence at a global issue summit or conference of the parties is, unquestionably, to gain access to a state delegation. And the swirl of NGO activism around high-profile events is not matched at the more mundane meetings where much of the business of governance is actually transacted. The third meeting of the Open-Ended Ad Hoc Committee for the Implementation of the Basel Convention (Geneva, June 1997) was attended by sixty-nine state parties to the Basel Convention, two nonparty states, five UN bodies, and six "nongovernmental organizations," that is, five industry groups and Greenpeace.

More generally, sovereignty carries with it the presumption of a complex *bundle* of rights: equality among states, nonintervention, exclusive territorial jurisdiction, the presumption of state competence, restrictions on binding adjudication without consent, exclusive rights to wield violence, and the embeddedness of international law in the free will of states.[23] Gaining ground along one or a few of these dimensions, such as standing or competence, does not in itself elevate the nonstate to an equivalent position of authority.

In other words, there is a critical difference between the creation of political space for influence and the constitution of authority. Within most environmental regimes, nonstate actors are agents with some capacity to move the institutions of governance through political pressure, the wielding of knowledge, the pressing of moral claims, or various other means. But they are not understood to govern, in the sense of bringing together a sufficient marriage of power and legitimacy to establish, operationalize, apply, enforce, interpret, or vitiate the regime's behavioral rules. In other words, the regime approach typically casts nonstate actors as influences on authority rather than as potential or actual authoritative agents.

Authority in Transnational Civil Society

A mounting body of evidence suggests the need to move beyond these static presumptions about the authoritative state and the supplicant nonstate. This is particularly evident in what may be the greatest challenge of global environmental governance: addressing those physically localized but globally cumulative problems that have been particularly resistant to the reach of interstate diplomacy, such as soil erosion, deforestation, coastal zone degradation, the loss of wetlands, or the assault on watersheds. Simply put, regime theory's presumption of state authority misreads what is often a very different reality around these localized natural resources and ecosystems. Frequently, "the state" lacks the uncontested ability to control local access to or uses of nature; efforts to exert such control become part of larger struggles to consolidate and legitimize state power. Historically, the ability to control rules of access to nature—to define who may alter which specific natural materials, systems, and processes—has been a central component of state power.[24] Conversely, where that power is lacking, authority is not fully consolidated. Consider the following testimony of a veteran field researcher in the Amazon:

> Wherever one looks in the Amazonian economy, the state is in retreat: unable to finance tax breaks or build highways without the aid of multilateral banks, unable to include more than one per cent of the rural population in official colonization schemes, unable to control land titling or land conflicts, unable to register or tax the greater part of the Amazonian economy, unable to enforce federal law on more than a sporadic basis.[25]

The contrast between this state of affairs and the way in which the Brazilian state is constituted in interstate environmental regimes—as the central delivery mechanism for "sustainable development"—could not be more striking.[26]

At the same time, there are also many circumstances under which nonstate actors have at least some authoritative ability to establish such controls. The growing rhetoric in established national and international institutions about incorporating "stakeholders" is partly a concession to the ability of local actors to gum up the works of business as usual. But it is also an acknowledgment that, on the ground, local societal organizations are often better positioned than the state to mediate the process by which people gain access to nature. So-called "joint forest management" initiatives in India provide an interesting example. In Canada's western province of British Columbia, the relative weakness of the state vis-à-vis various societal actors in implementing and administering land-use planning had by the early 1990s produced what Michael Mason describes as a "legitimation deficit" for public policy.[27] In Colombia, independently organized cooperatives for urban waste recycling have flourished while state recycling initiatives flounder.[28] Questions abound on the meaning of participation and the particular responsibilities that devolve to societal organizations under these arrangements.[29] Yet the very existence of such endeavors is a concession by the state to the local reality that local-level organizations are at least as authoritative as the centralized bureaucracies of the administrative state (see chapter 6).

If the regime approach is problematic in its uncritical, inflexible stance toward state authority, then one obvious place to look for conceptual alternatives is the nonstate, the rich array of networks, coalitions, and transnational campaigns created by a global panoply of citizens' organizations and protest groups. Not surprisingly, this work lacks the shared conceptual core that defines the regimes literature; scholars have taken many different approaches in seeking to make conceptual sense of a heterogeneous array of actors, campaigns, and ideas. Some conceptualize transnational nonstate processes in terms of networks of individuals or small groups that are well positioned to influence state policy via technical expertise.[30] Other network models stress the role of more oppositional forms of social organization, finding the transnational effects of the nonstate in social movements, protest campaigns, and loosely coupled networking processes. Here the emphasis is less on elite forms of knowledge power and more on the power emanating from the nonstate's explicit value stances and mobilizing potential.[31]

On one level, these models of networked agency fueled by knowledge-as-power or the pressing of moral claims do challenge the presumptions of the authoritative state in the international regimes literature. They find a basis for authority that the state cannot monopolize, be it grounded in expertise or ethics.[32] Yet, on another level, the idea of the state as the authoritative agent of governance is reinforced, in that state policies remain the ultimate target of epistemic communities, knowledge brokers, and transnational advocacy networks.

Other scholars of the nonstate go much further in the deconstruction of state authority. Thom Kuehls argues that environmental problems create challenges not simply to sovereign borders but also to the prevailing modalities and instrumentalities of government, creating a crisis not simply of sovereignty but also of "governmentality." As the modern project of creating "opulent and completely happy" states collides with the limits and vulnerabilities of the natural world, the state's ecologically destructive and socially coercive practices become increasingly exposed, generating a legitimation crisis.[33] One result is to draw political conflict outside the "smooth" space of the state and into the "striated" space of transnational relations—a space populated by a heterogeneous array of transnational actors such as Greenpeace. For Paul Wapner, this striated space constitutes the realm of an emergent world civic politics, in which the global-scale dissemination of new ideas, practices, values, and techniques challenges us to acknowledge a "politics beyond the state."[34]

What lies beyond the crisis of state governmentality and an emergent transstate politics? For Ronnie Lipschutz, it is the politics of individual sovereignty in a newly emerging historical era that lies "after authority."[35] He suggests that processes of globalization have replaced the state with the individual as the focal point for the construction of sovereignty: "If there is a single central "unintended consequence" of the international politics and economics of the past fifty years, it is the replacement of the sovereign state by the sovereign individual as the subject of world politics."[36] Others have stressed not individualization but rather new forms of community, in variants as heterogeneous as a highly idealized global ecumenical citizenry or a cartoonish politics of civilizational tribes.[37]

These forays into the politics of the nonstate reveal a wide array of approaches to governance, many of which offer reconceptualizations that challenge the monocultures of authority embedded in the interstate regime approach. But we should be careful not to overstate the degree to which state authority is actually transcended in these cases. Tellingly, most of the examples of global civil society in action emanate from two very different types of domains, one in which state authority is at its strongest, the other where it is weakest. In the former instance, stable states in pluralistic societies guarantee the existence of at least semidemocratic space for civil society to operate. In the latter instance, civil society fills a void left by the retreat of weak, illegitimate, and often postcolonial states—states which were never really there to be transcended. In these cases, the "global" in global civil society usually means that domestic political mobilization is drawn toward international interactions by material and normative resources emanating from the international system (be they human rights protections, financial assistance, Internet linkages, or symbolic frames). In other words, the conceptual premise of global civil society relies on the creation of a political space in domestic society that in most examples is guaranteed either by the state itself or by external conditions that emanate from the interstate system.

Another striking aspect of research on the nonstate is how little its chroniclers have had to say about the *institutionalization* of what are presumed to be fundamentally new authority relations. The emphasis is on movements, actors, networks, and relationships but not on embedded, enduring sets of roles and rules that give shape and form to a whole array of struggles over time. In the realm of global civil society, every struggle seems to be an independent reinvention. Highly general concepts of sustainability and democratic accountability may survive as organizing principles across individual episodes and campaigns, as do some specific network relationships among individuals or organizations. But when reading this literature one is left with the distinct impression that the process must be rebuilt each time, essentially from scratch.

Perhaps this is no surprise. Networks built around the politics of expertise or the value orientations of well-placed activists are by definition difficult to institutionalize or to translate across particular issue areas. Campaigns spearheaded by key transnational organizations depend on the survival and continuity of those organizations, which cannot be taken for granted. Social movements, too, are notoriously impermanent—the lack of staying power of environmental social movements in Eastern Europe in the 1990s is a cautionary tale for global governance strategies rooted in citizen activism and "global civil society."[38] But these observations should caution us against assuming that we are seeing the institutionalized authority of the nonstate, when we may in fact be seeing nothing more than episodic instances of the temporary convergence of the requisite amounts of power and legitimacy.

The Contestation of Authority in Global Environmental Governance

To be sure, there are issue domains in world politics where sovereign bargaining among plausibly authoritative states has generated meaningful environmental governance. Examples include the ozone accord, several regional seas agreements, and arrangements governing ocean dumping or the international trafficking in endangered species. We can also identify social networks or market relations that govern aspects of ecosocial life from which the state is largely absent, by choice or necessity. Yet neither the regime approach nor the civil society approach is particularly representative of an array of more complex mechanisms of international environmental governance that have begun to emerge in the past decade or two. The most fertile ground for such mechanisms has been a cluster of physically localized but globally cumulative and socioeconomically transnationalized environmental challenges, including watershed protection, biological conservation, toxics management, coastal zone protection, and efforts to protect critical ecosystems. These environmental challenges often exhibit dramatically different political dynamics than the transboundary pollutant flows or internationally shared commons that have been the stuff of the most significant international environmental treaties.[39] Environmental governance in the context of these problems is indeed growing increasingly transnationalized, routinized, and embedded. Yet the resulting institutional forms often bear little resemblance either to a formal interstate treaty or a global civil society that transcends the state.

One critical feature of the sort of institution building to which I am referring is that state authority is neither consolidated nor transcended. Rather, it occupies a more ambiguous status that we might refer to as contested. There are at least three reasons to view the state's authority in these settings in more complex terms. One is the multiplicity of sources from which transnational norms are emerging. Many scholars of international relations equate the idea of governance with an authoritative inscription of norms that impose constraints on state behavior. But for an increasingly wide swathe of transnational environmental problems, institution building is not centered on a single authoritative source of norms (such as an interstate accord might provide). Instead, the transnationalization of environmental governance is occurring at the *intersection* of several influences, including international law, transnational advocacy, the activities of expert networks, market relations, and stakeholder bargaining processes that seek to mediate social conflict.

Authority is contested under such circumstances because, as a general rule, no single set of stakeholders can consolidate a preferred institutional form such as an interstate accord, an autonomous expert network, or a market-based allocation mechanism. This in turn means that governance is not simply a process of operating within a single institutionalized strand but rather a process of navigating across strands that can vary dramatically in their normative content. States (and other actors) seeking to govern a resource, ecosystem, or environmental problem sitting at the intersection of these increasingly embedded but heterogeneous influences are likely to be neither the authoritative bargainers sometimes depicted in the international regimes literature nor the irrelevant distractions often depicted in the global civil society literature.

A second reason for the enduring contestation of authority is the particular kind of conflictual political dynamic at the heart of this class of environmental governance problems. Simply put, the essence of what we are seeing is international institution building in the context of transnationalized state-society conflicts. The push to manipulate local ecosystems and extract or "develop" natural resources has long had a strong transnational dimension, given the role of international funding and the participation of multinational firms in the construction and operation of major projects. A more recent development has been the transnationalization of opposition, through growing linkages among local affected peoples' organizations and the emergence of a global advocacy network linking environmentalists, human rights activists, indigenous peoples' groups, and grassroots development advocates. These linkages have been aided by the communications revolution and the expansion of space for political opposition in many countries during the 1990s.[40]

As a result, many localized ecosystems and resource bases lying beyond the formal reach of international law and interstate diplomacy are subject to intense, conflicting transnational pressures. Conflicts between "developmental" states and their societal opponents no longer remain contained within the bounds of the sovereign sphere of domestic politics. This projection of localized conflicts into the international domain entails, by definition, a partial loss of the state's uncontested authority, not simply because societal actors reject the state's initiatives but because the dispute can no longer be framed credibly as nobody's business outside the state.

Finally, it makes sense to think of authority as contested in these settings because some aspects of state power have eroded much more quickly and completely than others. The nature of effective power varies across the cumulative strands of law, diplomacy, expertise, and advocacy that frame these complex, emergent institutional forms, in part because of their often divergent normative content. Knowledge may be a central currency of power in expert networks, for example, but a lesser factor in diplomatic bargaining. The capacity to mobilize social protest may be a major force in a multistakeholder bargaining process, but a less direct form of power in a conference of the parties to an international accord. In this context, new aspects of state power grow in importance even as old ones fade. States may lose their grip—be it in terms of agenda-setting power, control of implementation, or the capacity to declare exceptions—much more quickly in some domains than in others.

The Hybridization of Authority: Protected-Areas Networks and Watershed Governance as Emergent Institutional Forms

One consequence of the contestation of authority appears to be its growing hybridization. As discussed in the ensuing examples, emergent institutional relationships have created some unconventional divisions of labor between state-centered and nonstate-centered loci of authority. Consider the norms, strictures, and power relations surrounding the governance of watersheds. Watershed practices have been pushed and pulled simultaneously by several incongruous forces: the international law of shared watercourses, suffused with a sovereign-rights-and-responsibilities approach; neoliberal structural adjustment, with its attendant values of privatization, marketization, and commoditization; elite networking among water policy experts, who seek to elevate technocratic norms of "integrated water resource management"; and increasingly transnationalized activism for the rights of local communities, with attendant norms of human rights, grassroots democracy, and the preservation of local cultures and ecosystems.

Watershed Governance

Each of these sets of forces is thoroughly transnationalized; none has generated a hegemonic normative frame governing watershed practices. To the extent that watershed governance is being "normalized" across national boundaries, the process is unfolding at the intersection of these heterogeneous forces. An illustration of the hybrid, even heterodox, roles that can be inscribed under such circumstances is the World Commission on Dams (WCD), an unusual mixed-membership body that emerged from contentious bargaining among stakeholder groups surrounding the global controversy over large dams.[41] Born out of political impasse in a highly polarized and contentious debate, the WCD included both vocal proponents and ardent opponents of dam construction among its thirteen commissioners. Its mandate was to review the "development effectiveness" of large dams, assess alternatives for water resources and energy development; and develop "internationally acceptable criteria, guidelines, and standards" for dam construction and operations.[42] The commission's recommendations, based on an unprecedented, multifaceted, and detailed assessment of the performance of large dams around the world, were twofold: (1) to shift the focus away from dams as ends in themselves and toward comprehensive options assessments for water and energy needs; and (2) to establish "core values" of equity, efficiency, participatory decision making, sustainability, and accountability in all decisions related to dams and their alternatives.

Whether the functioning of the WCD is seen as an act of framing, an exercise in political bargaining, or the process of constructing putatively authoritative global norms, there are some reasons to view it as a process of decentering state authority.[43] The subject under deliberation—the appropriateness of constructing large dams—constituted an essentially domestic matter that had been seized and dragged into a global forum. The thrust of the final recommendations, including ideals of human rights, watershed-scale democracy, and transnational accountability, essentially vested a set of traditional state responsibilities outside the sphere of the state. State actors enjoyed no particular pride of place alongside the activists, academics, technical experts, and industry representatives who sat as commissioners. Throughout the process, transnational corporate interests interacted directly with transnationally networked environmental, human rights, and indigenous peoples' advocates. The balance they struck between principles of economic efficiency and social justice may or may not be attainable in practice. Yet what is striking is the extent to which *both* sides transcended the traditional framework of state-provided public goods that has anchored more than half a century of water development projects around the world.

Nonetheless, states retained some traditional roles in this drama. Although funds were solicited from corporate donors and nonprofits, state funding sources (including both bilateral aid agencies and intergovernmental organizations) were central to the WCD's ability to deliver on its ambitious work plan.[44] States were also the single most important source of authoritative data, in the form of the economic statistics that allowed the commission to fashion its skepticism about large dams' performance. Indeed, the WCD was never intended to be more than an authoritative voice—its findings lacked any binding legal power, and one of its first decisions was to put itself out of business when it finished its report rather than seek to implement its recommendations.

More significantly, one consequence of *decentering* the state in the WCD process appears to be a countervailing reaction in which states are newly *recentered* in important ways. Given the relatively narrow foundation on which such a heterogeneous commission was able to craft its consensus, an explicit intent of the WCD process was to reinject the commission's findings back into the same local and national conflicts over which it asserted a temporarily global form of authority.[45] In other words, one consequence of elevating state-society conflicts to a broader, global level of norm construction was to reinject and reinvigorate those conflicts at the domestic level. Antidam activists gained an important set of arguments, but the state was reinscribed as the ultimate arena in which the struggles were to be played out.

The state may also be recentered in the context of norm legitimation. Authority for nonstate actors in the international environmental arena is typically grounded in some combination of knowledge and ethics, discursive forms that state actors cannot monopolize.[46] These authoritative platforms not only create enough power to herd states to the bargaining table; they also play a crucial "downstream" function in legitimizing or delegitimizing the protonorms that emerge from bargaining processes that those rounded-up states engage in. Yet in this case, the embrace of the WCD recommendations by some important donor governments and the rejection by some major dam-building states has been far more important in framing the legitimation struggle around the WCD's protonorms than the pronouncements of human rights advocates, environmentalists, or dam-building professional associations. Another example of this norm-validating role reversal can be seen in the specific way that some dam-building states have rejected the WCD findings, pressing their claims not only in the diplomatic terms of national sovereignty but also in the moral tones of legitimate development aspirations and the basic water needs of impoverished local communities.

Protected-Areas Governance

A very different but equally interesting example of the hybridization of authority is the increasingly transnationalized governance of national parks and protected areas. The World Conservation Monitoring Centre lists more than 30,000 protected-areas sites around the world, covering an area equivalent to almost 9 percent of the Earth's land surface (substantially more if one were to include the even larger number of protected areas of uncertain or marginal status or under private control).[47] The formation, validation, governance, and management of these protected areas are shaped by processes that are extensively transnational in scope and increasingly institutionalized in character.

Once again, however, there is no definitive international accord such as the Montreal Protocol or the Basel Convention on hazardous waste to define states' rights and responsibilities. Instead, the world's system of protected areas has grown in an ambiguous political space. A long history of interstate accords that tangentially address protected areas, dating back to the colonial era, has created a fragmented international legal-diplomatic framework.[48] One reason for this is that the central purpose performed by protected areas is far from clear. The idea of protecting natural areas masks the wide range of purposes toward nature (and people) that permeate the histories of particular protected areas. Even when conceived in relatively narrow environmental terms, these purposes may include wilderness preservation, landscape protection, natural resource conservation, herd and game management, protection of particular species, protection of biodiversity more generally, scientific research, environmental education, and nature-based recreation and tourism. Moreover, these environmental goals have been closely entwined, inevitably, with struggles over property rights, access to nature, control of territory, nation building, national or cultural identity, and the delineation of the public and private domain. Far from being the manifestation of a common purpose thrust upon states by interdependence, the global protected-areas network operates more like an institutionalized container for a wide array of shifting and only partially overlapping purposes.

Within this ambiguous political space, most states are less than fully authoritative over their protected areas and the increasingly dense transnational linkages that influence the governance of those spaces. As an important aspect of the legacy of colonialism, many important protected areas across the global South were born from the deeply transnationalized logic of an earlier era. A large number actually predate the states in which they are situated, and several have had postcolonial boundaries etched through their terrain. More recently, states have ceded some (though by no means all) governing authority to a transnational network of protected-areas experts centered on several nodes: the World Commission on Protected Areas of the World Conservation Union (IUCN), UNESCO's Man and the Biosphere Program, the nongovernmental World Wildlife Fund, and a series of increasingly high-profile and institutionalized world congresses that play a crucial role in defining progress and charting new directions in protected-areas governance and management. The result has been a palpable convergence over the past few decades in several core processes of protected-areas governance, including agenda setting, resource mobilization and allocation, knowledge validation, and the standardization of management practices and techniques.[49]

A full assessment of how transnational protected-areas practices affect state authority is beyond the scope of this chapter and could not be made outside the context of specific cases. But two sets of effects are worth highlighting. First, there does appear to be a genuine loss of agenda-setting power on the part of states. The absence of a formal codification of norms in a protected-areas "regime" shifts the center of agenda setting to institutionalized channels—specifically, the world congresses and the IUCN-based experts' network—in which states wield less influence than they would in a typical conference of the parties to an interstate accord. Informality also makes the regime more prone to capture by this season's intellectual fashion in international environmentalism or international political economy. This can be seen in several themes stressed in the action plan emerging from the Fourth World Congress on National Parks and Protected Areas, held in 1992. These themes include the rise of "global change" rhetoric, the growing focus on nonstate actors and local communities, and the neoliberal emphasis on steering funds toward institutional reform rather than specific projects.

Under these circumstances, even the most legitimate and powerful of states are challenged by the existence within their borders of protected areas as, literally, a type of ecological embassy. Tellingly, the strongest areas of growth in the global protected-areas business over the past decade or two have been in domains where state authority is often less fully consolidated, including marine protected areas and remote transborder zones often dubbed "peace parks."[50]

But there are also identifiable ways in which the transnationalization of protected-areas governance may enhance state authority. The history of protected areas shows quite clearly that creating parks and reserves is a way to assert particular forms of control over territory, natural resources, and people.[51] Even as they face mounting pressures to broaden and strengthen protection, governments retain broad latitude to mold the location and operation of protected areas to a range of underlying geopolitical, economic, or other purposes. Certain features of the process of transnational institutionalization have enhanced this latitude. The global network of protected-areas advocates has placed great symbolic emphasis on expanding the total global area under protection and extending coverage in all identifiable biogeographic zones. As a result, states willing to make parks are met at the border (so to speak) by actors bearing material and political resources that can be useful for a range of other agendas.

A second potential extension of state authority comes from the opportunity to build green legitimacy. A functional, regime-theoretic approach would view the pulse of additions to the global protected-areas network during the 1970s as the response of states to a perceived need to strengthen protection. But listing sites can also be a relatively easy and low-cost way to create the appearance of responding to environmental problems. The rising popularity of so-called "integrated conservation-development projects" (ICDPs) adds a new wrinkle, in that it may create new opportunities for states to reconcile the twin goals of environment and development, or at least to claim to be doing so.[52]

Conclusion

In both the watershed and protected-areas examples, some of the core processes of governance have become increasingly transnationalized. Critical resources are created and deployed across borders, including money, skilled people, information, ideas, technology, and persuasive imagery and rhetoric. Global agendas are established, legitimized, and actively changed over time. Authoritative knowledge is created, legitimized, and wielded to shape national policies. Management practices and objectives begin to be drawn toward convergence as standards and techniques come to be universalized and externally legitimized.

States are not displaced from these governance processes so much as they are decentered and recentered. They are decentered by the heterogeneous, multisourced, and often contradictory character of the increasingly embedded "rules" under which they must operate; by emergent wielders of authority that can (partially) usurp traditional state roles; and by a palpable loss of agenda-setting power. They are also recentered in some important ways. States continue to be the primary source of the often ambiguous knowledge that surrounds environment-development controversies. Informal mechanisms are probably more easily bent toward various agendas of state having little to do with environmental protection. Stakeholder approaches to global governance have some notable similarities to traditional corporatist models at the national level—an approach which, far from displacing the state, puts it at the center of political bargaining among sectoral or factional interests.[53]

How should we feel about these trends? Generalization is difficult; a central premise of this chapter has been that we need to notice and imagine a wide range of emergent institutional forms of global environmental governance that sit in various places between the familiar conceptual poles of interstate regimes and global civil society. Both of the cases sketched here are, in part, cautionary tales. In the watershed case, we may be seeing an instance of "corporatism going global," with potentially troubling ramifications for representation and participation.[54] In the protected-areas case, the history of parks and reserves is littered with "solutions" built on exclusion and coercion.

Still, in a world where governments have manifestly failed to come together effectively on a wide array of physically localized but globally cumulative environmental problems, more flexible and hybridized approaches to authority in institutional arrangements would seem to be the only game in town. Realizing the promise of such arrangements entails challenges for scholars. We need a much more carefully grounded understanding of what states can and cannot do in the more complex but increasingly common policy settings of the sort sketched in this chapter. More fundamentally, we must allow ourselves to conceive of institutions that construct more complex, heterogeneous, or fluid spaces for the exercise of authority, and to see them emerging in practices related to a wide range of ecological problems.

Notes

1. Kapstein (1994); John Gray (1998); and Linda Weiss (1998).

2. United Nations Environment Programme (2001).

3. Krasner, ed. (1982).

4. On global civil society and environmental governance, see Lipschutz and Mayer (1996); Princen and Finger, eds. (1994); and Wapner (1995a).

5. Krasner, ed. (1982).

6. Kuehls (1996).

7. Deudney (1995).

8. See, for example, Lipschutz and Conca, eds. (1993).

9. See, for example, Levy, Keohane, and Haas (1993).

10. On the concept of ecological modernization, see Mol and Spaargaren (2000).

11. David A. Lake (2003, 304).

12. Scheppele and Soltan (1987, 194), quoted in David A. Lake (2003, 304).

13. David A. Lake (2003, 304–305).

14. Lukes (1974).

15. Krasner (1982).

16. Rittberger (1993, xii).

17. The idea that agents and structures are mutually constituted, and the centrality of roles and rules in that process, are central themes of the constructivist school of international relations theory. See Wendt (1992); Wendt (1999); and Adler (1997).

18. Oran R. Young, Agarwal et al. (1999, 14, emphasis added).

19. According to Oran R. Young, Levy, and Osherenko (1999), "Regimes sometimes operate at the constitutive level, shaping the identities (and therefore the interests) of actors and, in the process, influencing the way actors behave as occupants of the roles to which they have been assigned."

20. See, for example, Edith Brown Weiss and Harold K. Jacobson, eds. (1998); Bernauer (1995); Miles and Underdal, eds. (2000); and Oran R. Young, ed. (1999).

21. For a discussion of these foundations of nonstate influence in the context of changing norms of sovereignty, see Litfin (1997).

22. Chayes and Chayes (1995, x).

23. Lapidoth (1992).

24. See Lipschutz and Mayer (1993).

25. Cleary (1993).

26. This theme is discussed in Conca (1995).

27. Mason (1999, 104).

28. Montes (1996).

29. See Ribot (1999).

30. Haas (1992); Haas (1990); and Litfin (1994).

31. See, for example, Keck and Sikkink (1998).

32. Litfin (1997).

33. Kuehls (1996, 71–72).

34. Wapner (1995a).

35. Lipschutz (2000).

36. Lipschutz (2000, 3).

37. Kung (1998); Huntington (1996).

38. See Dawson (1996).

39. This distinction among types of environmental problems is similar to that suggested in Turner et al. (1990).

40. Keck and Sikkink (1998).

41. See World Conservation Union (IUCN) and World Bank (1997).

42. World Commission on Dams (2000, xxx).

43. A brief earlier version of this interpretation of the WCD is presented in Conca (2002).

44. Dubash et al. (2001). See also the WCD Web site at <http://www.dams.org/>.

45. I am grateful to Navroz Dubash for this observation.

46. Litfin (1997).

47. Green and Paine (1997).

48. Some of the more important treaties and conventions that bound the space for international protected-areas politics include the 1933 London Convention for the Protection of Flora and Fauna of Africa; the 1940 Washington Convention on Nature Protection and Wild Life Preservation in the Western Hemisphere; the 1971 Ramsar Convention on Wetlands of International Importance; the 1972 World Heritage Convention; the 1973 Convention on International Trade in Endangered Species of Wildlife Fauna; the 1982 UN Convention on the Law of the Sea; the various regional-seas agreements negotiated under the auspices of the UN Environment Program, and the Convention on Biological Diversity signed at the 1992 UN Conference on Environment and Development.

49. Conca (1996).

50. World Conservation Union (IUCN) (1990). See also World Commission on Protected Areas (1997).

51. See, for example, Marks (1984); Guha (1997).

52. On ICDPs, see Wells, Brandon, and Hannah (1992).

53. Ottaway (2001).

54. Ottaway (2001).

10

The Republican State: An Alternative Foundation for Global Environmental Governance

Steven Slaughter

Contemporary global governance is pervasively colored by liberalism and the capitalist social forces that have encouraged the development and extension of neoliberalism and the promotion of globalized capitalism. In this context environmental degradation, transborder pollution, and environmental harm to vulnerable people around the world have become increasingly prevalent. This degradation resists moderation by contemporary global governance because of the very routine nature of the environmental harm and the fundamentally dominant nature of the liberal and capitalist values that underpin the global political economy. The purpose of this chapter is to provide a compelling counterpoint to liberalism, in the form of the neo-Roman approach of republicanism. While neo-Roman republicanism has its own limitations in addressing global environmental governance, considering its overt humanism and emphasis on the operation of the state, it does provide the possibility of global governance that uses the power of the state to limit rather than permit environmental degradation. Republicanism contrasts with liberalism in that it takes the role of the state to be one of promoting nondomination—to enable people to "live in the presence of people but at the mercy of none."[1]

In this chapter, I advance the normative argument that republican-inspired states provide a sounder foundation for global environmental governance than liberal global governance does. Neo-Roman republicanism asserts that the state, rather than being shaped by liberalism and global capital, should be an institution that embeds a concern for its citizens' common interests that surely include the manner in which environmental issues transcend time and space. There are three parts to the argument that republicanism can offer a solid basis for environmental governance. The first part briefly examines how contemporary global governance is interlaced with the ethical foundations of liberal states and neoliberal policymaking, which combine to narrow the ability of global governance to address environmental degradation. The second part outlines the neo-Roman strand of republicanism and the ways the republican state could create a new political space where people take responsibility for their state and direct the state toward the protection of its citizens. The last part turns to the extent and type of concern that the metavalues and potential practices of republican governance would have for global environmental governance.

The Production and Reproduction of Ecological Harm

In order to examine how republican values could influence global governance it is necessary to examine the values that shape contemporary global environmental governance and the condition of the global ecosystem. Global environmental governance refers to the various forms of international cooperation, international organizations, and nongovernmental organizations (NGOs) that bear upon environmental concerns.[2] Such governance has risen to prominence in world politics because of the awareness that human populations have placed immense and relentless pressure upon the global ecosystem. Far from existing within nature, humankind in the modern period has, via processes of science, industrialism, and capitalism, pushed at and broken fundamental ecological limitations. As a result, ecological problems have occurred in various parts of the world and have been transferred across state boundaries and generations, thereby ushering in a process of global environmental change. The course of global environmental change creates ongoing ecological harm in the shadow of an impending danger of ecological collapse. Together these processes entail an environmental crisis that has occurred because of "the *normal and mundane practices of modernity.*"[3] At the present time, we are faced with the simultaneous development of neoliberalism, which accentuates and deepens this crisis, and a broadening public concern regarding this environmental crisis, which is evident in the proliferation of environmental movements and a concern for environmental governance.

Many observers take global governance to encompass the process of solving issues that states cannot effectively address in isolation from other states or other actors in global civil society.[4] Within the context of global environmental governance, questions arise as how best to manage the global commons and transborder pollution in order to "manage" ecological harm. However, global governance can better be understood not just as a process of problem resolution but also as a process of political constitution.[5] Yet it is a constitution that actually produces problems. The way ecological harm has been constructed has enormous implications for the practice of global governance because this deeper view of global governance leads to the observation that "these power structures systematically *produce* environmental change in the first place, rather than simply preventing successful responses to that change."[6] This is especially evident in the way groups such as the World Trade Organization (WTO) focus narrowly on economic liberalization regardless of the broader social or ecological costs.[7] The form of global governance that prevents the formulation of robust responses to environmental change and thereby actually reproduces the circumstances that allow environmental crisis and change is politically constructed by the normative structure of liberalism as embedded within the liberal state and international institutions supportive of global capitalism.

The norms of liberalism have clearly been deeply constitutive of contemporary world politics.[8] Even with the post–World War II proliferation of non-Western states the norms of legitimate state agency have developed around liberalism. Christian Reus-Smit's examination of the metavalues that have shaped the mutual constitution of fundamental international institutions and the state asserts that in the modern period "the moral purpose of the modern state lies in the augmentation of individuals' purposes and potentialities, in the cultivation of a social, economic, and political order that enables individuals to engage in the self-directed pursuit of their interests.[9] This reflects the close historical and normative linkage of liberalism with free enterprise and capitalism.[10] This purpose is also reflected in the liberal norm of noninterference—the ideal that the state ought not restrain individuals except when such restraint would prevent greater restrictions on individual choice and action.[11] This norm can also be understood in the terms of "negative liberty" and paves the way for individuals to act on their individual interests minimally restrained by law,[12] because "law is always a 'fetter,' even if it protects you from being bound in chains that are heavier than those of the law, say, arbitrary despotism or chaos."[13] This reluctance to intervene in the choices of entrepreneurial agents has been dramatically augmented in the wake of the ascendancy of neoliberalism. Stephen Gill claims that within the context of economic globalization the liberal reluctance to intervene in capitalistic activity is being codified into law.[14] This "new constitutionalism" and neoliberalism are broadly underpinned, he writes, by the belief that "private forms of power and authority in capitalist society are only fully stabilized when questions of economic rule (e.g., workplace organization, the rights of investors) are removed from politics (that is, from democracy)."[15] In sum, the liberal norm of noninterference is the core problem of liberal governance because of the institutionalized reluctance to interfere in economic processes that affect the conditions in which people live. In the absence of such rules, those with power and mobility reign without regularized restraint.

The consequence of liberal states and global governance is a context defined by reluctant and minimal regulation. This consequence is also evident in a significant gap between discourse and actual regulation, with many environmental regimes either not being adequately enforced or else "enforced" by nonbinding targets. As Andrew Hurrell remarks, "The agreements negotiated at Rio on Global Climate Change and Biological Diversity are peppered with caveats, qualifications, and escape holes, and lacking in clear measurable commitments."[16] While pragmatic politics and the desire of states to control "their" affairs are largely responsible for this weak enforcement, the liberal reluctance to interfere in economic affairs provides an ethicopolitical backdrop for this reluctance to impede economic actors. Consequently, with respect to global environmental governance, there appear to be two levels of priority. On the higher level we have forms of global economic governance that enable economic globalization. On the lower level we have forms of environmental governance that seem to work around the prevalence of economic regimes and organizations, which generally promote transnational capitalism and systematically affect the environment. In sum, the higher level of global governance creates the framework on which a global environmental crisis is formed and where agents are allowed to create various forms of environmental harm as part of their "normal" economic practice.

It may be argued that defining global governance as a process that actually constitutes environmental harm is overly critical and understates the development of environmental regimes over the last couple of decades. My response is that these regimes do demonstrate that states can cooperate on complex issues of common interest even if states do sometimes defect from or cheat on the instituted rules.[17] However, these regimes do not demonstrate that the liberal basis underpinning this institutional development is able to provide an underlying *moral rationale* that consistently and legitimately regulates private market actors that produce environmental harm. In addition, there are clearly institutional and technological measures afoot that do promote sustainability and address at least some forms of ecological harm.[18] The question is how these possibilities can be enhanced and accentuated. It is my contention that republicanism can provide a rationale for a comprehensive and systematic public interference authored by the state into forms of ecological harm as well as promote positive efforts to avoid ecological harm. But first, the neo-Roman strand of republicanism must be expounded.

Republicanism

In recent years there has been a revival of neo-Roman republicanism, a way of thinking about liberty and good government. Republicanism draws inspiration from the Roman period but only gained coherence in the Italian Renaissance and later in the revolutions in England, France, and the American colonies. The foremost contemporary articulators of the neo-Roman strand of the republican tradition are Quentin Skinner, Philip Pettit, and Richard Bellamy.[19] The central claim of these writers is that before the ascendancy of liberalism, the neo-Roman view of liberty was a prominent political conception that "slipped from sight" during the nineteenth century.[20] This disappearance also occurred in thinking about politics in an international sense.[21] Central to the historical legacy of republicanism are the figures of Charles de Secondat Montesquieu, Niccoló Machiavelli, Jean-Jacques Rousseau, and James Harrington. The contemporary revival of republicanism distinguishes it from both liberalism and communitarianism.[22]

The guiding aspiration of republicanism is the construction of liberty through the exercise of public power. Public power is the state's authoritative capacity, which is controlled by the public and limited in the aims it is able to pursue but focused on the common aims it must fulfill in order to constitute the liberty of the public. Republicanism makes the claim that the only way to avoid domination is to include as many voices as possible into the political sphere and to divide power to promote the common good and to prevent any single interest from dominating. The ideal of preventing domination has historically been conducted within a republican state shaped and controlled by a politically aware society, the members of which feel responsible for the state. The neo-Roman conception of republicanism differs considerably from liberalism's concern for negative liberty, or noninterference of the state, claiming that nonarbitrary state intervention actually assists in the constitution of liberty rather than being a necessary evil in need of restraint.[23] The interpretation of the republican tradition drawn from the Roman account also differs markedly from the contemporary communitarian republican position heralded by Hannah Arendt and continued by neo-Aristotelian authors such as Michael Sandel and David Miller.[24] A clear distinction is drawn between communitarian republicanism, evident within the tradition of Aristotle, and the neo-Roman view of republicanism, which stems from Machiavelli.[25] Pettit, Skinner, and Bellamy hold that there is a distinction between the belief that participation in a political community is the development of liberty in the sense of positive liberty and the neo-Roman republican conception that political participation is the only means to establish a condition where society is free from domination. That is, "rather than trading on a moralistic conception of positive liberty . . . Machiavelli urged civic involvement to avoid the domination of tyrants or elites."[26] Consequently, Pettit refers to the republican conception of liberty as being "nondomination."[27] Political activity on the part of citizens in this sense is a crucial step in the construction of liberty.

The neo-Roman strand of republicanism emphasizes three key themes. The first is the constitutive relationship between the idea of nondomination and the state. According to republican thought, liberty is not a natural attribute but rather a civic achievement that requires a context where citizens are the masters of their own destiny.[28] The republican conception of liberty, understood as nondomination, "consists not in the presence of self-mastery, and not in the absence in interference by others, but in the absence of mastery by others: in absence . . . of domination."[29] Pettit claims domination is defined by a relationship where one person is dominated by another, so I shall assume, to the extent that the other person has the capacity to interfere in their affairs, in particular the capacity to interfere in their affairs on an arbitrary basis. . . . In the most salient case it is the capacity to interfere as the interferer's wish or judgment—their *arbitrium*—inclines them. . . . If freedom means nondomination, then such freedom is compromised whenever a person is exposed to the arbitrary power of another, even if that power is not used against them.[30]

Therefore republican nondomination is a condition that is defined by the diminution or elimination of the act of arbitrary intervention *and* the capacity to arbitrarily interfere in a person's life.[31]

Nondomination reflects a concern with the ways powerful interests can corrupt the body politic and usher in vulnerability, domination, and a dependence on the goodwill of the powerful, as well as potentially silencing voices in the political process. Nondomination is understood as the avoidance of subordination and vulnerability (rather than the liberal fear of restraint) and depends not upon the level of noninterference but the "extent that there exist institutional protections against interference" of an arbitrary kind.[32] Thus law enables nondomination, in contrast to the liberal view that law entails restraint only justifiable by lesser overall restraint by the presence of law.[33] Republicanism stresses that the existence of transparent, publicly governed, nonarbitrary law constitutes liberty defined as nondomination because such liberty "comes about only by design"—it is the "freedom of the city, not the freedom of the heath."[34]

Enacting nondomination in practice requires a republic. A republic is a state defined and constrained by the principle of sovereign self-government, which is thereby publicly controlled and focused on the common or public good of its citizens.[35] The intent is for individuals to be free from both *imperium*, domination by the state, and *dominium*, domination by powerful interests in society.[36] Thus the state and the publicly controlled and thus nonarbitrary interference it imparts do not cause liberty but rather "constitute" it,[37] thereby acting as a form of antipower aimed at curtailing domination.[38] Essentially, republicanism argues, "A state would not itself dominate its citizens—and could provide a unique protection against domination based on the private power or internal or external enemies—provided that it was able to seek only ends, and employ only means, that derived from the public good, the common weal, the *res publica*."[39] Indeed, as Bill Brugger has written, "At the center of republican thought is a strong constitutional state based on the rule of law and opposition to arbitrariness and with a clear notion of the common good or the public interest which is not simply the result of group pressure."[40]

The second republican theme is the public good, understood not as a prepolitical conception of the good life nor as an aggregation of individual interests but rather as a common interest in goods that are not able to be obtained individually—particularly a shared liberty.[41] This observation is underlined by Pettit's claim that nondomination is an "egalitarian good" and a "communitarian good" in that it is only realizable if the nondomination is enjoyed more or less equally and has a "common and social" character—it "is not the atomistic good associated with noninterference."[42] The common good of liberty is only possible if constituted collectively and institutionalized by a state that is principally designed to track all the common interests held by the citizenry.[43] Nonetheless, while the republican conception of the public good develops from actual ongoing forms of common association, it is neither a bloodless conception of shared interests nor an ethnic or nationalist conception.[44] Rather, republicanism is underpinned by patriotism, or "constitutional patriotism" as Jürgen Habermas calls this particularist public sentiment,[45] which is "sustained by shared memories of commitment to liberty, social criticism, and resistance against oppression and corruption."[46] Ultimately, then, republicanism does not embed any ethnic or nationalistic norms or conceptions of the good life other than norms that entail public responsibility and oversight—norms that reflect the social nature of the morality that constitutes nondomination.[47]

The third theme central to republicanism is that political participation is a crucial element in the promotion of the public good and the avoidance of domination. Instead of direct participation in the operation of all government decisions, republican thought emphasizes the importance of various avenues for the contestation of decisions that are made by public representatives to ensure that public decisions reflect the common good and do not promote particular interests.[48] Thus citizenship is a virtuous concern in the public good evident by an active interest in public affairs that sees "the people as trustor both individually and collectively: and sees the state as trustee: in particular, it sees the people as trusting the state to ensure a dispensation of nonarbitrary rule."[49] This trust is backed up by a state structure that ensures the dispersal of power over a range of institutional bodies and a virtuous practice of citizenship that involves vigilance and a concern for the common good that transcends individuals' own pecuniary or particular interests.[50] Thus, rather than being a necessary evil, the state is a crucial artifact of and for the people who are its citizens.

Republicanism provides a powerful statement of the potential of an appropriately designed state to achieve a similar but distinct liberty to that of liberalism. Both liberalism and republicanism agree that the state should aim at liberty, but whereas liberalism claims this is possible by ensuring noninterference in citizens' chosen decisions, republicanism

maintains that this can never be sufficient, since it will always be necessary for the state to ensure at the same time that its citizens do not fall into a condition of avoidable dependence on the goodwill of others. The state has the duty not merely to liberate its citizens from such personal exploitation and dependence, but to prevent its own agents, dressed in a little brief authority, from behaving arbitrarily in the course of imposing the rules that govern our common life.[51]

The scope of concern extends, as Skinner explains, not just to wariness of the state but to private sources of domination as well. Nondomination is a more demanding standard of freedom than noninterference in the sense that it guards against the potential, not just the exercise, of arbitrary interference in the creation of vulnerability or subjection. Republicanism is intent on protecting against the potential of powerful or wealthy groups in society from dominating the political process in a way that the liberal account of noninterference allows. Republicanism also asserts a commitment by the state to promote protection from vulnerability "by giving the powerless protection against the resources of the powerful, by regulating the use that the powerful make of their resources, and by giving the powerless new, empowering resources of their own."[52]

The neo-Roman vision of republicanism articulated here departs from romantic accounts of republicanism or democracy to the extent that Pettit refers to it as "gas-and-water-works republicanism."[53] The practical establishment of nondomination does not require a step back to the positive liberty or the "liberty of the ancients" even though republicanism does demand public virtue and concern on the part of citizens in order to contest power and construct institutions that secure the protection of citizens from domination.[54] The republican state is *empowered* to prevent certain people's becoming dominated by others; it is *designed* to avoid corruption by sectional interests within society; and it is itself legally and morally *constrained* from dominating people. This balancing requires people—citizens—to be actively concerned about political affairs and institutional mechanisms in which government action can be transparent and open to public discipline. So, republicanism is concerned with controlling power by the state. But how can this public control of power act upon global concerns such as the environment?

Republican Global Governance and the Environment

In order to act effectively to minimize ecological harm, republicanism needs to assert the efficacy of the state and state cooperation to act on global concerns. While there have been many ecologically based arguments for substate locales or suprastate cosmopolitan governance, these alternatives can be seen to leave the neoliberal state intact.[55] An alternative to these paths is to reframe the state[56] or to argue for a green state.[57] Even if the liberal state were to be replaced by a citizen-guided republic, there still needs to be clarification of how republicanism could act to avoid ecological harm and provide a foundation for global ecological governance superior to the one shaped by liberalism. After all, it could be argued that republicanism is too humanistic, too dependent upon a monolithic regulatory state, and too state-centric to act upon global environmental concerns. In the remainder of this chapter I address these three ostensible impediments to republicanism's being a fruitful approach to global ecological governance.

Nondomination and Ecology

The first challenge is to clarify the motivation for republicanism to act upon ecological issues. Because republicanism is clearly focused on obtaining the civic liberty of its citizens, it falls short of a green state that expressly emphasizes the importance of green values and policies. Republicanism is only concerned with ecological issues insofar ecological issues relate to the domination of its citizens. The emphasis on humans beings and the state may pose difficulties in addressing ecological concerns that are inherently global and transspecies. Nevertheless, the express humanism of republican thought does not exhaust the possibility of environmental regulation and protection. Indeed, the focus of the republican state on the nondominated condition of the citizens, while humanistic, does offer grounds for the state to interfere in society and the economy to promote commonly held goals and to protect people from the conditions and consequences of ecological domination.

After all, the environment is not just an issue concerning the relationship between humans and nature but also an issue where people exercise power over other people. It is possible to see the effects of ecological crisis and harm as consisting of a particular form of domination that persists across time and space. As Paul Wapner has noted, "Environmental degradation is not simply about how people treat nature but includes, in almost every instance, how they treat each other."[58] However, this behavior occurs across both time and space via forms of ecological "displacement"[59] Examples of these forms of displacement include forms of pollution that are transmitted by air or water and affect other people, and toxic wastes having consequences that extend across time to include future generations. One just has to contemplate the long-term consequences of the estimated 3.6 million tons of toxic waste transferred to developing countries from 1986 to 1988, or nuclear waste generated by power consumed by people in the present.[60] Similarly, the consumption of resources, especially non-renewable resources, has implications for people in the future. While the depletion of renewable resources will also affect people across time, the actual diminution of resources such as fish stocks has consequences for people in other places who rely upon the same resource. In all these cases, people are affected by the actions of other people in other places or times.

Living in the "presence of people but at the mercy of none" takes on a whole new complexion in this context. When humans beings affect the ecology, the idea of presence extends across time and space in ways that produce vulnerability and thereby conditions the capacity of people to be free from domination. Ecological harm therefore can be understood as a process of domination through ecology. This form of domination occurs when the unchecked utilization of resources diminishes the capacity of people in other places or in the future to be free from vulnerability. This can be either a discrete act or a systematic process that produces vulnerability and subordination whereby some people can arbitrarily affect the liberty and security of others—that is, the domination of people by other people whose presence has been extended and sustained by their impact on the ecosystem.

For our purposes, the focus is on the latter, more diffuse situation of systematic processes of domination through ecology. As argued earlier, contemporary global politics is defined by a systematic and ongoing degradation of the environment, a process framed by an assemblage of global governance shaped by practices of neoliberalism and the norms of liberalism. While by no means globally uniform in effect, such environmental degradation is a systematic process that produces the condition of domination for certain people. The assertion therefore is that global politics is defined by people acting through institutional and market-based practices to systematically dominate people living in other places, people living in the future, and potentially themselves if ecological effects of particular types escalate. This form of domination is defined by a vulnerability borne by some people because of the choices of others that significantly restrict and condition the liberty of the vulnerable.

Referring to ecological harm as being a process of domination through ecology is not merely a semantic sleight of hand. If we can claim that ecological effects wrought by environmental change are a form of domination, then republicans can claim that the ground is cleared for republican states to interfere in society to rectify and restrain such a condition and to protect dominated parties. The idea of public regulation as a condition of liberty is beyond the liberal approach to governance but not that of republicanism. The concern for people being affected by ecological effects and the countervailing action of the republican state are not motivated by the ideal of enabling future generations to enjoy the same standard of living but rather to prevent those people from being dominated—that is, to remove or moderate the shadow of constantly living at the mercy of people who did not fully consider the ramifications of their actions on other people. But while this motivation provides the *moral rationale* for republican action, it is clearly the case that republican states cannot enact such interference without having a capacity to affect the operation of capitalism or enable complex forms of cooperation between states.

The Republican State and Economic Regulation
The second challenge facing republicanism is whether this regulatory ideal incorporates a willingness to affect the operation of capitalism. As claimed earlier, republicanism is responsive to *dominium*, domination that is exercised by powerful individuals and groups in society. The act of

preventing *dominium* involves a state capable of enacting law and policies that *identify* the practice of domination and the legislative ability to *intercede* in such activity and thus minimize domination. The aspiration of republican structures and policies is to constitute individual independence either by protecting individuals and dampening the flows of power or by augmenting the capacity of individuals to protect themselves from subjection. In a practical sense, Pettit claims that "we may consider the introduction of protective, regulatory and empowering institutions."[61] The protective and empowering functions of a republican state are directed toward ensuring a common level of security. The former relate to rather standard forms of criminal law that promote a basic sense of security, and the latter relate to welfare state mechanisms that promote social security as well educational and medical services.[62] These types of functions are going to play a small role in avoiding ecological effects that cut across time and space. In contrast, the regulatory institutions of republicanism will play a significant role. Regulatory institutions attempt to reduce domination by "regulating the resources of the powerful, in particular, the resources whereby the powerful may subjugate others."[63] Indeed, "those in economically privileged positions will also dominate certain others—they may dominate employees, customers, or shareholders, for example—unless the way they exercise their resources is regulated."[64] This necessitates familiar regulations that protect workers from unfair treatment or dismissal, unsafe working conditions, misleading advertising, inside trading, and abuse of monopoly positions, for instance.[65] Of course, such domination can also have an ecological dimension in the form of pollution and the depletion of resources. This necessitates forms of law that restrict these forms of action where they can be seen to dominate other people in other places and in the future.

This endorsement of regulation lends itself to two practical consequences for republican policymaking. First, it becomes apparent that republican willingness to regulate decisively shifts economic policy away from deregulated regimes and opens the door for ecological concerns to be embedded in economic policymaking. Nicholas Onuf makes the point that "conspicuously missing from republican thought throughout its long and complex history is any conception of economic activity, of the economy as a sphere of activity that can (if given a chance) operate according to its own logic."[66] Nonetheless republicanism also falls short of a socialist agenda by protecting private property, promoting economic prosperity, and promoting the socioeconomic independence of people.[67] Cass Sunstein succinctly maintains that "free markets are a tool, to be used when they promote human purposes, and to be abandoned when they fail to do so."[68] Thus, according to republican thought, capitalism cannot trump the liberty of citizens in the name of property rights or profit. Rather, the republican state's highest concern is the liberty of its citizens, even if it requires regulating aspects of capitalism that allow domination or vulnerability, as long as the processes of state interference are consistent and nonarbitrary. Thus we can see that a republican state encourages capitalism to operate *but* on the terms dictated by the "priority of democratic goals" and the common interests of its citizens, which include avoiding potential ecological limitations on their liberty.[69]

Second, the integration of ecological concerns into economic policy-making underpins a fundamental shift in aspiration of policymaking. In particular, because we cannot know who might be affected by a given ecological risk in the future, policymakers must err on the side of caution and avoid ecological risks. The republican desire to ensure the liberty of people in other places and other times entails a confirmation of the precautionary principle. Moreover, the policies that stem from this republican impulse are not limited to regulation that *restricts* people's capacity to pollute or squander resources. While republicanism is willing to use the power of the state to curtail actual or future domination, republican policymaking can be open to market mechanisms in environmental issues, such as tradable pollution permits,[70] in the hope of enabling efficiency and decreasing forms of ecological displacement. But, as Sunstein emphasizes, such market mechanisms are not utilized as an article of faith and can be readily rejected if they do not operate to reduce the transmission of ecological harm. Republicanism supports the encouragement of efforts already under way that emphasize the economic advantages of increasing the efficiency by which economic actors use resources and produce wastes.[71]

Ultimately, then, republicanism supports a strong form of ecological modernization in that it endorses institutional mechanisms and democratic methods of policy consideration rather than a reliance on technology and technocratic forms of policy coordination.[72] Yet a strong rendering of ecological modernization and effective regulation of the environment and economy require significant forms of interstate cooperation and negotiation to be effective in practice.

Interstate Cooperation

Consequently, the last challenge facing republicanism is the contention that republicanism is ultimately a philosophy that defends an inward-looking state. While it is true that republicanism asserts the importance of a particularist political community, and forms of patriotism and political responsibility that are located in a specific country, republicans do not believe that this negates interstate forms of cooperation. Maurizio Viroli points out that patriotism is motivated by the desire to live in a country characterized by liberty, but the "love of a particular liberty . . . is not exclusive: love of the common liberty of one's people easily extends beyond national boundaries and translates into solidarity."[73] Thus while there is not an ascriptive global public in republican sense,[74] various publics around the world could still potentially direct their respective states to develop global forms of institutional collaboration to guard against domination, including a republican regulation of capitalism that necessarily includes ecological concerns.

What would a world of states infused with the metavalues of republican governance look like? While the "gas-and-waterworks" vision of republicanism would necessarily fall considerably short of a world state, the potential interactions between republican states would have a different quality than the contemporary relationships between existing states. The common desire of citizens within republican states to achieve the condition of nondomination requires global governance to promote forms of peaceful cooperation and comity. However, as liberty is a civic achievement obtained by the public control over public power, global governance cannot in itself legislate for liberty. Rather, it must develop the constitutive conditions that enable *states* to achieve the civic liberty particular to each society's political articulation of its public good. To enable states to prioritize the pursuit of their public goods, the infrastructure of global governance must address those goods that are beyond the jurisdiction of the state. Just as the values of the republican state license intervention in an individual's affairs if that individual is involved in relations of domination, the goal of nondomination and the pursuit of the global common good would license rules of intervention in the affairs of a state involved with domination within or beyond the territory of that state. As Onuf observes, "In a purely liberal world, sovereignty entails nonintervention; the republican legacy of concern for the common good affirms the propriety of intervention inspired by larger motivations than the intervenor's immediate advantage."[75] In order to maximize effective state autonomy, states have to forgo types of action that actually or potentially dominate other states or individuals and participate in forms of intervention or mutual aid that transcends borders.[76] The goal of nondomination necessitates systematic intervention and regulation of those human activities that enact or potentially enact conditions of domination, including the potential danger of ecological harm.

Global governance inspired by republicanism would be underpinned by sovereignty that would have a different quality. As Onuf does, Pettit claims that republican sovereignty is not sacred, thereby opening up the possibility that the enactment of nondomination could be handled with more efficacy in a body that is more distantly connected to the state.[77] Therefore the realization of the republican goal of nondomination requires the "multinational cooperation and institutionalization" that Pettit points to.[78] As Pettit explains, "While the republican state represents an indispensable means of furthering people's nondomination . . . there are some domestic issues on which it may be better from the point of view of promoting freedom as nondomination to give over control to those [external] bodies and thereby to restrict the local state."[79] This form of institutionalization applies to issues, such as environmental change, where the ability to enact the public good of the state fades in relation to the scale of the issue or the potential of other states to create circumstances of domination. Interstate cooperation stems from the goal of promoting nondomination and a maximal autonomy for each state rather than absolute autonomy. As such, interstate institutions would be shaped by republican states and by the norms of nondomination explicitly designed to interfere with agents who engage in various forms of domination. The aim is to produce lawlike conditions in international politics without consecrating a world government because within the multiple levels of governance the republican state's emphasis on constituting liberty remains. Ultimately, while the state remains the primary site of public power, the delegation of that power to interstate organizations and regimes is required to enable states to constitute liberty in an increasingly global context.

At the very least, this type of association of states entails a commitment to common rules and may entail a confederation of states as suggested in the writings of Montesquieu.[80] It could be claimed that this is a move toward the *civitas maximus* that Christian Wolff outlined over two hundred years ago, as colorfully detailed by Onuf.[81] However, the confederation would be more like Onuf's characterization of Emmerich de Vattel's confederation of states: less natural than Wolff's and more consciously constructed.[82] Thus republicanism entails the potential for a significant institutionalization of global politics, albeit one that falls short of the political and institutional cosmopolitanism of Richard Falk or David Held, for example,[83] even if republicanism does embed the need to be morally cosmopolitan in the sense of being globally aware and enabling other people in other parts of the world to develop institutional forms appropriate to their own public constitution of nondomination. In light of the developing threat of ecological crisis, republicanism offers a compelling rationale for states to cooperate to facilitate nondomination. In order for this to occur, international institutions would have to take a wider view of what constitutes a threat to liberty than the prevailing array of international institutions such as the WTO, which systematically promote capitalistic-liberal values that eschew a substantial regulation of economic life.

Conclusion

Republicanism provides foundational principles for global governance that provide strong reasons and suitably powerful means to regulate practices that can dominate others. As an approach to governance, republicanism seeks to reclaim the state in order to fashion a liberty against powerful interests that in a liberal world are allowed to create conditions of domination, including those forms of subordination and vulnerability that are transmitted through ecological ramifications. Republicanism provides a far superior rationale for global environmental governance than that of liberalism and neoliberalism because it discards the deep-rooted liberal reluctance to interfere in the decisions of individuals, particularly private property holders whose actions directly or indirectly dominate other people. Such rules would regulate and structure capitalism with nondomination and risk aversion at the forefront of policy deliberation. This intervention could only be enforced and justified by appealing to a state empowered and controlled by citizens to enact nondomination by developing institutions within and beyond the state. Global governance constituted by republican states would express greater commitment to minimizing the displacement of environmental harm because such harm is seen to be a process involving an arbitrary and reckless exercise of power.

In perceiving the exercise of environmental harm or the potential of environmental risk to be an issue of domination and power, republicanism involves a rethinking of not only the existence of such power but also the *normative response* of taking such power seriously. Ultimately it requires a rethinking not just of the ways humans treat nature but how they exercise the ability to dominate other humans. If such domination is to be minimized, only a counterbalancing exercise of public power and intervention will develop an effective institutional response to such domination. Republican political theory therefore reconstitutes citizenship and the state so that they can be seen as resources for environmental movements' attempts to regulate global economic activity and minimize environmental harm.

This chapter has argued that the prevailing and underlying values of liberalism and neoliberalism are central to the developing ecological crisis. In essence, the norm and practice of liberal noninterference, with its reluctance to regulate the displacement of domination across time and space, perpetuates ecological harm. By contrast, the interpretation of neo-Roman republicanism drawn here asserts the importance of public intervention in matters of ecological harm that have the potential to dominate others. This moral and political concern prompts citizens to direct their states toward the protection of their public interest that in the area of ecological governance will also require interstate cooperation consistent with the concerns of other states. The republican requirement of having a state able to intervene to avoid domination offers solid grounds for global governance capable of regulating human affairs and providing protection from ecological domination that stems from environmental change wrought by humankind.

Notes

I am grateful for the helpful advice of those attending the workshop The Nation-State and the Ecological Crisis: Sovereignty, Economy and Ecology at the European Consortium for Political Research Annual Joint Sessions, Grenoble, France April 6–11, 2001. I would also like to thank Robyn Eckersley, John Barry, and Philip Pettit for their constructive advice.

1. Pettit (1999a, 80).

2. Paterson (1999b, 794–796).

3. Saurin (1993, 62). Emphasis in original.

4. Commission on Global Governance (1995); Reus-Smit (1998).

5. Paterson (2000b, 254–255).

6. Paterson (2000b, 255).

7. Conca (2000b).

8. Reus-Smit (1999, ch. 6); Richardson (2001, 55–65).

9. Reus-Smit (1999, 123).

10. Pettit (1999a, 132).

11. Pettit (1999a, 40–43).

12. Pettit (1999a, 17–18).

13. Berlin (1958, 8).

14. Gill (1998).

15. Gill (1998, 23).

16. Hurrell (1994, 152). See also Smith (1993).

17. Oran R. Young (1990).

18. Christoff (1996).

19. Skinner (1992); Skinner (1990); Skinner (1998); Pettit (1999a); Bellamy (1999); and Bellamy (2000). See also Viroli (1995). *For Love of Country* (Oxford: Clarendon Press, 1995).

20. Skinner (1998, ix).

21. Onuf (1998, 2–3).

22. Pettit (1999a, 7–8); Skinner (1992, 222–223).

23. Pettit (1999a, 22–23).

24. Bellamy (2000, xii). See also Brugger (1999, 12–14).

25. Bellamy (2000, xii).

26. Bellamy (2000, xii).

27. Pettit (1999a, 51).

28. Bellamy (1999, 120).

29. Pettit (1999b, 165).

30. Pettit (1999b, 165).

31. Pettit (1999a, ch. 2).

32. Brugger (1999, 6–7).

33. Brugger (1999, 6).

34. Pettit (1999a, 122).

35. Skinner (1992, 217).

36. Pettit (1999a, 13).

37. Pettit (1999a, 108).

38. Pettit (1996).

39. Pettit (1999a, 287).

40. Brugger (1999, 20).

41. Pettit (1999a, 284).

42. Pettit (1999a, 125).

43. Pettit (1999a, 290).

44. Viroli (1995, 11–13).

45. Habermas (2001, 74).

46. Viroli (1995, 13).

47. Pettit (1999a, 8). See also Viroli (1995).

48. Pettit (1999a, 296) forwards "contestatory democracy" where people have both "authorial" and "editorial" powers and avenues in relation to government decisions. See also Skinner (1981, 65–67).

49. Pettit (1999a, 8).

50. Skinner (1992, 217).

51. Skinner (1998, 119).

52. Pettit (1996, 589–590).

53. Pettit (1999a, 239).

54. Pettit (1999a, 18).

55. Hurrell (1994, 154).

56. See four models in Eckersley (2000b).

57. See Eckersley's contribution to this volume (chapter 8).

58. Wapner (1997a, 214).

59. Wapner (1997a, 217).

60. Wapner (1997a, 219–220).

61. Pettit (1996, 589–590).

62. Pettit (1989, 156).

63. Pettit (1996, 590).

64. Pettit (1996, 590).

65. Pettit (1996, 591); Sunstein (1997, 9).

66. Onuf (1998, 247).

67. Pettit (1999a, 158–163).

68. Sunstein (1997, 7).

69. Sunstein (1997, 386).

70. See Moran (1995).

71. Christoff (1996, 207–211).

72. Christoff (1996, 222).

73. Viroli (1995, 12).

74. See Habermas (2001, 108–109) and Miller (1999).

75. Onuf (1998, 140).

76. Onuf (1998, 139–140).

77. Pettit (1999a, 152). See also Onuf (1998, 137–138, 140).

78. Pettit (1999a, 152).

79. Philip Pettit (1999a, 152).

80. Montesquieu (1748, 183).

81. Onuf (1998, 58).

82. Nicholas Onuf (1998, 60, Chs. 3 and 4).

83. Falk (1995); Held (1995).

11

In Defense of International Environmental Cooperation

John Vogler

To those involved in environmental diplomacy the idea that international cooperation should need defending may seem bizarre. It is, surely, a self-evidently beneficial activity to be promoted and perfected. The outputs, as represented in the framework of international environmental governance erected by states, are impressive. Over five hundred multilateral legal instruments now relate to environmental matters, and the 1990s witnessed an unprecedented period of innovation in international environmental law and organization. To this may be added a dense network of less formal understandings and contacts between governments, and a complex and extensive architecture of international scientific cooperation.

Although an underlying agreement on the importance of such activities and achievements may represent the consensus in the policy community and among mainstream students of international environmental politics, there are also critics. It is the burden of this chapter that there is now a sustained critique of international cooperation that cannot be neglected. What is at stake here reflects a key international dimension of the central question considered in this book: whether the state remains "the preeminent institution with the requisite political authority and steering capacity to tackle ecological problems." The attack upon the utility of international cooperation is thus a subset of the wider critical debate on the functions of states in an era of globalization and perceived failures of environmental governance. If the state can no longer be regarded as an effective instrument of public environmental purpose, then international cooperation—the making of multilateral agreements between states—is a trivial or even bogus activity in terms of confronting the global ecological crisis. In the face of this, it is incumbent upon advocates of international cooperation both to explain and defend their position. This, in a small way and in the spirit of countering the political resignation that may arise from considering the manifold inadequacies of interstate environmental cooperation, the present chapter attempts to do.

It commences by considering mainstream and more radical views on international environmental governance and then attempts to draw out and respond to four significant criticisms made by the latter. They involve, first, the ontology and epistemology of those who study international cooperation; second, the functions of international environmental cooperation; and third, the related question of its effectiveness. En route an attempt will be made to respond by considering what an advocate of international environmental cooperation might regard as the key functions of the activity, something that is often taken for granted. This can hardly be said of the fourth and final part of the chapter, which considers the critical question, upon which much of the rest of the debate turns, as to whether the state may be seen as in any way a capable instrument for bringing about ecologically beneficial change.

Differing Views of Environmental Governance

In advance of the 2002 World Summit on Sustainable Development (Johannesburg) the UN Secretary General proclaimed the continuing need to strengthen the system of international governance for sustainable development "to ensure coherence, integrate policies, limit overlap and strengthen implementation."[1] Formalized cooperation between the governments of sovereign states remains at the heart of this endeavor even though it may be rebranded as international or even global environmental governance. The latter concept is potentially capable of comprising a whole range of actors and governance processes within and beyond the sovereign state. Indeed, the use of the term *governance* in international relations denotes not only the need for the performance of government-like tasks in the absence of a central world authority but also a sense of the inadequacy of interstate cooperation and the involvement of many other actors.[2]

Nonetheless, it is probably not too much to say that in the day-to-day discourse of policymakers, *governance* typically amounts to little more than a synonym for international organization. Witness, for example, the discussions on international environmental governance initiated by the UN Environment Programme (UNEP) Governing Council. Issues under discussion were the upgrading of UNEP to specialized agency status, improved coordination between the various MEAs (multilateral environmental agreements) and within the UN system generally, and better non-governmental organization (NGO) access to the UNEP Governing Council. Much also depended upon "technology support and capacity building" to assist developing countries.[3] Above all, there is scant consideration of the functions of international environmental governance or of the continuing utility of the international architecture of conventions, organizations, and programs. Rather, they are simply assumed to be necessary but in need of better coordination or status. Thus attention is directed toward improving performance, extending integration between the various organizations and conventions, and creating new overarching forms of international authority as, for example, in the proposal to transform the moribund UN Trusteeship Council into an organ of supreme environmental stewardship. While it is impossible to deny the huge increase in NGO participation, which should now be regarded as one of the principal outcomes of the United Nations Conference on Environment and Development (UNCED, Rio deJaneiro, 1992)—and the various official and semiofficial commentaries do not deny it—the focus is still determinedly intergovernmental. "Civil society dialogue" represents another means of improving and extending global governance, which fundamentally remains a matter of cooperation between the governments of sovereign states.

The academic study of the international relations of global environmental change overlaps substantially with the policy discourse. There is a very large and growing literature on international environmental law, institutional design, and implementation issues. Not all of it is state-centered. There has been a burgeoning interest in the role of NGOs and "epistemic communities," indicating extensive dissatisfaction with a purely state-centered approach. However, such work probably does not mark a decisive break with underlying assumptions about international cooperation. NGOs in practice and theory remain in a highly symbiotic relation with state governments and international institutions, working to improve and redirect rather than supplant the latter. In the tradition of the study of international organization, most work has been concerned not so much with the efficacy of international cooperation as with the circumstances under which it may occur in a system that is still assumed to have an anarchical character. Since the mid-1970s the dominant concept in the study of international cooperation has been that of international regimes. International lawyers had long used the term to refer to a corpus of law, but now it was employed to denote the principles, norms, rules, and decision-making procedures that applied to the governance of a specific issue area in the international system. A regime could include elements of international law and organization, but the intent was to provide a more encompassing conception of governance institutions, particularly those for global economic management.[4]

When in the latter part of the 1980s global environmental issues rose to prominence, they were mainly incorporated into this preexisting theoretical apparatus. The reduction of transboundary air pollution or the restoration of the stratospheric ozone layer were essentially represented as problems of international cooperation in the same way as achieving monetary order had been. Mainstream regime-based scholarship could therefore be characterized as a subset of a wider debate between neorealist and liberal institutionalist accounts of the bases for interstate cooperation. In the study of environmental questions, as Steve Smith observes, the liberal institutionalist line has tended to predominate.[5] Utilizing this perspective, work on international environmental regimes flourished, particularly in the United States.[6] In terms of the purposes of this chapter, the essential point is that the significance of international cooperation for global environmental governance continued to enjoy mainstream acceptance.

European analysts often followed the U.S. lead and focused on international regime construction. However, certainly in Britain, there has also been another debate which, in questioning the efficacy of interstate cooperation, was perhaps more reflective of wider currents in green political thought. It derives from a radical challenge to the whole business of international cooperation and both the objects and assumptions of those who spend most of their time studying international environmental regimes. It is really about the relevance of the international dimension of global environmental change. This is dangerous territory because questions inevitably arise about the relevance of international relations as a discipline, at least as currently constituted. In concrete terms it may even affect research funding, where it often seems expedient to argue that international relations has something distinctive to say about global environmental change and that its research is worth funding alongside other well-established claimants: environmental economics and geography, and a newly globalized sociology. In response, an effective strategy was to align the solution of global environmental problems with the central problematic in orthodox international relations: the maintenance of order in a world fragmented into separate state sovereignties. By representing global environmental problems as collective action problems between states, the special competence of international relations scholarship could be asserted.

The challenge to such ideas and to a preoccupation with international cooperation was in part fueled by green politics. As for so much else, the Rio process provided a catalyst. Disillusionment with mainstream international cooperation and demands for a radical rethinking emerged most strongly in critical accounts written in the wake of that great diplomatic and NGO jamboree.[7] The Rio conference was oversold at the time and constituted an unmissable target: the pieties of its declaration and Agenda 21, the toothlessness of the UN Framework Convention on Climate Change (UNFCCC), the sinister influence of the World Bank and the role given to its Global Environmental Facility (GEF), the absence of a forestry convention, the machinations of the Business Council on Sustainable Development, and so forth. Perhaps most insidious of all, the rhetoric of green politics was adopted by those responsible for the degradation of the earth—governmental and business elites. As Wolfgang Sachs writes, "Ecology—understood as the philosophy of a social movement—is about to transform itself from a knowledge of opposition to a knowledge of domination."[8]

Such disillusionment provided the background to the more specific critique of international environmental cooperation. Not all the critics would necessarily describe themselves as adherents of radical political ecology, but I hope they will forgive the use of this label to denote a particular political and academic critique of the liberal institutionalist mainstream that developed during the 1990s. Radical political ecology starts from a very different problematic from that which is conventional among liberal institutionalists. The essential question concerns the environmental degradation that is a direct consequence of globalized capital accumulation rather than the absence of effective governance in an anarchic system. Its approach is structuralist rather than agent-oriented and critical rather than problem-solving.

One may well stigmatize these approaches as incommensurable, leaving a situation in which adherents simply "talk past each other." It is nonetheless the contention of this chapter that despite some of its uncomfortable implications (not least for research funding) the radical critique cannot be ignored, and that it is incumbent upon those who study international environmental cooperation to engage with it. In the process they will have to provide, among other things, a more convincing and specific account of the functions of international cooperation and its environmental effectiveness. My discussion is organized around what seem to me to be four key criticisms made by the opponents of international cooperation. The first is fundamental in that it raises questions about the character of international relations as a discipline. The second queries the functions of international cooperation, and the third contests the effectiveness of multilateral environmental agreements. Finally, there is the matter of the role and capabilities of the contemporary state. This is the issue that underlies all the others.

The Ontological and Epistemological Character of International Relations

As Julian Saurin, Matthew Paterson, and others have argued, orthodox international relations, which takes the anarchical state system as its problematic, is incapable of comprehending the global socioeconomic phenomenon of environmental change.[9] A profound contradiction exists between a proper understanding of global political ecology and the discipline as currently constituted. While global environmental change can be seen as a pervasive and complex set of processes intimately connected to globalization, international relations remains fixated upon the ways in which states and international organizations have responded to the impact of environmental change, "where the change is taken as given and relatively unproblematic," whereas "a thorough analysis of *causes* and of the *diffused* processes which engender environmental change should be regarded as the *sine qua non* of this field of enquiry."[10]

This is a persuasive argument, and it is true that international relations as a discipline fails to fully comprehend, still less explain, the global change problem. The easy response would be to retreat into disciplinary specialization of labor and argue that there is little point in international relations specialists attempting to transform themselves into climate scientists, anthropologists, or even global social theorists, although we should be open to such influences. The field as currently constituted does, however, have a great deal to say about the political context of global change, its potentially violent consequences, and governance and efforts to coordinate solutions. Part, but only part, of the approach to stemming global degradation must involve working through the existing international political system with all its inadequacies. For example, one frequently comes across the work, say, of environmental economists who, having developed an elegant scheme for emissions trading or carbon taxation, conclude with a sigh, "If only politics allowed this to happen or if only national governments were less short-sighted." The concentration of scholars of international relations of the environment on the forms and bases of international cooperation, however marginal to some recent developments in the discipline as a whole, may thus be justifiable in terms of the much larger picture of international global change research.

However, radical critics are certainly correct in their view of the narrowness of a concentration on the study of international cooperation per se. Divorced from a wider understanding of the functioning of the international political economy, and of the causes and consequences of environmental degradation, it can rapidly become a sterile exercise. It is, for example, impossible even to begin to evaluate the environmental effectiveness of international agreements without an appreciation of the socioeconomic and ecological circumstances within which they operate.

However, this is not really the point at issue. For theorists of radical political ecology, the state and interstate institutions are indissolubly bound up with the processes of capitalist accumulation and domination. The fundamental error of orthodox students of international cooperation, shared with exponents of ecological modernization, is that they hold to a false assumption about the independence of state structures and the possibilities of reform. At root these arguments take a Marxist form:

Because of the necessity of economic growth for capitalism to survive, those organizing such growth, defined generally as capital, gain a great deal of power with respect to state decision making. In this context, therefore, the state's fundamental purpose is to secure the conditions under which capital accumulation (economic growth) can proceed smoothly.[11]

The state is not irrelevant to global environmental degradation; it is necessarily an agent of that degradation. This constitutes an axiomatic point that non-Marxist international relations scholars will simply deny.

The epistemological challenge posed by radical political ecology is closely related. In this view, contemporary international relations is founded on an atomistic positivism that inhibits proper ecological understanding. From this perspective, the attachment to rationalistic and instrumental science is seamlessly related to the emergence of the capitalist state and thus inherently suspect. In the attack on international cooperation, this view chimes in with a broader ecological and feminist critique of environmental science and "rational" management of ecosytems.[12]

It is true that most regime analysts adopt a positivist stance and utilize the tools of rational choice analysis. This need not always be the case, and there have been significant contributions to the study of international cooperation that do not fit into this mold. Karen Litfin's discourse analysis of the ozone regime or the cognitive approach of epistemic community theorists provide examples.[13] Just as the state and the constitution of the international system have been subject to constructivist analysis, there is no inherent reason that the same approach should not be applicable to international environmental cooperation.[14]

The attack on positivism could, of course, be directed to the bulk of global change research, dominated as it is by the physical sciences. Indeed, an advantage of maintaining a positivist epistemology is that it unites social scientists with the climate modelers, economists, and other members of the global change scientific community. Rightly or wrongly, the adoption of a positivist approach may represent a criterion of acceptability among research funding agencies and even those mainly concerned with the social sciences. This was, however, not the case with the British social science program that ran throughout the 1990s.[15] What does tend to distinguish the research that was funded was its perceived policy relevance. This is usually the other key criterion of acceptability and may bring policy-focused researchers into collision with radical critics who adopt Cox's famous distinction between problem solving and critical research.[16] There is no question that the overwhelming bulk of work on the international relations of the environment falls into the problem-solving category; it does not stand outside the system and exercise a radical and independent critique. Researchers may respond that given the immediacy and magnitude of the problems to be solved, this is entirely justifiable, but in a wider perspective such policy-driven concern with aspects of institutional design and implementation will serve to substantiate radical charges of cooption. Once again, the critical divergence between radical political ecology and the orthodox study of international cooperation is over whether the latter is ever capable of independence.

The Functions of International Cooperation

One of the most telling charges made by academic critics and activists is that, in Tony Evans's memorable phrase, international environmental cooperation involves "doing something without doing anything."[17] The sense is that intergovernmental activity may have a number of functions, but a serious attempt to address environmental degradation is not demonstrably among them. It is indeed easy to establish the heavily politicized and rhetorical functions of international cooperation. Almost any major document emerging from UN environmental conference diplomacy will suffice to illustrate this point. Take, for example, the Rio +5 meeting held in New York in the summer of 1997. Its review document was, as ever, a nice exercise in compromise drafting:

> To foster a dynamic and enabling international economic environment favorable to all countries is in the interest of all countries. And issues, including environmental issues, that bear on the international economic environment can be approached effectively only through a constructive dialogue and genuine partnership on the basis of mutuality of interests and benefits, taking into account that in the view of the different contributions to global environmental degradation, states have common but differentiated responsibilities.[18]

Further verbiage, no doubt meaningful to insiders but requiring extensive deconstruction for the uninitiated, is continually produced in the UN system. It is grist to the mill of those who argue that international meetings involve an expensive and environmentally damaging charade. Perhaps an environmental impact assessment of international environmental diplomacy since 1992 ought to be undertaken. The results would no doubt be shameful in terms of the contribution to global warming of the millions of air miles traveled and to deforestation of the mountains of paper consumed.

Yet this is not the whole story. It is merely to say that one important function of international environmental cooperation is the legitimation of governments and the pursuit of status at the international level. Such activity is universally recognizable across the whole spectrum of international relations and does not necessarily mean that there can be no substantive outcome. It is thus important to obtain a clear view of the limits and potentialities of international cooperation. Too often the argument is conducted in partisan black-and-white stereotypes in which the significance of international action is either uncritically defended or rejected out of hand.

The relevance of particular types of international environmental cooperation will be problem-dependent. In their simplest form, agreements involve the coordination of the classic functions of states in guarding their frontiers. Hence the role of international cooperation in suppressing trade in environmentally undesirable goods, for example, the Convention on International Trade in Endangered Species (CITES) or the Basel Convention on hazardous waste, is fairly self-evident. To this may be added the rather more complex provisions of the Cartagena Protocol 2000 on the transboundary movement of living modified organisms—products of the new biotechnology. This erects a system of "advanced informed agreement" between governments to regulate such trade in the interests of maintaining biosafety.

At the other end of the spectrum lies the climate change regime (perhaps as indication of a trend, the United States, although involved in both biosafety and climate protocol negotiations, is a party to neither). Although the UN Framework Convention on Climate Change and its Kyoto Protocol are intergovernmental agreements, there should be few illusions about what is achievable solely at the international level. Tackling climate change will clearly involve multilevel governance, and Kyoto will be only one part of the structure.

What generalizations can be made as to the functions of international cooperation with respect to environmental governance? There are at least four that can be observed across a range of environmental regimes.

Norm Creation   This is a self-proclaimed function of many international conferences, and it is easy to sneer at the declaratory pretensions of Rio and its successors. Equally, it is always difficult to establish the provenance of phenomena that lack a concrete and measurable existence. However, in retrospect, it is clear that the first great international meeting at Stockholm, the UN Convention on Humans and the Environment

(UNCHE, 1972) did have a range of significant consequences, including the dissemination of the basic notion that governments had environmental responsibilities. In the next decade most major states established ministries of the environment. In Europe, the Treaty of Rome of 1958 had been famously silent on environmental matters, but the UNCHE provided a stimulus to the creation of the European Community's successive environmental action plans. Similar points could be made about the UNCED's Agenda 21 on sustainable development. It has evidently been influential in the creation of large numbers of local Agenda 21 programs, leading to direct implementation of some of its recommendations. Another example of international norm and standard setting is provided by the mass of "soft law" generated by UNEP in such areas as its Regional Seas Programes. Alternatively, one might point to the dissemination and adoption of concepts such as the precautionary principle. It is obviously not possible to identify a particular moment or meeting when this very significant norm gained currency, but it is a reasonable assumption that its propagation over the years owes much to the processes of international cooperation.

Generation and Dissemination of Scientific Knowledge   In terms of the orthodox positivist approach to environmental management, effective policy is necessarily related to scientific knowledge, although the interface between the two is frequently complex and controversial (this is not to say that other knowledges are irrelevant). International scientific collaboration has a long and distinguished history dating back to the beginning of the twentieth century and such pioneering bodies as the International Council for the Exploration of the Seas (ICES). There is no need here to recount the important internationally organized scientific investigation that lay behind the ozone protocol or the climate change regime. The scale of the international scientific effort focused on the Inter governmental Panel on Climate Change (IPCC) is truly awe-inspiring and unprecedented. The essential point about all this activity is very simple. Unlike, for example, pharmaceutical research, the overwhelming bulk of investigation into the science of large-scale natural systems is publicly funded by governments. There really are no viable alternatives, and it is therefore an important and continuing function of international cooperation to organize the various national programs into a coherent effort and to disseminate the results. To this may be added the generation of scientific consensus and the legitimation of findings so as to make them the basis for international agreement (one might put this more negatively and say that clear and authoritative science removes a convenient excuse for inaction). The various levels at which the appositely named Inter*governmental* Panel on Climate Change operates provide a good example of a mechanism for translating scientific findings into a politically usable product. They also, of course, provide evidence of the interplay of special interests and politicization.[19]

Capacity Building   This is an element of most recent multilateral environmental agreements. It recognizes the fact that the economic disparities between different societies and the corresponding gap between the capabilities of governments are extraordinarily wide. It is also a matter of practical politics within the UN system that many developing states will not participate in agreements unless there is an element of financial assistance and redistribution between North and South. The underlying bargain is expressed in the formal title of the 1992 Earth Summit; it was a conference on environment and development. Individual agreements will often not be negotiable without an element of compensation for the disadvantaged, involving technology transfer. A well-known example is provided by the 1990 London Agreement to an interim ozone fund, which allowed India and China to become parties to the Montreal Protocol through funding their acquisition of an environmentally safer chemical technology. At an even more basic level, the reporting and other requirements of multilateral agreements are beyond the scientific and administrative capabilities of a great many states. Capacity building in terms of international funding is thus a sine qua non of their participation. A salient example is provided by the assistance given with the drawing up of national greenhouse gas emission inventories in the climate change regime.

Once again, it is difficult to envisage the private sector having the incentives or resources to effect such transfers (although in the administration of aid NGOs have become increasingly significant). Overall capacity building and transfer of funds and technology continue to be important intergovernmental functions, usually exercised through the multilateral development banks and particularly through the Global

Environmental Facility of the World Bank. In a series of moves that were unsuccessfully opposed by many developing nations, the latter has been designated the funding mechanism for the UN Climate Change Convention and various other contemporary agreements.

Provision of Multilateral Regulatory Frameworks   This is perhaps the most evident function of international cooperation. The argumentation is very well known. In a decentralized system of sovereign states lacking any central authority, there is need to cope with the problems arising from unavoidable interdependence. The classic responses to economic, security, and more recently ecological interdependence have been through multilateral cooperation between the governments of sovereign states. The extent of such cooperation can range from restricted forms of policy coordination through the most intense and complex attempts at international management. The formal output of all this activity is a vast and ever-expanding corpus of international public law.

In terms of the environment there is a clear requirement to develop some form of governance for the global commons, areas and resources that do not fall under sovereign jurisdiction. In its absence, as graphically illustrated by the fate of the great whales or by the more recent decline of high seas fisheries and "straddling stocks," there is likely to be an unregulated exploitation of "open access." The avoidance of such "commons tragedies" requires the creation of a regulatory regime with the consent of the various national authorities. The Antarctic Treaty system, the UN Law of the Sea regime for the deep seabed, and the stratospheric ozone or climate change regimes provide examples. A key consideration here is that governments are loath to increase taxation or impose controls if these are seen to put national economies at a disadvantage in increasingly competitive markets. International regimes provide a framework of reassurance to allow such action to be taken in a coordinated manner.

There is some limited evidence of regime building by corporate actors, especially in standard setting beyond formal international organizations such as the International Telecommunication Union. However, this remains marginal to the overarching regulatory role of multilateral cooperation between governments. Only they have the authority to make international law and to represent and bind their subjects. The fact that in many instances such formal authority is not matched by an actual ability to deliver results emphasizes the capacity-building activities just discussed.

The Effectiveness of International Cooperation

The radical case cannot deny the existence of the mass of multilateral policy coordination, but it does contest that its functions can be effectively fulfilled. Indeed, as Paul Wapner has pointed out, it would be possible for the cynic to establish a strong positive correlation between the volume of international environmental diplomacy and the increasing scale of environmental degradation.[20]

One line of attack is to emphasize that effective environmental agreements depend upon enforcement, which is (beyond the terms of Chapter 7 of the UN Charter or the dispute procedures of the World Trade Organization) impossible between sovereign states.[21] Effective commons management in particular cannot occur at the nation-state level—the numbers are too great and observation of others' behavior, upon which compliance rests, cannot be assured. Governments will, in any case, not bind themselves to do things that contradict their short-term interests or the interests of influential national business corporations.

To this it may be responded that there exists a mass of empirical evidence demonstrating that 99 percent of international law is observed and that there are subtle "horizontal" means of enforcement resting upon reciprocity and reputation.[22] However, it may more convincingly be argued that governments will not sign treaties that, although environmentally desirable, contradict their interests. Witness, for example, the U.S. record on climate change. Here radical critics may join forces with realists in denigrating the possibilities of international cooperation. Colin Gray, for example, commented on the provisions of the Antarctic, outer space, and seabed regimes, "In all three cases the High Contracting Parties solemnly agreed not to do what they saw no good reason to do anyway."[23] This may well be true, but it does not mean that international cooperation will always be condemned either to triviality or ineffectiveness. A profound point of difference between liberal institutionalists and both radical and realist critics is the contention by the former that involvement within an institution, whatever the reason for initial entry, can have significant implications for the shaping of both attitudes and behavior. Thus, to take the case of Antarctic cooperation, it is quite possible to accept that lack of overriding national interests would militate against collaboration, particularly while the costs of exploiting the hydrocarbons of the Antarctic continent remain uneconomically high. And yet it is also demonstrable that the policies of the Antarctic Treaty consultative parties have been molded by over forty years of involvement. The continuing record of the Antarctic Treaty regime, through the 1991 Madrid Protocol, is one of a tightening and extension of environmental regulation.

Effectiveness is not easy to establish. There is a lawyer's view in which agreements become effective when they are duly ratified and states are in formal compliance, and there is the view, often found in the study of international organization, that effectiveness can be measured in terms of a transfer of authority from the national level. More relevant is the test not just of formal treaty compliance but of the actual modification of behavior and ultimately physical measurement of alterations in the natural world. There are long and sometimes complex chains of causation here that are as yet imperfectly understood.[24] One prominent critic of contemporary regime analysis concludes her study of effectiveness in the transboundary air pollution and Mediterranean regimes as follows: "The social and structural origins of environmental degradation need to be studied in order to understand, on the one hand, the constraints under which policymaking operates and, on the other, the complexity that underlies the study of effectiveness."[25] Note that this conclusion relates to the failings of contemporary regime analysis and to the shortcomings of its concept of effectiveness rather than to the inevitable impotence of international agreements themselves.

There are, of course, many obvious failures of international environmental cooperation. World fisheries are subject to a calamitous decline, but sustainable management either at the world or regional level appears impossible. The disaster of rainforest destruction continues unabated despite numerous attempts under the auspices of the Biodiversity Convention and elsewhere to organize international action to arrest it. While I reject the assumption that state activity and environmental degradation are necessarily related, it is possible to see that some of the critical drivers of global environmental change may be positively encouraged rather than restrained by governments. This is evident in the priority given to the expansion of trade and investment in the absence of effective environmental safeguards. Of course, there are arguments that trade and environmental protection can be mutually supportive, especially in promoting economic development, which is, according to proponents of the "environmental Kuznets curve," positively related to better air and water quality. But there are also numerous ways in which increasing volumes of trade can give rise to degradation through the externalities associated with transport and production processes. At the moment it would be fair to say that while governments have moved substantially toward implementing free trade in manufactures within the WTO regime, there has been minimal progress toward ensuring the sustainability of trade or toward ending agricultural subsidies. The latter appear as outrageous to the apostles of free trade as they do to proponents of sustainable development but weighty domestic constituencies in the United States and a number of European Union states have the ear of their governments.[26]

Whereas the development of the international and legal architecture has been "an area of real progress in pursuing the goals of Agenda 21" there have been significant problems of implementation at national level: "While countries must comply with an increased number of treaty obligations, there is often a lack of coordination and integration in meeting obligations. Moreover, in many cases the work is not directly linked with economic and trade policies and financing strategies."[27] These comments merely address the more restrictive definition of effectiveness. If our effectiveness criteria are set in terms of behavioral and physical change, as they ought to be, it becomes extremely difficult to assert with confidence that particular international agreements are effective.

There are certainly some indications of success—in atmospheric pollution, in the Mediterranean and the increasingly stringent Antarctic rules. Above all the Montreal Protocol is usually seen as the paradigm case of successful regime building. Here it is possible to find indicators of physical effectiveness in recent findings that atmospheric concentrations of CFCs are in decline—although the ozone layer itself will not be restored until the middle of the century. For climate change the road towards ratification of the Kyoto Protocol has been one of extraordinary slowness and difficulty and the greenhouse gas reductions to which Parties are committed (approximately 5% from a 1990 baseline for developed countries excluding the United States) fall pathetically short of the 60–80% estimates of what would be required to achieve climate stabilisation. The usual response by proponents of the Protocol, such as the EU Commission, is that it represents the beginning of a process and that it is better to make a start than remain inactive. Yet it is also important to remember that if the Protocol were to fail completely this would hardly end the contribution of international cooperation to the management of climate change. Scientific awareness of the extent of the problem and available remedies relies upon the IPCC and the reporting mechanisms of the FCCC, while mitigation of the predicted effects of climate change would require inter-state collaboration—if states remain the primary authorities with the capacity to mobilise the necessary human and material resources.

The Problem of the Contemporary State

The advocate of international cooperation is confronted with two contradictory arguments to the effect that the contemporary state is either weak and supine before the forces of globalization or, alternatively, dedicated to the ruthless pursuit of national interest defined as economic growth. In the latter view ecology becomes the plaything of *realpolitik*: "The rhetoric, which ornaments conferences and conventions ritually calls for a new global ethic but the reality at the negotiating tables suggests a different logic. There, for the most part, one sees diplomats engaged in a familiar game of accumulating advantages for their countries, eager to outmaneuver their opponents, shrewdly tailoring environmental concerns to interests dictated by their country's economic position.[28]

It is difficult to generalize about the contemporary state. The rhetoric of globalization and, indeed, governance paints a picture of state incapability. The very use of the term *governance* implies the declining legitimacy and effectiveness of state governments, yet can it seriously be argued that viable nonstate alternatives have arisen? Globalization has been encouraged by state action in liberating trade and communication, but as Christoff argues, it may encourage a transfer of attention to environmental welfare policies (see chapter 2). Developed states with high gross domestic product per capita still deploy enormous resources (often above 40 percent of total GDP) and have the capability to engineer major changes in their surroundings. Some of the major functions of international cooperation, in the generation of scientific understanding and capability building, rely upon the willingness of state governments to use their revenues. The problem lies with mobilizing such resources when green issues appear to have low political salience and when the consequences of ecological interdependence are either disputed or apparently distant. As critics point out, democratic governments have a notoriously short time horizon, often extending little further than the date of the next election, and are prone to adopt a definition of the national interest predicated on the necessity for continued economic growth.

The mobilization of state capabilities for other purposes will typically depend upon "securitization."[29] Essentially this means moving an issue up the political agenda and thereby justifying major new expenditure by associating it with threats to the integrity of the state and its physical survival (classically it is the state rather than individual citizens or even whole societies that has been the object of securitization). The reaction and expenditures of the United State and other governments in pursuit of the "war on terrorism" after September 11, 2001, demonstrates the full extent of what remains possible when the security of the state comes under threat. It is thus very understandable that environmental activists have toyed with notions of "environmental security" as a means of increasing the salience of what must and indeed should be represented as the ultimate existential threat. Yet this would be an impossible speculation for citizens of the majority of resource-poor states of the international system that lack even basic governmental capability. Inevitably included among their number would be those most immediately threatened by the likely impact of climate change and sea-level rise.

For radical political ecology, state incapacity, whether associated with the "failed states" of the South or the high-consumption states of the North, represents a single phenomenon. State incapacity can be read deterministically as the inevitable result of the capture of national political systems by globalized capital. The important question in terms of political action concerns the potential independence of state structures and the extent to which they can be the vehicles for the achievement of human purposes beyond or in contradiction to capital accumulation (always assuming that the latter is necessarily the motor of environmental degradation).

Advocates of international environmental cooperation would necessarily contend that the functions of the state are neither fixed nor determined but that, in Karen Litfin's words, "no a priori reason exists for saying that environmental protection cannot become one of the state's primary objectives, and there is evidence that it is doing just that."[30] Matthew Paterson's response is that there are indeed very good a priori reasons for denying this: "Sustainability cannot become a structural requirement for the reproduction of state rule and thus the system must be transformed."[31]

If we move away from a priori assertion, there is most certainly a great deal of depressing evidence for this thesis, ranging all the way down from the fossil fuel industry–inspired climate policy of the Bush administration. It would be tedious to reproduce this story across a wide spectrum of multilateral environmental agreements. The pivotal role of Dupont, Atochem, and ICI in setting national priorities in the stratospheric ozone negotiations and the huge influence of the biotechnology companies, which essentially defined the position of the Miami group of countries in the biosafety negotiations leading to the 2000 Cartagena Protocol, would certainly merit inclusion. Yet the critical question for international environmental cooperation and a great deal more besides is whether the capture and incapacity of state authorities is to be considered an *inevitable* consequence of capitalist globalization. There are grounds for thinking that it is not or at least that the situation is rather more complicated than radical critiques might suggest. Some instances of international environmental cooperation exist that cannot simply be explained by reference to the dictates of global capital. The substance of many negotiations, particularly on climate change, reveals rather brutally the conflict between conceptions of national economic interest. Yet it is difficult to explain everything on this basis—the very creation of the IPCC, for example, while it may serve the interests of organized science, does not obviously betray the influence of capital.

Importantly, there is no single undifferentiated global corporate interest. Thus it may be possible to observe how, even within the energy sector, conceptions of economic advantage are continually shifting. In these circumstances, as Robert Falkner has argued, a business conflict model applies under which substantial space opens up for state governments to play a brokerage role.[32] For many international environmental negotiations this may well provide a more convincing account of the policy of major developed states. Above all, it suggests that there is a role for state agency expressed through international cooperation.

Those who despair of the state and international cooperation envisage an alternative global political system. Ecological survival must attend the restructuring of the global political system, abandoning the moribund nation-state structure and relying upon new forms of transnational political action or resistance and new sources of governance. This aspiration helps to explain much of the recent interest in the international relations literature over burgeoning NGO environmental activity and epistemic communities. These are privileged simply because they are not states or international organizations. Global problems thus require a new global politics. The full implications of this alternative have barely begun to be investigated.[33] One plausible scenario is that state structures would not entirely wither away. They would remain necessary to the maintenance of minimal order and to provide the basic institutional conditions under which economic activity can continue. However, their capacity to intervene and to articulate public concerns would be much diminished. In these circumstances the new political actors of global civil society are most unlikely to be able to provide a bulwark against the exercise of corporate power.

The nongovernmental sector has been of extraordinary importance in recent international environmental politics, but it can be argued that it represents an important adjunct to state-based environmental cooperation rather than a replacement for it. NGOs devote enormous efforts to influencing state policies and proselytizing at international meetings. They also increasingly operate at ground level in disbursing funds and monitoring implementation. While these tasks often have to be performed by them because local state authorities are incapable or nonexistent, their activities are usually within the context of broader international action and GEF or EU funding.

In the theoretical literature their role has been extensively recognized and studied, particularly in relation to the role of epistemic communities in engendering the cognitive shifts that underpin regime change.[34] However, just as NGOs themselves may seem to have been drawn into day-to-day international environmental politics, analysis of epistemic communities is now conventionally incorporated into the prevalent institutionalist approach to the understanding of international cooperation.

From a radical political ecology standpoint, such cooption, although easy to explain, must represent false consciousness on the part of activists. If radical propositions hold, then a reformist program of collaboration with the state and international cooperation cannot advance the cause of ecological survival. The only alternative is a strategy of active resistance that challenges existing power structures and evolves an alternative political economy.[35]

Conclusion

Radical political ecology certainly destabilizes some conventional assumptions about international environmental cooperation. This chapter has argued that this is to be welcomed insofar as exponents of regime analysis and of international relations of the environment should be prepared to think through and defend their position. It stimulates questions about an ontological position that gives pride of place to an anarchical state system rather than to the processes of global environmental change and degradation. At the same time, there are problems with the acceptance of a positivist epistemology, even though this may facilitate research funding and an acceptance of the place of international relations in the wider global change research community. It is often difficult to respond to attacks on the more manifest absurdities and failures of the Rio process and other international enterprises. With so much time and energy spent on considering the circumstances under which international cooperation may occur, there has been insufficient consideration of its precise functions in relation to the multilevel tasks of environmental governance. Much the same can be said about measuring the effectiveness of international cooperation.

It is possible, as this chapter has attempted to demonstrate, to defend the theory and practice of international cooperation from such criticisms. However, there is one crucial point to which this cannot apply and to which time and again the theorists of radical political ecology return. It is of course their axiomatic position on the nature of the state, its responsibility for environmental degradation, and the consequent impossibility of political action utilizing the apparatus of intergovernmental coordination. An acceptance of this position could lead either to fatalism or, as we have seen, to the search for new forms of nonstate governance or resistance, none of which appear to be very realistic propositions in the near future. In the absence of independent and effective interstate cooperation, the power of global corporate interests is likely to be unrestrained.

Such a pessimistic conclusion is avoidable if propositions about the inevitability of and ecologically destructive characteristics of the contemporary state are challenged. They are grounded upon one version of Marxist state theory that we are not bound to accept. Indeed, we may find some grounds for optimism in recent developments. Just as striking as the rise of NGOs has been the capacity of states to reconstruct and reinvent themselves in new combinations. The inherent constructedness and malleability of statehood has become a very significant theme of recent international relations literature.[36]

In international environmental politics the most remarkable instance of this has been provided by the European Union. The Union is not a state, but it has a continuing basis in the statehood of its members and a pooling of their capabilities. Since the 1970s the European Community has acquired very extensive environmental competences that have been translated into a diverse and highly significant role as an actor in international environmental politics.[37] Since the negotiation of the Montreal Protocol in the mid 1980s, the United States has shown an increasing reluctance to engage fully in environmental regime building and has more recently adopted an openly destructive and unilateralist approach. It would not be an exaggeration to say that the EU has self-consciously assumed the mantle of environmental leadership. It provided much of the impetus behind the Basel Convention on trade in hazardous wastes and was centrally involved in negotiating the Biosafety Protocol. At the WTO it has championed such causes as ecolabeling. This is not to say that its record is unblemished, and there are huge shortcomings in the area of the Common Agricultural and Fisheries policies, as critics are never slow to observe. Most notably, however, it has championed the cause of the emergent climate regime and through considerable diplomatic effort rescued the Kyoto Protocol, the terms of which were finally agreed at Marrakesh in 2001. At the time of writing the Protocol remains unratified, but the EU has developed ambitious plans for an emissions trading system. Its example may at least give us pause for thought about the supposedly predetermined character of both the actors and the outcomes in international environmental cooperation.

In evaluating the possibility of effective international action our view of the capacity of state government appears fundamental. This is not only because there are evident difficulties with many multilateral environmental agreements at the level of national implementation. It is also because there may be doubt as to whether contemporary states are capable of organizing remedial action in the face of the forces of economic globalization. Clearly this was possible in the ozone case under quite favorable circumstances, which are not replicated in other areas, notably, climate change. Radical critiques of the failings of the FCCC have at their heart a profound pessimism as to the possibility of the independent agency of states, trapped within the structure of contemporary global capitalism. The alternative view is that despite the difficulties standing in the way of achieving and evaluating effective international agreements, there is evidence that states still have the capacity to engineer collective responses to environmental threats.

Notes

1. United Nations Economic and Social Council (2002, 233).

2. According to the Commission on Global Governance (1995), "Governance is the sum of the many ways which individuals and institutions, public and private, manage their common affairs. It is a continuing process through which conflicting or diverse interests may be accommodated and cooperative action may be taken. It includes formal institutions and regimes empowered to enforce compliance, as well as informal arrangements that people and institutions either have agreed to or perceive to be in their interest" (2). Despite the diversity of actors in global governance—transnational corporations, local voluntary associations—the commission acknowledges that 'states and governments remain the primary public institutions for constructive responses to issues affecting peoples and the global community as a whole" (4).

3. Summary of Third Global Ministerial Environment Forum (2002).

4. It is also worth mentioning that regime analysis was a U.S. -inspired undertaking and that in the beginning it was addressed to the problems of international economic management and most specifically to solving how stable international cooperation could be maintained in the absence of a hegemonic monetary power. The precise circumstances were those following the abandonment of fixed parities tied to the dollar in 1971. The regime definitions are from Krasner, ed. (1982). Robert O. Keohane (1984) provides a revealing discussion of the political significance of regimes.

5. Smith (1993).

6. See in particular the extensive and influential work of work of Oran R. Young, for example, *International Governance* (1994) *Global Governance* (1997).

7. See, for example, Sachs, ed. (1993); *Ecologist* (1993).

8. Sachs, ed. (1993, xv).

9. Saurin (1993); Saurin (1996); Paterson (2000a).

10. Saurin (1996, 79).

11. Paterson (2000a, 46).

12. See, for example, Plumwood (1993).

13. Litfin (1994). The idea of transnational epistemic communities of scientists, activists, and policymakers as instigators of international cooperation was developed in Haas (1990).

14. The best-known example of a social constructivist approach to international relations is provided by the work of Wendt (1999), but see also my attempt to develop a social constructivist account of environmental regimes: Vogler (2003).

15. Studies that did not rely on a positivist epistemology were in evidence at the U.K. Economic and Social Research Council's Global Environmental Change Programme, which spanned the 1990s. Most, however, were seen as having "policy relevance." For an account of the program and some of its implications, see Berkhout, Leach, and Scoones, eds. (2003).

16. Cox (1981).

17. Evans (1998).

18. United Nations General Assembly (1997, para. 28).

19. For the operation of the IPCC, see Skodvin (2000). A number of studies by Sonia Boehmer-Christiansen have considered the IPCC from the perspective of scientific interest groups, for instance, Boehmer-Christiansen (1996).

20. Wapner (1995b, 47).

21. Chapter 7 of the Charter of the United Nations contains provisions under which the Security Council may, when it has established that a threat to the peace exists, authorize enforcement action, usually involving "all necessary means" against a state. At the WTO the situation is rather different. The successful litigant in a trade dispute panel at Geneva is permitted to impose punitive duties upon the exports of the offending state party or parties.

22. Henkin (1979) provides the classic statement of this view.

23. Colin S. Gray (1983, 200–201).

24. This is a brief summary of the argument contained in chapter 7 of Vogler (2000).

25. Kutting (2000, 131). Recent years have witnessed a rising concern among environmental regime analysts about effectiveness and enforcement. See, for example, Victor et al., eds. (1998).

26. This discussion relates to a major ongoing debate about trade and environment that can be sampled in any economics textbook that covers green issues or on the Web sites of the WTO or hostile NGOs. For critics of the WTO, there has been a problem with its rule that prohibits the use of trade measures to combat the environmentally damaging process and production methods of others (see, for example, the infamous tuna-dolphin dispute rulings of 1991 to 1994). While the WTO, since setting up its Committee on Trade and the Environment in 1995, has recognized that there may be difficulties at the interface of the two, it has so far mainly restricted itself to considering the use of trade instruments by multilateral environmental agreements.

27. United Nations Economic and Social Council (2002, 153).

28. Sachs, ed. (1993, 12).

29. The concept is developed in Buzan, Waever, and de Wilde (1998).

30. Cited in Paterson (2000a, 45).

31. Paterson (2000a, 45).

32. Falkner (2001).

33. For some serious analyses of the potential alternatives, see Lipschutz (1997) and Wapner (1997b).

34. The term was coined in Haas (1990).

35. Paterson (2000a, 149–161) makes this point with particular clarity.

36. See, for example, Hobson (2000).

37. Vogler (1999).

12

W(h)ither the Green State?

John Barry and Robyn Eckersley

Despite claims about the "hollowing out of the state" and its diminished or weakened role in the face of economic globalization, the contributors to this volume conclude that the state is not defunct and should not simply be bypassed or rejected as having nothing to offer progressive green politics. The strategic choice facing the green movement is not a simplistic one between pursuing political projects within the state or opposing the state. Rather, the question seems to be, What sort of state ought the green movement seek to create and engage with, while at the same time deepening its roots in civil society? As Dryzek and co-workers have noted in *Green States and Social Movements*, "Naive antistatism and naive statism both fail because they lack any sense of context and historical dynamics in the political economy."[1] The terrain between these two poles—statism, which is usually linked to a reformist, "light-green," business-as-usual position, and anti-statism, which is usually linked to radical green demands for the rejection or complete transformation of the state, economy, and society),—is what the chapters volume in this explore, looking in different ways state's at the potential for green politics and for facilitating local and global sustainability.

One of the common themes of the chapters is that there is much to be gained from focusing on the greening of the state as a way to constrain, contain, and where necessary oppose corporate power and the destructive dimensions of neoliberal capitalism. While particular states are certainly implicated in advancing this neoliberal agenda and therefore ought to be challenged, it is strategically damaging and theoretically unhelpful to reject or ignore the state as "irredeemable" from a green point of view. As John Gray argues, "The truth is that free markets are creatures of state power, and persist only so long as the state is able to prevent human needs for security and the control of economic risk from finding political expression."[2] State legal systems play a pivotal role in generating and upholding property rights, contracts, the rules of commerce, taxation, accounting, employee-employer relations, and liability that shape patterns of investment, production, consumption, and reproduction.[3] Whether by means of domestic policy initiatives or multilateral agreements, ensuring that the rules of economic activity are compatible with environmental protection and justice is a task that can only be carried out on a systematic basis by states. Of course, consumer and shareholder vigilance, corporate self-regulation, and initiatives by nongovernmental organizations (NGOs) can all play a significant role in promoting more ecologically responsible economic activity. However, these initiatives cannot compete with the steering capacity of states in terms of scale and scope.

For those concerned with making positive changes toward a less unsustainable world, the state has to be engaged with, its positive potentials explored and developed, its flaws examined for signs of possible improvement, and its dynamics and characteristics understood in their particularity. In short, sustainability this side of the next millennium has to involve the creation of greener state systems, particularly if the challenge of global warming is to be met. We have to work within what we have and, to paraphrase Rousseau, "take states both as they are and how they might be."

In this concluding we chapter, draw together the main themes that have been raised in the book, point to possible future areas of inquiry in critical green theory, and highlight some of the major political and economic challenges to greening the state.

Toward a Green Theory of the State

A concern to develop a critical green theory of the state is something this book shares with recent work in green politics.[4] Equally, our concern with the state, green or otherwise, needs to be placed in the context of existing debates about the state in other fields; the impacts of globalization on the state and the state system in both its local and transnational dynamics; new modes of civil society engagement; state-corporate relations; and fiscal and taxation pressures on the state (particularly the welfare state), which are often expressed in terms of the shift from government to governance, where the state no longer "rows" but "steers" economic and social development.

However, some of the recent work in green politics differs from our book in terms of approach, aims, and prescriptions. For example, Juan Martinez-Alier in *The Environmentalism of the Poor* distinguishes what he calls "wilderness preservation" environmentalism from "environmentalism of the poor" in terms of their relationships to the state: "The wilderness movement relies almost everywhere on the state for the designation of natural parks, sometimes against the wishes of local populations, while popular environmentalists act against the state in cases of oil extraction, mining or dams, or they operate totally outside the state, as in the agroecological movements."[5] Given his identification with local, indigenous environmentalist movements, it is not surprising that Martinez-Alier adopts an antistatist position (although he does not quite endorse an anarchist arrangement).

Similarly, *Green States and Social Movements*, by Dryzek et al. (some of whose main arguments are outlined in chapter 4 in the present volume), enlists the state's "core imperatives," identified as economic growth and legitimation, as key analytical tools to distinguish between different forms of environmentalism:

An emerging connection of environmental values to both economic and legitimation imperatives could help establish a green state with a conservation imperative. There are, however, two paths to ecological modernization, likely to attract different sorts of environmental groups. Moderate mainstream groups seek the connection of environmental concerns only to the economic imperative of the state. More radical groups in the public sphere . . . raise legitimation questions. Such groups both highlight issues of environmental risk and promote the more participatory aspects of modernization.[6]

Martinez-Alier objects to "wilderness preservation" environmentalism as collaborating with reformist state action that is sometimes contrary to the needs of local people, whereas Dryzek and co-workers point out that an ecological modernization approach can combine well with a reformist state strategy. However, the latter write about developed states (Norway, United States, United Kingdom, and Germany), whereas Martinez-Alier writes about the developing world, where wilderness preservation and biodiversity conservation have been more urgent imperatives (often externally imposed) than in the developed world.[7] Yet one must be wary of generalizations. Developed countries such as Canada, the United States, Australia, and New Zealand have also had their share of wilderness preservation and biodiversity conservation battles and have raised radical new ecophilosophical questions as well as challenging state developmentalism and resource extraction industries.[8] Bryant and Lawrence (see chapter 6) paint a more complicated picture of biodiversity conservation, in the Philippines. They show that the push for protected areas may initially be driven by external pressures but may later be appropriated by local people for local benefit under the right conditions. More generally, policy transfer and the sharing of sustainability best practice between jurisdictions can be an important part of social and institutional learning and the capacity-building process that is central to achieving sustainability.

These different examples highlight two insights about the state. The first is that context is everything, as Hunold and Dryzek emphasize in their comparative histories of four states (see chapter 4). The second, underscored by Christoff (see chapter 2), is that the state is a fragmented entity. Different agencies and departments are often allied with different social forces in civil society and the corporate world. These insights suggest that there are likely to be different entry points into the state on the part of the green movement in different state/society complexes. Only a close historical analysis of particular states (and their societies and economies) can reveal where these might reside.

Against our argument, recent work in green political economy suggests that the ecological degradation produced or sponsored by states is characteristic of, or inherent in, states rather than being simply the result of mistakes, ignorance, or contingent factors. In *Understanding Global Environmental Politics*, Matthew Paterson maintains that "through the promotion of accumulation, military competition, practices of ecological displacement and rationalized rule, states systematically produce environmental degradation."[9] It follows that "the state is not only unnecessary from a green point of view, it is positively undesirable" and that greens should continue to pursue their commitment to the decentralization of power and "to communities much smaller in scale than nation-states."[10]

However, the creation of an anarchistic federation of locally based political and economic communities requires a surrender of existing state power, and it is difficult to imagine how this might take place without the agreement and support of the state. Something like the state would also have to be reinvented at the regional level to maintain minimum welfare conditions in all localities via transfer payments, uphold basic civil and political rights, maintain corporate accountability across all communities in the federation, and represent the broader interests of the federation on the international stage. In any event, the further democratization, decentralization, and devolution of political power for the purposes of promoting sustainability is something that can take place within the framework of existing states. Again, discovering to what extent such moves are desirable and feasible requires studies of actual states, including the political and economic dynamics, contexts, and pressures within which and against which they operate. In this respect, Paterson is right to urge green political theorists to pay more attention to political economy questions. We take this opportunity briefly to map out the contours of a green political economy and to highlight some of the more significant domestic and global economic challenges that any critical green theory of the state must confront.

Domestic Challenges: Beyond Ecological Modernization

A critical green theory of the state presupposes a critical green theory of political economy that challenges the assumptions and limited analyses of neoclassical economics (including its environmental offshoots). Here most green political theorists draw inspiration from the new discipline of ecological economics, which (unlike neoclassical environmental economics) proceeds on the basic insight that the economy should be managed in ways that respect the ecological integrity and carrying capacity of the parent ecosystem in which it operates.[11] The role of the state is crucial in this regard: to establish democratically the ecological parameters within which all economic activity is to take place, and to protect the health and safety of human and nonhuman species. The fulfillment of such a role depends upon the production of a rich body of ecological knowledge (scientific and local/vernacular) that is continually and publicly tested and revised. The fulfillment of such a role also requires new systems of public accounting to enable the setting of targets and the development and review of strategies, within an overall context of the political regulation or steering of the market economy. This includes a critical examination of the technical and analytical questions associated with developing new forms of multicriteria measurements and indicators of sustainability and unsustainability, especially those related to measuring improvements in well-being and quality of life.

More generally, a green political economy would need to focus not only on investment and production but also on reproduction, distribution, and consumption—three areas that are often neglected in existing sustainability strategies. For example, understanding the role of unpaid household labor, the distribution of goods (wealth and income, urban amenity) and bads (pollution, disease), and patterns of consumption (and the waste generated from such consumption) are all crucial if the economy is to be managed in ways that produce both environmental protection and environmental justice. On the question of corporate accountability, a green political economy would need to reexamine private property regimes, corporate liability regimes, and the more general question of the transparency and accountability of corporations not only to shareholders but also to other stakeholders and affected parties (such as suppliers, employees, consumers, local communities, local ecosystems).

A number of the contributions to this volume focus on ecological modernization as an important new dynamic in the general quest for sustainability (see chapters 2, 3, 4, and 8). However, when set against the foregoing sketch of the issues that need to be addressed by any critical green political economy, a strategy of ecological modernization appears as merely a helpful but ultimately inadequate means of meeting the sustainability challenge.

Ecological modernization is in many respects a coping strategy adopted by states in the face of demands both for better environmental protection, and for continuing economic growth. Successful strategies of ecological modernization have also enlisted environmental regulation "to drive the process of industrial innovation with environmental and economic gains realized as a result."[12] Indeed, much of the modernization aspect of ecological modernization rests on the central emphasis on innovation, both technological and in production processes and management and distribution systems. Smart production systems, "doing more with less," applying novel scientific breakthroughs (for example, in renewable energy, biotechnology, and information and communication technology, such as nanotechnology), and developing and utilizing "clean" technologies are all hallmarks of the modern, dynamic, forward-looking, solutions-focused character of ecological modernization.[13] While the state enables and supports innovation, it is left to the private sector to develop, test, and market these new ecologically efficient innovations and production methods.

Ecological modernization may be seen as an attempt to politically regulate production in response to the socialization (externalization) of the (environmental) costs of production. This typically entails setting emissions standards, enlisting market-based instruments (such as green taxes and charges, and tradable pollution permits), encouraging voluntary self-regulation, enacting "polluter pays" legislation, upholding the precautionary principle, providing mandatory environmental impact assessments, and prescribing the use of best available technology. In this sense, ecological modernization follows the prescriptions of neoclassical environmental economics in seeking the internalization of the negative ecological costs of production and in highlighting the economic usefulness and value of environmental goods and services. Collective ecological problems are thus turned into selective economic opportunities for market actors (aided by the state). Indeed, the prescriptions of environmental economists (unlike those of ecological economists) are increasingly an accepted part of the state's bureaucratic/administrative response to environmental problems. All of this confirms Hunold and Dryzek's insight that ecological modernization works because it attaches green demands to the core economic imperative of the state, which is to promote capital accumulation.

Yet ecological modernization also serves the legitimation imperative of states, providing an ecological dimension to the modern state's crisis management function. As Christoff has explained, ecological modernization is "a discursive strategy useful to governments seeking to manage ecological dissent and to relegitimize their social regulatory role."[14] The attractiveness of ecological modernization to governments, as a policy response to environmental problems, lies in the basic fact that ecological modernization offers a relatively painless win-win policy choice.

However, for the most part, simple win-win strategies of ecological modernization fail to confront the full range of issues that we suggest require attention by green political economists. This kind of ecological modernization does not require major structural changes in the economy.

It does not challenge the organization and principles of ownership, the structure and practice of corporate governance, or the limitations of market mechanisms. Nor does it challenge the idea of progress or the commitment to an increasing aggregate output of goods and services. Rather, it primarily addresses the means (ecological, technological, and economic) by which these goals are pursued. It merely seeks to improve environmental productivity (the production of goods and services with less energy, materials, and wastes) by enlisting more environmentally friendly technologies and production methods. In short, it seeks more environmentally efficient ways of expanding output.

Secondly, win-win ecological modernization focuses on production rather than consumption, seeking to "make more with less." In this sense, ecological modernization is primarily a supply side rather than a demand side approach to environmental policy. It does not seek to challenge or regulate the demand for goods and services in the economy nor to address issues concerning the distribution of consumption and waste within society.[15] Like all supply side policies, ecological modernization attempts to downplay or avoid issues of social or distributional justice and equality. Politically regulating or addressing demand side and consumption dynamics is, in these post-Keynesian times, simply not on the cards for most governments. It goes against the grain of the hands-off styles of modern governance. At the same time, adopting a supply side approach reduces the sustainability challenge to either an energy or resource shortage problem or overproduction of environmental externalities (pollution). This supply side focus of ecological modernization also overlooks the need to address the problem of excessive demand and consumption as a necessary part of the transition to sustainability. Sustainability is as much about dealing with overconsumption (in the North) as it is about resource and energy efficiency. Addressing the demandside of the causes of unsustainability is a challenge that no state or society has adequately even begun to address, but one that any putative green state will have to tackle.

While win-win ecological modernization appears to provide a creative way of simultaneously managing the state's accumulation and legitimation functions, it still papers over very real tensions between these functions. A serious deficit on either side of this equation can pull the state more in one direction than the other. For example, serious legitimation deficits or crises (stemming, say, from major ecological disasters) have the potential to prompt stronger versions of ecological modernization that move in the direction of more public participation and openness in environmental decision making and policymaking, more preventive action, and greater institutional reflexivity. To the extent that this occurs, we can expect to see a move away from the neoliberal competition state, for which the overriding and constitutive imperative is to ensure that economic activities located within the nation-state are successful in terms of competitive advantage in the global market. Strong ecological modernization opens up the possibility of greater social learning and more chances of political, cultural, economic, and social changes toward sustainability, whereas weak ecological modernization remains a new but discrete policy subissue subsumed within the overarching state imperative of economic growth and capital accumulation in the increasingly competitive economy. However, strong ecological modernization is likely to risk generating accumulation problems unless carefully phased and managed, and even then there are limits in the ability of any single state to go it alone. The transition to strong ecological modernization therefore seems to require an explicit transnational level of governance, cooperation, and social learning.

Global Challenges: Economic versus Ecological Governance

One of the most significant challenges facing fledgling green states in the current neoliberal economic climate is the increasing influence of transnational corporations on global economic and environmental policy and governance. A vivid example of the changing power relations between states, corporations, and NGOs was the World Summit on Sustainable Development (WSSD), held in Johannesburg in August/September 2002. The primary purpose of the WSSD was to review progress in implementing Agenda 21 and to develop plans for further implementation of sustainable development. One of the most notable features of the summit was the increasing presence and influence of corporate representatives in government delegations compared to previous summits. Whereas previous major environmental summits at Stockholm in 1972 and Rio de Janeiro in 1992 had produced new declarations, action plans, financial mechanisms, and in the case of the Rio summit, two new framework environmental conventions, the main outcomes of the WSSD were a set of voluntary undertakings by corporations and a set of voluntary partnerships between corporations, other nonstate actors, and states.[16] However, environmental NGOs have always questioned the effectiveness of voluntary agreements—a view broadly endorsed in a study by the OECD.[17] The outcomes of the previous summits had been welcomed in cautiously optimistic terms by many environmental NGOs, but the outcomes of the WSSD have been uniformly condemned as inadequate to meet the sustainable development challenge. No new major summits are planned in the foreseeable future, and it appears that the practice and potential of earth summitry has, for the time being, been exhausted. As Rutherford observes, while the power of business in policymaking and politics is generally acknowledged by most observers, "at the WSSD this power was more visible. Business seems to have gained an unprecedented level of 'public' legitimacy as a pivotal environmental actor."[18] The confidence with which corporate interests could portray themselves as "good environmental stewards" is evidence of a shift (as much discursive as actual) in the balance of power between corporations and environmental NGOs in shaping global ecological governance.

However, at the major institutions of global economic governance, such as the World Trade Organisation, the International Monetary Fund, and the World Bank, environmental NGOs have even less influence. Not surprisingly, these institutions have become major sites of political confrontation by the antiglobalization movement, which includes (prominently) the environmental movement. As Dan Esty puts it, "The whole world is now watching the WTO and asking questions about the organization's purpose, structure, representation, decision procedures, and legitimacy."[19] That NGOs, along with international organizations such as the United Nations Environment Program are frozen out of international trade negotiations is all the more noticeable when set against the increasingly influential role of environmental NGOs in negotiation of multilateral environmental agreements. Here, environmental NGOs have played a major role in agenda setting and norm development in environmental treaties by identifying and publicizing ecological problems, developing policy-relevant knowledge and new ways of framing problems, negotiating policies and rules (sometimes as members of official delegations), and monitoring and implementing environmental treaties.[20]

Yet it is ultimately states that sign, ratify and via domestic legislation and policies, implement such treaties. Moreover, it appears that those states that act as green leaders in environmental treaty negotiations also tend to have better domestic environmental records. For example, the European Union (EU) has played a leadership role in the international climate change negotiations, and many states within the EU (notably the Netherlands and Germany) have taken active steps to promote ecological modernization. It is perhaps no accident that the member states of the EU have also experimented with bold new forms of ecological democracy, as illustrated by the Aarhus Convention (see chapters 7 and 8). The hypothesis emerging from these developments is that more environmental democracy and more reflexive modernization at the domestic level produces greener citizens at the international level on the part of both states and their civil societies. Only further research can bear this hypothesis out.

Although we have defended the argument that states provide the best means of resistance to corporate environmental irresponsibility, this still leaves open a range of strategic questions for the green movement concerning exactly where opposition and engagement should be focused in relation to the state and the state system. If the modest headway that has been gained through improved domestic and international environmental regulation is undermined by the new rules of trade forged by the WTO, then the question arises as to whether multilateral effort should be directed toward the creation of a World Environment Organization (WEO) to match the global reach and disciplinary power of the WTO.[21] The catch-22 is that such a new body would, of course, require the active support of a critical mass of states in order to succeed in upholding environmental norms against commercial ones, and this presupposes nothing short of a sea change in the hierarchy of economic and environmental goals currently pursued by states.

However, if green movements continue to grow; if the influence of green parties at the local, national, and regional levels deepens; and if the harmful consequences of environmental degradation (such as climate change) become more apparent and more costly, then it is not inconceivable that the hierarchy of economic and environmental goals will undergo realignment and environmental protection will emerge as a central and defining rather than merely incidental or contingent feature of an increasing number of states. Ironically, to the extent that this occurs, a WEO may become redundant.

In the meantime, most of the contributors to this book seem to agree on at least a strategic-instrumental attitude toward the state, although a few offer more principled defences (see chapters 7, 8, and 10). As noted, states are the only legal-political institution capable of offering systematic resistance (largely through regulation) to the forces of globalization. This in no way deflects from the fact that states and the state system are also implicated in organizing and facilitating globalization, and that this strategic-instrumental view of the state is not without dangers and pitfalls, as the chapters in part I indicate. Sometimes, resistance can be fertile, not futile.[22] However, equally, this should not blind us to the state's positive (or at least defensive) potentials.

Faced with the unregulated (but not unorganized) forces of economic globalization, it is perfectly understandable and sensible (on a case-by-case basis, it has to be stressed) for the green movement to gravitate toward the state as a protective mechanism. It may be that just as some view social justice as a remedial virtue (necessary only because of scarcity and lack of solidarity), the state on this account is a remedial institution, signifying, as Marx pointed out, a seriously flawed and divided society. However, one does not have to go as far as the "humanist" Marxian critique of the state to have a critical but strategic-instrumental account of it. The state is certainly flawed, but it has its uses.

In particular, the state can perform social and environmental protective functions, as James Meadowcroft points out in his historical-theoretical analysis of the evolution of the ecostate (see chapter 1). These protective functions are particularly important to consider given the various harms, risks, and vulnerabilities that economic globalization has created and transmitted. It is perhaps inevitable that some green thinkers and activists (including most of the contributors to is book), coming as they do from a green discourse concerned with coping with risks, threats, and limits, should move in the direction of one of the remaining institutions capable of protecting people and the planet from the predatory attentions of the market, namely, the state. In much the same way as Karl Polanyi pointed out the dangers to society of a market-based economic system that was "disembedded" from social and political restraints or contexts in his seminal work, *The Great Transformation*, and the importance of self-defense mechanisms such as the democratic/welfare state for social well-being, an argument can be made for the green state.[23] Again, the key issue is whether these protective functions of the state can become defining rather than contingent or minor.

This strategic-instrumental view of the state as a self-defense mechanism for society against the "disembedded" self-regulating market is something that others have examined from a broadly green perspective. John McMurtry, for example, in his wonderfully titled book, *The Cancer Stage of Capitalism*, suggests that the welfare state and civic commons be viewed as society's "immune system," protecting it from the "corporate pathogens" of economic globalization. McMurtry puts it in these terms:

> As one considers in overview increasing state and public sector mediations of every aspect of our lives by complexly articulated systems of life-protection circulation and regulation of our social intercourse and functions, one begins to recognize that—despite its continuous errors, oversights, and dogmas—this historically evolved ordering and organization of civilized communities and states for the healthful survival and reproduction of their members is a social immune system of ever more developed complexity and importance to human survival and reproduction.[24]

This strategic-instrumental view of the state has also been a preoccupation of work by green political economists such as Michael M'Gonigle. For M'Gonigle, "Only a strong state can, for example, confront the movements of multinational capital, ensure the broad (intraterritorial) respect for the principles of social justice, manage the impacts of increasing technological complexity, maintain interregional equity, and provide support for and protection of local, self-governing spaces."[25] While the idea of a strong state is likely to raise concerns about how this fits with the emancipatory and decentralist democratic principles and aims of the green movement, this sober assessment of the political and economic forces ranged against the implementation of meaningful conceptions of sustainability also guides most of the contributions to this book.

Ultimately, this strategic-instrumental conception of the state enables focus to shift to the ultimate end—that of the creation/transition to a more sustainable society. After all, the greening of the state is not an end in itself. Just as Tocqueville long ago pointed out the difference between a democratic system and a democratic society, so must one be aware of the difference between a green state and a sustainable society.

A green state is only a step, but a crucial one we would hold, along the road to achieving sustainability.

Uneven Development and the Challenge of Green Proliferation

Judging by environmental standards, the density and sophistication of environmental legislation and taxation, and measurable outcomes in environmental quality, some states are clearly greener than others, as the chapters in this volume have shown. Thus it is possible to classify states along a continuum stretching from laggards to leaders in environmental protection, just as on the broader indicators of democratization, human rights, and social justice. Within the OECD, states such as the Netherlands, Sweden, and Germany are further along the path to sustainability than others, such as the United Kingdom, Australia, or the United States.[26] Understanding why some states are greener than others is obviously a prerequisite to understanding the potential for more states to become greener. However, these are not easy questions to answer, and they require detailed comparative histories of the kind conducted by Dryzek et al. in their study of states and social movements. Extensive comparative studies of the environmental capacity of different states have also helped to illuminate the conditions and factors that account for environmental performance.[27]

Capacity building is even more crucial for developing states, some of which (for a complex range of reasons) lack the basic infrastructure to pursue successful policies generally, not just in the environmental domain. However, it would be too complacent and crude simply to explain this simply in terms of differences in overall levels of economic development. Such a generalization does not explain significant differences in environmental capacity and policy innovation within OECD countries. Nor does it critically address the reasons for uneven development.

Of course, unevenness in environmental policy development among states has some benefits. For example, it enables experimentation and the development of policies that are tailored to suit the circumstances of different states. Where appropriate, it also enables the voluntary adoption and adaptation of successful models by other jurisdictions, either horizontally, via direct emulation, or vertically, when successful models are incorporated into multilateral environmental agreements. Environmental policy transfer between states is an important dimension of the institutional learning that is characteristic of strong ecological modernization.

Yet unevenness in environmental policy development also raises the controversial question of whether and to what extent environmental reforms should be "forced" on laggard states. This problem does not arise in the case of multilateral environmental agreements, which are based on the principles of liberal contractualism. The right to sign a convention is an attribute, not an abdication, of sovereignty. Nor is it a problem in the EU, where the notion of the self-governing, sovereign state has given way (by agreement) to the idea of pooled sovereignty within a federation of states, and where environmental directives have forced a ratcheting up of environmental standards on the part of laggard states within the EU. In both of these cases, agreements among states over common environmental standards and practices act as a corrective to the race to the bottom attendant upon the competition between states for investment, which often forces environmental (and labor protection) standards downward to make countries more attractive to footloose capital.

However, unevenness in environmental policy development is an acute problem in relations between developed states and developing states, many of which are still burdened by the legacies of colonialism. First, sovereignty is important to developing countries still struggling with the structural economic injustices in the world economy, not to mention crippling debt. Green conditionality attached to World Bank loans and even debt-for-nature swaps orchestrated by environmental NGOs are regarded as encroaching on hard-won sovereignty, just one more stanza in the same old imperialist song. The unequal terms of trade between developed and developing countries (another legacy of the colonial period) are seriously exacerbated by lack of access by commodity exporters in the South to lucrative markets in the North (worsened by agricultural subsidies in the United States and the EU). This dire situation has meant that many developing countries are resistant to arguments to improve both labor and environmental standards on the grounds that these would impose further costs on exporters and result in a loss of desperately needed export earnings. These general economic difficulties also explain why developing countries have been particularly resistant to the introduction of stronger environmental norms within the WTO, a point that is sometimes lost on anti-WTO environmental protestors. Focusing on the structural economic injustices facing developing countries must therefore be a prerequisite to addressing environmental performance.

Second, developing countries have different environmental and development priorities, a point that was made abundantly clear at the WSSD, where immediate issues such as lack of basic sanitation and access to potable water are far more important to local people than long-range problems such as global warming. Developing countries should be free to determine their own environmental priorities.

The problem, however, is that not all developing countries are self-determining in the democratic sense of the term, and all the evidence suggests that democracy is good for the environment as well as for governance.[28] Conversely, there are numerous examples where local ecosystems have suffered serious devastation at the hands of state elites practicing either crony capitalism or totalitarian economic planning, particularly in circumstances where corruption of state officials and political leaders is rife. It is fitting, therefore, to return here to Martinez-Alier's analysis in *The Environmentalism of the Poor* that strategies of resistance to the state may be more fertile than strategies of engagement in circumstances where local people have no or little say in development projects that directly affect their livelihoods and environmental well-being.

Although the purpose of this volume has been to highlight the (yet to be fulfilled) green potential of the state, we have avoided simple formulas and emphasized the importance of context. The state has and will continue to evolve and, to extend the metaphor, will be part of the "ecology of governance," not least in the area of the environment, for some time to come. For us, this suggests that the green movement should be continually revising its strategy toward the state, whether this be a strategy of resistance or engagement. Either way, the state cannot be *ignored*. The lessons from the chapters in this volume suggest that those interested in pushing for ecological sustainability should enlist the state where possible (while remaining critical of it) and also foster positive, new hybrid forms of ecological governance, some of which will involve the state, some of which may not.[29] Some of these hybrid forms of governance may require exploiting the fact that the state is a nonunitary entity.

Greener states will not spontaneously emerge but will have to be fought for, and no positive change within the state can be taken for granted, because history has shown how quickly progressive legislation and policies can be dismantled. Equally, this positive engagement with and assessment of the state's ecological potential does not mean that the green movement's focus and roots in civil society should be abandoned. One of the strategic issues for the green movement is to explore the potential for forging closer ties and alliances within and among sympathetic agencies and personnel in the state without sacrificing the right to criticize the state, and without depleting the supply of green activists in civil society (see chapter 4). It is the relationship between states and civil societies (both locally and globally), and alliances between (elements of the) state and civil society against the institutions, actors, and interests organizing economic globalization, that will constitute the terrain of ecological conflict and hope in the coming century.

Notes

1. Dryzek, Downes et al. (2003, 196).
2. John Gray (1998, 1).
3. See Sassen (1996, 25–26).
4. See Dryzek, Downes et al. (2003); Eckersley (2004); Gale and M'Gonigle, eds. (2000); and Martinez-Alier (2002). For a review of some recent work on green theories of the state, see Barry (2003b).
5. Martinez-Alier (2002, 203).
6. Dryzek, Downes et al. (2003, 193).
7. See also Peluso (1993) and Raymond L. Bryant and Sinead Bailey (1997).
8. Peter Hay (2002, 16–18); Hay and Hayward (1988).
9. Paterson (2000a, 45).
10. Paterson (2000a, 62).
11. See, for example, the journal *Ecological Economics*.
12. Murphy and Gouldson (2000, 43).
13. Popular examples of weak/technologically focused ecological modernization discourse include Von Weizäcker, Lovins, and Lovins (1998); Hawken, Lovins, and Lovins (1999). For a critical overview of this technocentric discourse, see White (2002).
14. Christoff (1996, 482).
15. See, for example Princen, Maniates, and Conca, eds. (2002).
16. The official WSSD Program of Implementation signed by states produced only two new specific targets (sanitation and marine parks). There were also provisions on good governance and corporate responsibility, but none of these

declarations contained specific targets, timetables, or details. No agreement was reached on renewable energy targets or energy policy in general.

17. Organisation for Economic Co-operation and Development (2003).

18. Rutherford (2003, 145).

19. Esty (2002, 12).

20. Newell (2000).

21. Biermann (2001).

22. See Paehlke (2001); Dryzek (2001).

23. Polanyi (1944).

24. McMurtry (1996, 88).

25. M'Gonigle (2000, 13).

26. We are aware that the spread of states discussed in this volume is very Western-oriented; most of the states discussed come from within the OECD. However, the plain fact is that most of the promising developments are emerging from the developed world. While we do not dismiss innovative work being carried out in developing states (especially in terms of local/community initiatives or in specific areas such as microfinance and waste), the strategic dimensions of, and political, policy, and intellectual debates around sustainable development as a (potential) state project are more advanced in the developed world. Indeed, it is an interesting issue, in terms of emerging norms and best practice around the effective governance and implementation of sustainable development and the global justice dimensions of sustainable development, that part of the latter obligation be delivered through governance learning/transfer from the North to the South (on its own terms, of course) in the same way as we talk about technology transfer from North to South. It is also desirable that this capacity building and learning be seen as a two-way flow, so that there may be lessons that developed states can (and should) learn from developing states in terms of sustainable development. One might go so far as to say that green states will be characterized by precisely this commitment to learning and openness.

27. Jänicke and Weidner, eds. (1997); Lafferty and Meadowcroft, eds. (2000).

28. A focus on democracy and good environmental governance is the dominant theme of the landmark report by the United Nations Development Programme et al. (2003), *World Resources 2002–2004: Decisions for the Earth: Balance, Voice and Power*.

29. An example of ecological governance by civil society is the Forest Stewardship Council, although its democratic and egalitarian character been attacked by corporations and states; see Gale (2000).

References

Acevedo, Mariana T. 2000. The Intersection of Human Rights and Environmental Protection in the European Court of Human Rights. *New York University Environmental Law Journal* 8 (2): 437–496.

Adler, Emmanuel. 1997. Seizing the Middle Ground: Constructivism in World Politics. *European Journal of International Relations* 3 (3): 319–364.

Anderson, Esther. 2000. *Victoria's National Parks, a Centenary History*. Melbourne: Parks Victoria/State Library of Victoria.

Anderson, Michael R. 1996. Individual Rights to Environmental Protection in India. In *Human Rights Approaches to Environmental Protection*, ed. Alan E. Boyle and Michael R. Anderson, 1–25. Oxford: Clarendon Press.

Anderson, Michael, and Duncan Liefferink, eds. 1997. *European Environmental Policy: The Pioneers*. Manchester: Manchester University Press.

Ashford, Douglas. 1986. *The Emergence of the Welfare States*. Oxford: Blackwell.

Ashley, Richard K. 1984. The Poverty of Neorealism. *International Organization* 38 (2): 225–286.

Australian Conservation Foundation/National Farmers Federation (ACF/NFF). 2001. *Repairing the Land*. Melbourne: ACF.

Axelrod, Richard J. 1984. *The Evolution of Cooperation*. New York: Basic Books.

Baker, Susan, Maria Kousis, Dick Richardson, and Stephen Young, eds. 1997. *The Politics of Sustainable Development: Theory, Policy and Practice within the European Union*. London: Routledge.

Balistier, Thomas. 1996. *Straßenprotest. Formen oppositioneller Politik in der Bundesrepublik Deutschland*. Münster: Westfälisches Dampfboot.

Barry, Brian. 1999. Sustainable and Intergenerational Justice. In *Fairness and Futurity: Essays on Environmental Sustainability and Social Justice*, ed. Andrew Dobson, 93–117. Oxford: Oxford University Press.

Barry, John. 1999. *Rethinking Green Politics*. London: Sage.

Barry, John. 2003a. Ecological Modernisation. In *Environmental Thought,* ed. Edward Page and John Proops, 191–217. Cheltenham, UK: Edward Elgar.

———. 2003b. Holding Tender Views in Tough Ways: Political Economy and Strategies of Resistance in Green Politics. *British Journal of Politics and International Relations* 5: 614–625.

Barry, John, and Matthew Paterson. 2004. Globalisation, Ecological Modernisation, and New Labour. *Political Studies.* 54(4).

Beck, Ulrich. 1992. *The Risk Society: Towards a New Modernity.* London: Sage.

———. 1997. *The Reinvention of Politics: Rethinking Modernity in the Global Social Order.* Cambridge: Polity.

———. 1998. *Democracy without Enemies.* Cambridge: Polity.

———. 1999. *World Risk Society.* Cambridge: Polity.

———. 2000. *What Is Globalisation?* Cambridge: Polity.

Beetham, David. 1991. *The Legitimation of Power.* Atlantic Highlands, N.J.: Humanities Press International.

Beja, Edsel L. Jr. 1999. *Environmental Non-governmental Organizations in Policymaking: The Case against Lifting the Export Ban on Lumber in the Philippines.* M.Phil. Thesis, Department of Geography, Cambridge University.

Bellamy, Richard. 1999. *Liberalism and Pluralism.* London: Routledge.

———. 2000. *Rethinking Liberalism.* London: Pinter.

Benton, Lisa, and John Rennie-Short. 1999. *Environmental Discourse and Practice.* Oxford: Blackwell.

Berkhout, Franz, Melissa Leach, and Ian Scoones, eds. 2003. *Negotiating Environmental Change: New Perspectives from Social Science.* Cheltenham, UK: Edward Elgar.

Berlin, Isaiah. 1958. *Two Concepts of Liberty.* Oxford: Oxford University Press.

Bernauer, Thomas. 1995. The Effect of International Environmental Institutions: How We Might Learn More. *International Organization* 49: 351–377.

Biermann, Frank. 2001. The Emerging Debate on the Need for a World Environment Organization: A Commentary. *Global Environmental Politics* 1 (1): 45–55.

Blair, Tony. 2000. Prime Minister's Speech to the CBI/ Green Alliance Conference on the Environment. October 24. <http://www.sustainable-development. gov.uk/ann_rep/ch4/brief1.htm>.

Boehmer-Christiansen, Sonia. 1996. The International Research Enterprise and Global Environmental Change: Climate-Change Policy as a Research Process. In *The Environment and International Relations,* ed. John Vogler and Mark Imber, 171–195. London: Routledge.

Bonyhady, Tim. 2000. *The Colonial Earth.* Melbourne: Miegunyah Press.

Bookchin, Murray. 1980. *Toward an Ecological Society.* Montreal: Black Rose Books.

———. 1982. *The Ecology of Freedom: The Emergence and Dissolution of Hierarchy*. Palo Alto, Calif.: Cheshire Books.

Boyle, Alan. 1996. The Role of International Human Rights Law in the Protection of the Environment. In *Human Rights Approaches to Environmental Protection*, ed. Alan E. Boyle and Michael R. Anderson, 43–71. Oxford: Clarendon Press.

Brandl, Ernst, and Hartwin Bungert. 1992. Constitutional Entrenchment of Environmental Protection: A Comparative Analysis of Experiences Abroad. *Harvard Environmental Law Review* 16 (1): 1–100.

Brick, Philip, Donald Snow, and Sarah Van De Wetering, eds. 2001. *Across the Great Divide: Explorations in Collaborative Conservation and the American West*. Washington, D.C.: Island Press.

British Government Panel on Sustainable Development. 2000. *Sixth Report*. <http://www.sd-commission.gov.uk/panel-sd/panel6/index.htm>.

British Medical Association (BMA). 1999. *The Impact of Genetic Modification on Agriculture, Food and Health: An Interim Statement*. London: BMA.

Broad, Robin, with John Cavanagh. 1993. *Plundering Paradise: The Struggle for the Environment in the Philippines*. Berkeley: University of California Press.

Brugger, Bill. 1999. *Republican Theory in Political Thought: Virtuous or Virtual?* New York: St. Martin's Press.

Bryant, Bunyan. 1996. *Environmental Justice: Issues, Policies, and Solutions*. Washington, D.C.: Island Press.

Bryant, Bunyan, and Paul Mohai, eds. 1992. *Race and the Incidence of Environmental Hazards: A Time for Discourse*. Boulder, Colo.: Westview Press.

Bryant, Raymond L. 2000. Politicized Moral Geographies: Debating Biodiversity Conservation and Ancestral Domain in the Philippines. *Political Geography* 19: 673–705.

Bryant, Raymond L., and Sinead Bailey. 1997. *Third World Political Ecology*. London: Routledge.

Bullard, Robert, ed. 1993. *Confronting Environmental Racism: Voices from the Grassroots*. Boston: South End Press.

Buzan, Barry, Ole Waever, and Jaap de Wilde. 1998. *Security: A New Framework for Analysis*. Boulder, Colo.: Lynne Rienner.

Camacho, David E., ed. 1998. *Environmental Injustices, Political Struggles: Race, Class, and the Environment*. Durham, N.C.: Duke University Press.

Caranta, Roberto. 1993. Governmental Liability after *Francovich*. *Cambridge Law Journal* 52: 272–297.

Carter, Alan. 1993. Towards a Green Political Theory. In *The Politics of Nature: Explorations in Green Political Theory*, ed. Andrew Dobson and Paul Lucardie, 39–62. London: Routledge.

Cerny, Philip. 1990. *The Changing Architecture of the State*. London: Sage.

Charter of Fundamental Rights of the European Union. <http://www.europarl. eu.int/home/default_en.htm>.

Chayes, Abram, and Antonia Handler Chayes. 1995. *The New Sovereignty: Compliance with International Regulatory Agreements.* Cambridge, Mass.: Harvard University Press.

Christoff, Peter. 1996. Ecological Modernisation, Ecological Modernities. *Environmental Politics* 5 (4): 476–500. Also in *The Emergence of Ecological Modernisation: Integrating the Environment and the Economy,* ed. Stephen Young. London: Routledge, 2000.

————. 1998a. From Global Citizen to Renegade State: Australia at Kyoto. *Arena Journal* 10: 113–128.

————. 1998b. Degreening Government in the Garden State: Environment Policy under the Kennett Government. *Environmental and Planning Law Journal* 15 (1): 10–32.

————. 1999. Regulating the Urban Environment. In *Serving the City: the Crisis in Australia's Urban Services,* ed. Patrick Troy, 34–59. Sydney: Pluto Press.

————. 2000. Environmental Citizenship. In *Rethinking Australian Citizenship,* ed. Wayne Hudson and John Kane, 200–214. Cambridge: Cambridge University Press.

————. 2002. *In Reverse: Australia's Environmental Performance 1992–2002.* Melbourne: ACF/ ACFOA/Greenpeace Australia-Pacific.

Churchill, R. 1996. Environmental Rights in Existing Human Rights Treaties. In *Human Rights Approaches to Environmental Protection,* ed. Alan E. Boyle and Michael R. Anderson, 89–109. Oxford: Clarendon Press.

Cleary, David. 1993. After the Frontier: Problems with Political Economy in the Modern Brazilian Amazon. *Journal of Latin American Studies* 25: 331–349.

Coates, David, and Peter Lawler, eds. 2000. *New Labour into Power.* Manchester: Manchester University Press.

Cole, Luke, and Sheila Foster. 2001. *From the Ground Up: Environmental Racism and the Rise of the Environmental Justice Movement.* New York: New York University Press.

Commission on Global Governance. 1995. *Our Global Neighbourhood: The Report of the Commission on Global Governance.* Oxford: Oxford University Press. <http://www.sovereignty.net/p/gov/gganalysis.htm>.

Conca, Ken. 1995. Rethinking the Ecology-Sovereignty Debate. *Millennium: Journal of International Studies* 23 (3): 701–711.

————. 1996. International Regimes, State Authority, and Environmental Transformation: The Case of National Parks and Protected Areas. Occasional Paper no. 15. Harrison Program on the Future Global Agenda, University of Maryland. <http://www.bsos.umd.edu/harrison>.

————. 2000a. Beyond the Statist Frame: Environmental Politics in a Global Economy. In *Nature, Production, Power: Towards an Ecological Political*

Economy, ed. Fred P. Gale and R. Michael M'Gonigle, 141–155. Cheltenham, UK: Edward Elgar.

———. 2000b. The WTO and the Undermining of Global Environmental Governance. *Review of International Political Economy* 7 (3): 484–494.

———. 2002. The World Commission on Dams and Trends in Global Environmental Governance. *Politics and the Life Sciences* 21 (1): 67–70.

Coronel, Sheila S., ed. 1996. *Patrimony: 6 Case Studies on Local Politics and the Environment in the Philippines*. Manila: Philippine Center for Investigative Journalism.

Coward, D. 1976. From Public Health to Environmental Amenity. In *Sydney's Environmental Amenity, 1970–1975: A Study of the System of Waste Management and Pollution Control*, ed. Noel Butlin, 4–26. Canberra: Australian National University.

Cox, Robert W. 1981. Social Forces, States and World Order: Beyond International Relations Theory. *Millennium* 10 (2): 126–151.

Crozier, Michel, Samuel P. Huntington, and Joji Watanuki. 1975. *The Crisis of Democracy: Report on the Governability of Democracies to the Trilateral Commission*. New York: New York University Press.

Daly, Herman. 1991. Elements of Environmental Macroeconomics. In *Ecological Economics*, ed. Robert Costanza, 32–46. New York: Columbia University Press.

Dawson, Jane. 1996. *Econationalism: Anti-Nuclear Activism and National Identity in Russia, Lithuania, and Ukraine*. Durham, N.C.: Duke University Press.

DeMerieux, Margaret. 2001. Deriving Environmental Rights from the European Convention for the Protection of Human Rights and Fundamental Freedoms. *Oxford Journal of Legal Studies* 21 (3): 521–561.

Dente, Bruno. 1988. Towards Sustainability: Instruments and Institutions for the Ecological State. Paper presented at the Fifth Workshop of EU Concerted Action, Florence.

Department of Communications, Information Technology and the Arts (DCITA). 2004. A Sustainability Strategy for the Australian Continent: Environment Budget Statement 2004–05, Statement by the Honourable Dr. David Kemp, MP, Minister for the Environment and Heritage. May 11. Canberra: DCITA.

Department for Environment, Food and Rural Affairs (formerly Department of Environment, Transport and the Regions). 2000. *Climate Change: The UK Programme*. <http://www.defra.gov.uk/environment/climatechange/cm4913/>.

———. 2003. *Emissions Trading Schemes*. <http://www.defra.gov.uk/environment/climatechange/trading/index.htm>.

Desgagné, Richard. 1995. Integrating Environmental Values into the European Convention on Human Rights. *American Journal of International Law* 89 (2): 263–294.

Deudney, Daniel. 1990. The Case against Linking Environmental Degradation to National Security. *Millennium* 19 (3): 461–476.

———. 1995. Ground Identity: Nature, Place and Space in Nationalism. In *The Return of Culture and Identity to International Relations Theory,* ed.Yosef Lapid and Friedrich Kratochwil, 129–145. Boulder, Colo.: Lynne Rienner.

———. 1998. Global Village Sovereignty: Intergenerational Sovereign Publics, Federal Republican Earth Constitutions, and Planetary Identities. In *The Greening of Sovereignty in World Politics,* ed. Karen T. Litfin, 299–325. Cambridge, Mass.: MIT Press.

Dobson, Andrew. 1998. *Justice and the Environment: Conceptions of Environmental Sustainability and Dimensions of Social Justice.* Oxford: Oxford University Press.

Doherty, Brian. 1999. Paving the Way: The Rise of Direct Action Against Road-Building and the Changing Character of British Environmentalism. *Political Studies* 47 (2): 275–291.

Doherty, Brian, and Marius de Gues, eds. 1996. *Democracy and Green Political Thought: Sustainability, Rights and Citizenship.* London: Routledge.

Doherty, Brian, Matthew Paterson, Alexandra Plows, and Derek Wall. 2002. The Fuel Protests of 2000: Implications for the Environmental Movement in Britain. *Environmental Politics* 11 (2): 165–173.

Douglas-Scott, Sionaidh. 1992. Environmental Rights in the European Union. In *Human Rights, Sustainable Development and the Environment,* ed. Edith Brown Weiss et al. San José, Costa Rica: Instituto Interamericano de Derechos Humanos.

Downing, Peter, and Kenneth Hanf. 1983. *International Comparisons in Implementing Pollution Laws.* Dordrecht: Kluwer-Nijhoff.

Driver, Stephen, and Luke Martell. 1998. *New Labour.* Cambridge: Polity.

Dryzek, John S. 1987. *Rational Ecology: Environment and Political Economy.* Oxford: Blackwell.

———. 1992. Ecology and Discursive Democracy: Beyond Liberal Capitalism and the Administrative State. *Capitalism, Nature, Socialism* 3 (2): 18–42.

———. 1995. Political and Ecological Communication. *Environmental Politics* 4 (4): 13–30.

———. 1997. *The Politics of the Earth: Environmental Discourses.* Oxford: Oxford University Press.

———. 2000. *Deliberative Democracy and Beyond.* Oxford: Oxford University Press.

———. 2001. Resistance Is Fertile. *Global Environmental Politics* 1 (1): 11–17.

Dryzek, John S., David Downes, Christian Hunold, and David Schlosberg, with Hans-Kristian Hernes. 2003. *Green States and Social Movements: Environmentalism in the United States, United Kingdom, Germany, and Norway.* Oxford: Oxford University Press.

Dryzek, John S., Christian Hunold, and David Schlosberg, with David Downes and Hans-Kristian Hernes. 2002. Environmental Transformation of the State: The USA, Norway, Germany, and the UK. *Political Studies* 50 (4): 659–682.

Dryzek, John, and David Schlosberg, eds. 1998. *Debating the Earth: The Environmental Politics Reader*. Oxford: Oxford University Press.

Dubash, Navroz K., Mairi Dupar, Smitu Kothari, and Tundu Lissu. 2001. *A Watershed in Global Governance? An Independent Assessment of the World Commission on Dams*. Washington: World Resources Institute.

Dunlop, Clare. 2000. GMOs and Regulatory Styles. *Environmental Politics* 9 (2): 149–155.

Dunstan, David. 1984. *Governing the Metropolis: Politics, Technology and Social Change in a Victorian City: Melbourne 1850–1891*. Melbourne: Melbourne University Press.

———. 1985. Dirt and Disease. In *The Outcasts of Melbourne*, ed. G. Davidson, D. Dunstan, and C. McConville, 140–171. Sydney: Allen and Unwin.

Eckersley, Robyn. 1992. *Environmentalism and Political Theory*. Albany: State University of New York Press.

———. 1996. Greening Liberal Democracy: The Rights Discourse Revisited. In *Democracy and Green Political Thought: Sustainability, Rights and Citizenship*, ed. Brian Doherty and Marius de Geus, 212–236. London: Routledge.

———. 2000a. Deliberative Democracy, Ecological Representation and Risk: Towards a Democracy of the Affected. In *Democratic Innovation: Deliberation, Association and Representation*, ed. Michael Saward, 117–132. London: Routledge.

———. 2000b. Disciplining the Market, Calling in the State: The Politics of Economy-Environment Integration. In *The Emergence of Ecological Modernisation: Integrating the Environment and the Economy*, ed. Stephen Young, 233–252. London; Routledge.

———. 2004. *The Green State: Rethinking Democracy and Sovereignty*. Cambridge, Mass.: MIT Press.

Ecologist, The. 1993. *Whose Common Future? Reclaiming the Commons*. Gabriola Island, B.C., Canada: New Society Publishers.

Elliott, Larry, and Dan Atkinson. 1999. *The Age of Insecurity*. 2d ed. London: Verso.

Enloe, Cynthia. 1975. *The Politics of Pollution in Comparative Perspective*. New York: David McKay.

Environmental Science for Social Change (ESSC). 1999. *Mining Revisited*. Manila: ESSC.

Esping-Andersen, Gosta. 1990. *The Three Worlds of Welfare Capitalism*. Cambridge: Polity.

Esty, Daniel C. 2002. The World Trade Organization's Legitimacy Crisis. *World Trade Review* 1 (1): 7–22.

European Commission. 2000. White Paper on Environmental Liability. COM(2000) 66 final, February 9. <http://europa.eu.int/eur-lex/en/com/ wpr/ 2000/com2000_0066en01.pdf>. See also <http://europa.eu. int/comm/ environment/liability/white_paper.htm> and <http://europa.eu.int/comm/ environment/ liability/>.

Evans, Anthony. 1998. Doing Something Without Doing Anything: International Environmental Law. In *Law in Environmental Decision-Making*, ed. T. Jewell and L. Steele, 207–227. Oxford: Clarendon Press.

Faber, Daniel, ed. 1998. *The Struggle for Ecological Democracy*. New York: Guilford.

Falk, Richard. 1995. *On Humane Governance*. Cambridge: Polity.

Falkner, Robert. 2001. Business Conflict and U.S. International Environmental Policy: Ozone, Climate and Biodiversity. In *The Environment, International Relations and US Foreign Policy,* ed. Paul Harris, 135–157. Washington, D.C.: Georgetown University Press.

Fernandez, José. 1994. State Constitutions, Environmental Rights Provisions, and the Doctrine of Self-Execution. In *Social Rights as Human Rights: A European Challenge*, ed. Krzysztof Drzewick, Catarina Krause, and Allan Rosas. Turku, Finland: Institute for Human Rights, Åbo Akademi University.

Finger, Mathias. 1994. Global Environmental Degradation and the Military. In *Green Security or Militarised Environment?* ed. Jyrki Käkönen, 169–191. Aldershot, UK: Dartmouth Publishing.

Finney, Colin. 1993. *Paradise Revealed: Natural History in Nineteenth-Century Australia*. Melbourne: Museum of Victoria.

Fisher, Elizabeth. 2001. Is the Precautionary Principle Justifiable? *Journal of Environmental Law* 13 (3): 315–334.

Flora, Peter, and Arnold Heidenheimer, eds. 1981. *The Development of Welfare States in Europe and America*. London: Transaction Books.

Fraser, Nancy. 1997. *Justice Interruptus: Critical Reflections on the Postsocialist Condition*. London: Routledge.

———. 1998. Social Justice in the Age of Identity Politics: Redistribution, Recognition, and Participation. In *The Tanner Lectures on Human Values*, vol. 19, 1–67. Salt Lake City: University of Utah Press. <http://www.tannerlec-tures.utah.edu/lectures/Fraser98.pdf>.

Frederick, Michel. 1999. A Realist's Conceptual Definition of Environmental Security. In *Contested Grounds: Security and Conflict in the New Environmental Politics*, ed. Daniel H. Deudney and Richard A. Matthew, 91–108. Albany: State University of New York Press.

Friends of the Earth. 2000. Response to the Draft Climate Change Programme. <http://www.foe.co.uk/campaigns/climate/resource/experts.html>.

————. 2001. Genetically Modified Foods: Adding to the Debate. <http://www.foe.co.uk/pubsinfo/briefings/html/20000208165641.html>.

Gale, Fred. 2000. Regulating Accumulation, Guarding the Web: A Role for (Global) Civil Society? In *Nature, Production Power: Towards an Ecological Political Economy*, ed. Fred Gale and Michael M'Gonigle, 195–214. Cheltenham, UK: Edward Elgar.

Gale, Fred, and Michael M'Gonigle, eds. 2000. *Nature, Production Power: Towards an Ecological Political Economy*. Cheltenham, UK: Edward Elgar.

Giddens, Anthony. 1985. *A Contemporary Critique of Historical Materialism.* Vol. 2: *The Nation State and Violence.* Cambridge: Polity.

————. 1998. *The Third Way.* Cambridge: Polity.

————. 2000. *The Third Way and Its Critics.* Cambridge: Polity.

Gill, Stephen. 1998. New Constitutionalism, Democratisation and Global Political Economy. *Pacifica Review* 10 (1): 23–38.

Glasbergen, Pieter. 1996. Learning to Manage the Environment. In *Democracy and the Environment: Problems and Prospects*, ed. William Lafferty and James Meadowcroft, 175–193. Cheltenham, UK: Edward Elgar.

Gore, Albert. 1992. *Earth in the Balance.* Boston: Houghton Mifflin.

Gould, Carol. 1996. Diversity and Democracy: Representing Differences. In *Democracy and Difference,* ed. Seyla Benhabib, 171–186. Princeton, N.J.: Princeton University Press.

Gray, Anne. 1998. New Labour—New Labour Discipline. *Capital & Class* 65 (2): 1–9 .

Gray, Colin S. 1983. Space Is Not a Sanctuary. *Survival* 5 (5): 194–204.

Gray, John. 1998. *False Dawn: Delusions of Global Capitalism.* London: Granta.

Gray, Vanessa Joan. 2000. Transnational Environmental Politics: The Case of U.S. NGOs in Colombia. Ph.D. dissert., University of Miami.

Green, Michael J. B., and James Paine. 1997. State of the World's Protected Areas at the End of the Twentieth Century. Paper presented at IUCN (World Conservation Union) World Commission on Protected Areas Symposium, "Protected Areas in the Twenty-First Century: From Islands to Networks." Albany, Australia, November 24–29. <http://www.wcmc.org.uk/ protected_areas/albany.pdf>.

Grove, Richard. 1995. *Green Imperialism: Colonial Expansion, Tropical Island Edens and the Origins of Environmentalism.* New York: Cambridge University Press.

————. 1997. *Ecology, Climate and Empire: Colonialism and Global Environmental History 1400–1940.* Cambridge: Whitehorse Press.

Guha, Ramachandra. 1997. The Authoritarian Biologist and the Arrogance of Anti-Humanism: Wildlife Conservation in the Third World. *The Ecologist* 27 (1): 14–20.

Gutierrez, Eric. 1994. *The Ties That Bind: A Guide to Family, Business and Other Interests in the Ninth House of Representatives.* Manila: Philippine Center for Investigative Journalism.

Haas, Peter M. 1990. *Saving the Mediterranean: The Politics of International Environmental Cooperation.* New York: Columbia University Press.

———. 1992. Banning Chlorofluorocarbons: Epistemic Community Efforts to Protect Stratospheric Ozone. *International Organization* 46 (1): 187–224.

Haas, Peter M., R. O. Keohane, and M.A. Levy, eds. 1993. *Institutions for the Earth: Sources of Effective Environmental Protection.* Cambridge, Mass.: MIT Press.

Habermas, Jürgen. 2001. *The Postnational Constellation.* Cambridge: Polity.

Hajer, Maarten A. 1995. *The Politics of Environmental Discourse.* Oxford: Oxford University Press.

Handl, Günther. 1992. Human Rights and the Protection of the Environment: A Mildly Revisionist View. In *Human Rights, Sustainable Development and the Environment,* ed. Edith Brown Weiss et al. San José, Costa Rica: Instituto Interamericano de Derechos Humanos.

Hanf, Kenneth, and Alf-Inge Jansen, eds. 1998. *Governance and Environment in Western Europe: Politics, Policy and Administration.* London: Longman.

Hardin, Garrett. 1966. The Tragedy of the Commons. *Science* 162: 1243–1248.

Harris, Thistle Y. 1956. *Naturecraft in Australia.* London: Angus and Robertson.

Hawken, Paul, Amory Lovins, and L. Hunter Lovins. 1999. *Natural Capitalism: Creating the Next Industrial Revolution.* London: Earthscan.

Hay, Colin. 1996. From Crisis to Catastrophe? The Ecological Pathologies of the Liberal-Democratic State. *Innovations* 9 (4): 421–434.

———. 1999. *The Political Economy of New Labour.* Manchester: Manchester University Press.

———. 2001. The Invocation of External Economic Constraint: A Genealogy of the Concept of Globalization in the Political Economy of the British Labour Party, 1973–2000. *The European Legacy* 6 (2): 233–249.

Hay, Colin, and Matthew Watson. 1998. Rendering the Contingent Necessary: New Labour's Neo-Liberal Conversion and the Discourse of Globalisation. Program for the Study of Germany and Europe Working Paper 8.4. Cambridge, Mass.: Harvard University, Center for European Studies.

Hay, P. R., and M. G. Haward. 1988. Comparative Green Politics: Beyond the European Context. *Political Studies* 36: 433–448.

Hay, Peter. 2002. *Main Currents in Western Environmentalism.* Sydney: University of New South Wales Press.

Hayward, Tim. 1997. Anthropocentrism: A Misunderstood Problem. *Environmental Values* 6 (1): 49–63.

———. 1998. *Political Theory and Ecological Values.* Cambridge: Polity.

————. 2002. Environmental Rights as Democratic Rights. In *Democracy and the Claims of Nature*, ed. Ben A. Minteer and Bob Pepperman Taylor, 237–256. Lanham, Md.: Rowman and Littlefield.

Held, David. 1995. *Democracy and the Global Order*. Cambridge: Polity.

Henkin, Louis. 1979. *How Nations Behave: Law and Foreign Policy*. New York: Columbia University Press.

Hirst, Paul. 1997. *From Statism to Pluralism*. London: UCL Press.

Hobson, John H. 2000. *The State in International Relations*. Cambridge: Cambridge University Press.

Hofrichter, Richard, ed. 1993. *Toxic Struggles: The Theory and Practice of Environmental Justice*. Gabriola Island, B.C., Canada: New Society.

Honneth, Axel. 1992. Integrity and Disrespect: Principles of Morality Based on the Theory of Recognition. *Political Theory* 20 (2): 187–201.

————. 1995. *The Struggle for Recognition*. Cambridge, Mass.: MIT Press.

Huber, Evelyne, and John D. Stephens. 2001. Welfare State and Production Regimes in the Era of Retrenchment. In *The New Politics of the Welfare State*, ed. Paul Pierson, 107–145. Oxford: Oxford University Press.

Hughes, David. 1995. Analysis [of *Duddridge* case]. *Journal of Environmental Law* 7 (2): 238–244.

Hunold, Christian. 2001. Environmentalists, Nuclear Waste, and the Politics of Passive Exclusion in Germany. *German Politics and Society* 19 (4): 43–63.

Hunold, Christian, and John S. Dryzek. 2002. Green Political Theory and the State: Context Is Everything. *Global Environmental Politics* 2 (3): 17–39.

Hunold, Christian, and Iris Marion Young. 1998. Justice, Democracy, and Hazardous Siting. *Political Studies* 46 (1): 82–95.

Huntington, Samuel. 1996. *The Clash of Civilizations and the Remaking of World Order*. New York: Simon and Schuster.

Hurrell, Andrew. 1994. A Crisis of Ecological Viability? Global Environmental Change and the Nation State. *Political Studies* 42: 146–165.

Jacinto, Eusebio R. 1995. Historical Narratives of Taytay, Northern Palawan. In *Compilation of CBCRM [Community Based Coastal Resources Management] Researches in Taytay Bay and Malampaya Sound Northern Palawan*, 1–9. Manila: Tambuyog Development Center.

Jacobs, Michael. 1999a. Sustainability and Markets: On the Neo-classical Model of Environmental Economics. In *Planning Sustainability*, ed. Michael Kenny and James Meadowcroft, 78–100. London: Routledge.

————. 1999b. *Environmental Modernization: The New Labour Agenda*. London: Fabian Society.

Jänicke, Martin. 1990. *State Failure*. Cambridge: Polity.

————. 1997. The Political System's Capacity for Environmental Policy. In *National Environmental Policies: A Comparative Study of Capacity-Building*, ed. Martin Jänicke and Helmut Weidner, 1–24. Berlin: Springer.

Jänicke, Martin, and Helmut Weidner. 1997. Germany. In *National Environmental Policies: A Comparative Study of Capacity-Building*, ed. Martin Jänicke and Helmut Weidner, 133–155. Berlin: Springer.

Jänicke, Martin, and Helmut Weidner, eds. 1997. *National Environmental Policies: A Comparative Study of Capacity-Building*. Berlin: Springer.

Jordan, Andrew. 2000. Environmental Policy. In *Developments in British Politics, Vol. 6*, ed. Patrick Dunleavy, Andrew Gamble, Ian Holliday, and Gillian Peele, 257–276. London: Palgrave.

———. 2001. Is There a Climate for Policy Change? The Contested Politics of a Low Carbon Economy. *Political Quarterly* 72 (2): 249–254.

Käkönen, Jyrki, ed. 1994. *Green Security or Militarised Environment?* Aldershot, UK: Dartmouth Publishing.

Kalaw, Maximo T. 1997. *Exploring Soul and Society: Papers on Sustainable Development*. Manila: Anvil.

Kapstein, Ethan. 1994. *Governing the Global Economy: International Finance and the State*. Cambridge, Mass.: Harvard University Press.

Kasa, Sjur. 2000. Policy Networks as a Barrier to Green Tax Reform: The Case of CO2-Taxes in Norway. *Environmental Politics* 9 (4): 104–122.

Kaufmann, Franz-Xavier. 2001. Towards a Theory of the Welfare State. In *Welfare State Futures*, ed. Stephen Leibfried, 15–36. Cambridge: Cambridge University Press.

Keck, Margaret, and Katherine Sikkink. 1998. *Activists Beyond Borders: Advocacy Networks and International Politics*. Ithaca, N.Y.: Cornell University Press.

Keohane, Robert O. 1984. *After Hegemony: Cooperation and Discord in World Political Economy*. Princeton, N.J.: Princeton University Press.

Kewley, T. H. 1973. *Social Security in Australia*. 2d ed. Sydney: Sydney University Press.

Kitschelt, Herbert P. 1986. Political Opportunity Structures and Political Protest: Anti-Nuclear Movements in Four Democracies. *British Journal of Political Science* 16 (1): 57–85.

Korten, Francis. 1994. Questioning the Call for Environmental Loans: A Critical Examination of Forestry Lending in the Philippines. *World Development* 22: 971–981.

Krasner, Stephen D. 1982. Structural Causes and Regime Consequences: Regimes as Intervening Variables. In *International Regimes*. Ithaca, N.Y.: Cornell University Press.

Krasner, Stephen D., ed. 1982. *International Regimes*. Ithaca, N.Y.: Cornell University Press.

Ksentini, Farma Zohra. 1994. *Final Report on Human Rights and the Environment*, UN Sub-Commission on Prevention of Discrimination and Protection of Minorities. E/CN.4/Sub.2/1994/9. July.

Kuehls,Thom. 1996. *Beyond Sovereign Territory*. Minneapolis: University of Minnesota Press.

Kummer, David M. 1992. *Deforestation in the Postwar Philippines*. Chicago: University of Chicago Press.

Kung, Hans. 1998. *A Global Ethic for Global Politics and Economics*. New York: Oxford University Press.

Kutting, Gabriela. 2000. *Environment, Society and International Relations: Towards More Effective International Environmental Agreements*. London: Routledge.

Kymlicka, Will. 1996. *Multicultural Citizenship: A Liberal Theory of Minority Rights*. Oxford: Oxford University Press.

——— . 2001. *Politics in the Vernacular: Nationalism, Multiculturalism, and Citizenship*. Oxford: Oxford University Press.

Kymlicka, Will, and Wayne Norman, eds. 2000. *Citizenship in Diverse Societies*. Oxford: Oxford University Press.

Labour Party. 2001. *Ambitious for Britain: Labour's Manifesto 2001*. London: Labour Party.

Lacey, Michael J. 1991. The Environmental Revolution and the Growth of the State: Overview and Introduction. In *Government and Environmental Protection: Essays on Historical Developments Since World War II*, 1–17. Washington, D.C.: Woodrow Wilson Center Press.

Laferriere, Eric. 1996. Emancipating International Relations Theory: An Ecological Perspective. *Millennium* 25 (1): 53–75.

Lafferty, William. 2000. Democracy and Ecological Rationality. In *Globalization: Governance and Identity*, ed. Guy Lachapelle and John Trent, 39–65. Montreal: University of Montreal.

Lafferty, William, and Oluf Langhelle, eds. 1999. *Towards Sustainable Development: On the Goals of Development and the Conditions of Sustainability*. London: Macmillan.

Lafferty, William, and James Meadowcroft, eds. 1996. *Democracy and the Environment: Problems and Prospects*. London: Edward Elgar.

——— . 2000. *Implementing Sustainable Development: Strategies and Initiatives in High Consumption Societies*. Oxford: Oxford University Press.

Lake, David A. 2003. The New Sovereignty in International Relations. *International Studies Review* 5: 303–323.

Lake, Robert. 1996. Volunteers, NIMBYs, and Environmental Justice: Dilemmas of Democratic Practice. *Antipode* 28 (2): 160–174.

Lapidoth, Ruth. 1992. Sovereignty in Transition. *Journal of International Affairs* 45 (2): 325–346.

Lawrence, Karen. 2002. Negotiating Conservation for Local Social Change, Malampaya Sound, Philippines. Ph.D. dissert., Department of Geography, King's College, London.

Lee, Charles, ed. 1992. *Proceedings: The First National People of Color Environmental Leadership Summit.* New York: United Church of Christ Commission for Racial Justice.

Lee, Kai N. 1993. *Compass and Gyroscope: Integrating Science and Politics for the Environment.* Washington, D.C.: Island Press.

Lehmbruch, Gerhard, and Philippe Schmitter, eds. 1982. *Patterns of Corporatist Policy-Making.* London: Sage.

Leopold, Aldo. 1949. *A Sand County Almanac.* Oxford: Oxford University Press.

Levy, Marc A., Robert O. Keohane, and Peter M. Haas. 1993. Improving the Effectiveness of International Environmental Institutions. In *Institutions for the Earth: Sources of Effective Environmental Protection,* ed. Peter M. Haas, Robert O. Keohane, and Marc A. Levy, 397–426. Cambridge, Mass: MIT Press.

Linklater, Andrew. 1996a. The Achievements of Critical Theory. In *International Theory: Positivism and Beyond,* ed. Steve Smith, Ken Booth, and Marysia Zalewski, 279–300. Cambridge: Cambridge University Press.

———. 1996b. Citizenship and Sovereignty in the Post-Westphalian State. *European Journal of International Relations* 2 (1): 77–103.

Lipschutz, Ronnie D. 1997. From Place to Planet: Local Knowledge and Global Environmental Governance. *Global Governance* 3 (1): 83–102.

———. 2000. *After Authority: War, Peace, and Global Politics in the 21st Century.* Albany: State University of New York Press.

Lipschutz, Ronnie D., and Ken Conca, eds. 1993. *The State and Social Power in Global Environmental Politics.* New York: Columbia University Press.

Lipschutz, Ronnie D., and Judith Mayer. 1993. Not Seeing the Forest for the Trees: Rights, Rules, and the Renegotiation of Resource Management Regimes. In *The State and Social Power in Global Environmental Politics,* ed. Ronnie D. Lipschutz and Ken Conca, 246–275. New York: Columbia University Press.

———. 1996. *Global Civil Society and Global Environmental Governance: The Politics of Nature from Place to Planet.* Albany: State University of New York Press.

Litfin, Karen. 1994. *Ozone Discourses: Science and Politics in Global Environmental Cooperation.* New York: Columbia University Press.

———. 1997. Sovereignty in World Ecopolitics. *Mershon International Studies Review* 41 (2): 167–204.

Litfin, Karen, ed. 1998. *The Greening of Sovereignty in World Politics.* Cambridge, Mass.: MIT Press.

Low, Nicholas, and Brendan Gleeson. 1998. *Justice, Society and Nature: An Exploration of Political Ecology.* London: Routledge.

Ludlam, Steve, and Martin J. Smith, eds. 2000. *New Labour in Government.* London: Palgrave.

Lukes, Steven. 1974. *Power: A Radical View.* London: Macmillan.

Lundqvist, Lennart. 1980. *The Hare and the Tortoise: Clean Air Policies in the United States and Sweden.* Ann Arbor: University of Michigan Press.

———. 2001. A Green Fist in a Velvet Glove: The Ecological State and Sustainable Development. *Environmental Values* 10: 455–472.

———. 2004. *Straddling the Fence: Sweden and Ecological Governance.* Manchester: Manchester University Press.

Marks, Stuart A. 1984. *The Imperial Lion: Human Dimensions of Wildlife Management in Central Africa.* Boulder, Colo.: Westview Press.

Martinez-Alier, Juan. 2002. *The Environmentalism of the Poor: A Study of Ecological Conflict and Valuation.* Cheltenham, UK: Edward Elgar.

Mason, Michael. 1999. *Environmental Democracy.* London: Earthscan.

Mathews, Freya, ed. 1996. *Ecology and Democracy.* London: Frank Cass.

McGinnis, Michael. 1999. *Bioregionalism.* London: Routledge.

McMurtry, John. 1996. *The Cancer Stage of Capitalism.* London: Pluto Press.

Meadowcroft, James. 1997. Planning, Democracy and the Challenge of Sustainable Development. *International Political Science Review* 18: 167–190.

———. 1999a. The Politics of Sustainable Development: Emergent Arenas and Challenges for Political Science. *International Political Science Review* 20: 219–237.

———. 1999b. Planning for Sustainable Development: What Can Be Learned from the Critics? In *Planning Sustainability*, ed. Michael Kenny and James Meadowcroft, 12–38. London: Routledge.

M'Gonigle, Michael. 2000. A Dialectic of Centre and Territory: The Political Economy of Ecological Flows and Spatial Relations. In *Nature, Production Power: Towards an Ecological Political Economy*, ed. Fred Gale and Michael M'Gonigle, 3–16. Cheltenham, UK: Edward Elgar.

Miles, Edward L., and Arild Underdal, eds. 2000. *Explaining Regime Effectiveness: Confronting Theory with Evidence.* Cambridge, Mass.: MIT Press.

Miller, Christopher. 1995. Environmental Rights: European Fact or English Fiction. *Journal of Law and Society* 22 (3): 374–397.

Miller, David. 1976. *Social Justice.* Oxford: Clarendon Press.

———. 1999. Bounded Citizenship. In *Cosmopolitan Citizenship*, ed. Kimberly Hutchings and Roland Dannreuther, 72–77. Basingstoke, UK: Macmillan.

Mishra, Ramesh. 1990. *The Welfare State in Capitalist Society.* London: Harvester Wheatsheaf.

Mol, Arthur P. J. 1996. Ecological Modernisation and Institutional Reflexivity: Environmental Reform in the Late Modern Age. *Environmental Politics* 5 (2): 302–323.

Mol, Arthur P.J., and Gert Spaargaren. 2000. Ecological Modernization Theory in Debate: A Review. *Environmental Politics* 9 (1): 17–49.

Monbiot, George. 2000a. *Captive State: The Corporate Takeover of Britain.* London: Macmillan.

———. 2000b. Car Workers Are Rightly Doomed. *Guardian.* April 27.

Montes, Margarita Pacheco. 1996. Colombia's Independent Recyclers' Union: A Model for Urban Waste Management. In *Green Guerrillas: Environmental Conflicts and Initiatives in Latin America and the Caribbean,* ed. Helen Collinson, 215–220. London: Latin America Bureau.

Montesquieu, Charles de Secondat. 1748. *The Spirit of Laws,* ed. David W. Carrithers. Berkeley: University of California Press, 1977.

Morales, Horacio. 1997. Interview with Horacio Morales. Manila: Philippine Rural Reconstruction Movement. May 30.

Moran, Alan. 1995. Tools of Environmental Policy: Market Instruments versus Command-and-Control. In *Markets, the State and the Environment: Towards Integration,* Robyn Eckersley, 73–85. Melbourne: Macmillan.

MORI. 1999. Poll Conducted for Greenpeace on GM Crops and Organic Food. June.

Moyal, Ann. 1986. *A Bright and Savage Land: Scientists in Colonial Australia.* Sydney: Collins.

Murphy, James, and Andrew Gouldson. 2000. Environmental Policy and Industrial Innovation: Integrating Environment and Economy through Ecological Modernisation. *Geoforum* 31 (1): 33–44.

National Integrated Protected Areas Program (NIPAP). 1997. *Annual Report for 1996.* Manila: NIPAP.

National Land and Water Resources Audit (NLWRA). 2002. *Australian Terrestrial Biodiversity Assessment 2002.* Canberra: NLWRA.

Newell, Peter. 2000. *Climate for Change: Non-State Actors and the Global Politics of Greenhouse.* Cambridge: Cambridge University Press.

Nozawa, Cristi. 1996. *Interview with Cristi Nozawa.* Manila: Haribon Foundation. October 28.

Nuffield Council on Bioethics. 1999. *Genetically Modified Crops: The Ethical and Social Issues.* Oxford: Nuffield Foundation.

O'Connor, James. 1973. *The Fiscal Crisis of the State.* New York: St Martin's Press.

Offe, Claus. 1975. The Capitalist State and Policy Formation. In *Stress and Contradiction in Modern Capitalism: Public Policy and the Theory of the State,* ed. L. N. Lindberg, R. Alford, C. Crouch, and C. Offe. Lexington, Mass.: Lexington Books.

———. 1980. The Attribution of Public Status to Interest Groups: Observations on the West German Case. In *Organizing Interests in Western Europe,* ed. Suzanne Berger, 123–158. Cambridge: Cambridge University Press.

———. 1984. *Contradictions of the Welfare State.* Cambridge, Mass.: MIT Press.

————. 1996. *Modernity and the State*. Cambridge, Mass.: MIT Press.

————. 1998. From Youth to Maturity: The Challenge of Party Politics. In *The German Greens: Paradox Between Party and Movement,* ed. Margit Mayer and John Ely, 165–179. Philadelphia: Temple University Press.

Onuf, Nicholas. 1998. *The Republican Legacy in International Thought*. Cambridge: Cambridge University Press.

Ophuls, William. 1977. *Ecology and the Politics of Scarcity*. San Francisco: W.H. Freeman.

Organisation for Economic Co-operation and Development (OECD). 2003. *Voluntary Approaches for Environmental Policy—Effectiveness, Efficiency and Usage in Policy Mixes*. Paris: OECD. <http://www1.oecd.org/publications/e-book/9703091E.PDF>.

Ostrom, Elinor. 1990. *Governing the Commons: The Evolution of Institutions for Collective Action*. Cambridge: Cambridge University Press.

Ottaway, Marina. 2001. Corporatism Goes Global. *Global Governance* 7 (3): 265–292.

Paehlke, Robert. 1988. Democracy, Bureaucracy and Environmentalism. *Environmental Ethics* 10: 291–308.

————. 2001. Environment, Equity and Globalization: Beyond Resistance. *Global Environmental Politics* 1 (1): 1–10.

Paehlke, Robert, and Douglas Torgerson, eds. 1990. *Managing Leviathan: Environmental Politics and the Administrative State*. Peterborough, Ont., Canada: Broadview Press.

Parliamentary Answer for Mr. Battle to Joan Whalley. 1999. *Hansard*, vol. 16, no. 13, June 28, col. 39.

Paterson, Matthew. 1996. Green Politics. In *Theories of International Relations,* ed. Scott Burchill, 252–274. London: Macmillan.

————. 1999a. Green Political Strategy and the State. In *Environmental Futures,* ed. N. Ben Fairweather, Sue Elworthy, Matt Stroh, and Piers H. G. Stephens, 73–87. London: Macmillan.

————. 1999b. Overview: Interpreting Trends in Global Environmental Governance. *International Affairs* 75 (4): 793–802.

————. 2000a. *Understanding Global Environmental Politics: Domination, Accumulation and Resistance*. London: Macmillan.

————. 2000b. Car Culture and Global Environmental Politics. *Review of International Studies* 26: 253–270.

————. 2001. Climate Policy as Accumulation Strategy: The Failure of COP6 and Emerging Trends in Climate Politics. *Global Environmental Politics* 1 (2): 10–17.

Pehle, Heinrich. 1998. *Das Bundesministerium für Umwelt, Naturschutz und Reaktorsicherheit: Ausgegrenzt statt integriert. Das institutionelle Fundament der deutschen Umweltpolitik*. Wiesbaden: Deutscher Universitätsverlag.

Peluso, Nancy Lee. 1993. Coercing Conservation: The Politics of State Resource Control. In *The State and Social Power in Global Environmental Politics,* ed. Ronnie D. Lipschutz and Ken Conca, 46–70. New York: Columbia University Press.

Pettit, Philip. 1989. The Freedom of the City: A Republican Ideal. In *The Good Polity,* ed. Alan Hamlin and Philip Pettit, 141–168. Oxford: Blackwell.

———. 1996. Freedom as Antipower. *Ethics* 106: 577–604.

———. 1999a. *Republicanism.* London: Oxford University Press.

———. 1999b. Republican Freedom and Contestatory Democratization. In *Democracy's Values,* ed. Ian Shapiro and Casiano Hacker-Cordón, 163–190. Cambridge: Cambridge University Press.

Philippine Council for Sustainable Development (PCSD). 1997. *Philippine Agenda 21: A National Agenda for Sustainable Development.* Manila: PCSD.

Pierson, Christopher. 1998. *Beyond the Welfare State? The New Political Economy of Welfare.* 2d ed. Cambridge: Polity.

Plumwood, Val. 1993. *Feminism and the Mastery of Nature.* London: Routledge.

———. 1998. Inequality, Ecojustice, and Ecological Rationality. In *Debating the Earth: The Environmental Politics Reader,* ed. John Dryzek and David Schlosberg, 559–583. Oxford: Oxford University Press.

Poggi, Gianfranco. 1982. The Modern State and the Idea of Progress. In *Progress and Its Discontents,* ed. G. Almond, M. Chodorow, and R. Pearce, 337–360. Berkeley: University of California Press.

———. 1990. *The State: Its Nature, Development and Prospects.* Stanford, Calif.: Stanford University Press.

Polanyi, Karl. 1944. *The Great Transformation.* Boston: Beacon Press.

Policy Innovation Unit. 2001. *Renewable Energy in the UK: Building for the Future of the Environment.* <http://www.strategy.gov.uk/files/pdf/renewanalytpap1nov.pdf>.

Porter, Gareth, Janet Welsh Brown, and Pamela S. Chasek. 2000. *Global Environmental Politics.* Boulder, Colo.: Westview Press.

Powell, Joe M. 1976. *Environmental Management in Australia 1788–1914.* Melbourne: Oxford University Press.

Price, Richard, and Christain Reus-Smit. 1998. Dangerous Liaisons? Critical International Theory and Constructivism. *European Journal of International Relations* 4 (3): 259–294.

Princen, Thomas, and Matthias Finger, eds. 1994. *Environmental NGOs in World Politics: Linking the Local and the Global.* London: Routledge.

Princen, Thomas, Michael Maniates, and Ken Conca, eds. 2002. *Confronting Consumption.* Cambridge, Mass.: MIT Press.

Productivity Commission. 1999. *Implementation of Ecologically Sustainable Development by Commonwealth Departments and Agencies: Inquiry Report.* Report No.5. Canberra: Productivity Commission.

Pulido, Laura. 1996. *Environmentalism and Social Justice: Two Chicano Struggles in the Southwest*. Tucson: University of Arizona Press.

Raschke, Joachim. 1993. *Die Grünen. Wie sie wurden, was sie sind*. Cologne: Bund-Verlag.

Rawls, John. 1971. *A Theory of Justice*. Oxford: Oxford University Press.

Redclift, Michael. 1987. *Sustainable Development: Exploring the Contradictions*. London: Routledge.

Redgwell, Catherine. 1996. Life, the Universe and Everything: A Critique of Anthropocentric Rights. In *Human Rights Approaches to Environmental Protection*, ed. Alan Boyle and Michael R. Anderson, 71–89. Oxford: Clarendon Press.

Rest, Alfred. 1997. Improved Environmental Protection through an Expanded Concept of Human Rights in Europe. *Environmental Policy and Law* 27 (3): 213–216.

Reus-Smit, Christian. 1998. Changing Patterns of Governance: From Absolutism to Global Multilateralism. In *Between Sovereignty and Global Governance: The State, Civil Society and the United Nations*, ed. Albert J. Paolini, A. P. Jarvis, and C. Reus-Smit, 3–28. London: Macmillan.

———. 1999. *The Moral Purpose of the State*. Princeton, N.J.: Princeton University Press.

Ribot, Jesse C. 1999. Integral Local Development: Authority, Accountability and Entrustment in Natural Resource Management. Working Paper prepared for the Regional Program for the Traditional Energy Sector (RPTES) in the Africa Technical Group (AFTG1—Energy) of the World Bank.

Richardson, James. 2001. *Contending Liberalisms in World Politics: Ideology and Power*. Boulder, Colo.: Lynne Rienner.

Rittberger, Volker. 1993. Editor's Introduction. In *Regime Theory and International Relations*, xii-xix. Oxford: Clarendon Press.

Rivera, Rebecca. 1997. Network Analysis of Palawan Fishers' Problems and Issues. *Lundayan Journal*. Special Issue: 7–19.

Robar, Stephen. 1999. Collaboration, Policy Perspectives, and Discursive Democracy: Public Land Management and the Colorado Plateau Forum. Ph.D. dissert., Department of Political Science, Northern Arizona University.

Robertson, John. 1898. Letter to Governor LaTrobe. September 20, 1853. In *Letters from Victorian Pioneers*, ed. T. H. Bride, 34–35. Melbourne: Brain, Govt. Printer.

Rood, Steven. 1998. NGOs and Indigenous Peoples. In *Organizing for Democracy: NGOs, Civil Society, and the Philippine State*, ed. G. Sidney Silliman and Lela Garner Noble, 138–156. Honolulu: University of Hawaii Press.

Ross, Michael L. 1996. Conditionality and Logging Reform in the Tropics. In *Institutions for Environmental Aid*, ed. Robert Keohane and Marc Levy, 167–197. Cambridge, Mass.: MIT Press.

————. 2001. *Timber Booms and Institutional Breakdown in Southeast Asia.* Cambridge: Cambridge University Press.

Royal Commission on Environmental Pollution. 2000. *Energy: The Changing Climate.* Twenty-second Report of the Royal Commission on Environmental Pollution. Cmnd 4749. London: Stationery Office.

Rucht, Dieter, and Jochen Roose. 1999. The German Environmental Movement at a Crossroads. *Environmental Politics* 8 (1): 59–80.

Rutherford, Paul. 2003. "Talking the Talk": Business Discourse at the World Summit on Sustainable Development. *Environmental Politics* 12 (2): 145–150.

Sachs, Wolfgang, ed. 1993. *Global Ecology.* London: Zed Books.

Sagoff, Mark. 1993. Animal Liberation, Environmental Ethics: Bad Marriage, Quick Divorce. In *Environmental Philosophy: From Animal Rights to Radical Ecology,* ed. Michael Zimmerman, 84–94. Englewood Cliffs, N.J.: Prentice Hall.

Sassen, Saskia. 1996. *Losing Control? Sovereignty in an Age of Globalization.* New York: Columbia University Press.

Saurin, Julian. 1993. Global Environmental Degradation, Modernity and Environmental Knowledge. *Environmental Politics* 2 (4): 46–64.

————. 1996. International Relations, Social Ecology and the Globalisation of Environmental Change. In *The Environment and International Relations,* ed. John Vogler and Mark F. Imber, 77–98. London: Routledge.

Saward, Michael. 1998. Green State/Democratic State. *Contemporary Politics* 4 (4): 345–356.

Scheinin, Martin. 1994. Direct Applicability of Economic, Social and Cultural Rights: A Critique of the Doctrine of Self-Executing Treaties. In *Social Rights as Human Rights: A European Challenge,* ed. Krzysztof Drzewick, Catarina Krause, and Allan Rosas. Turku, Finland: Institute for Human Rights, Åbo Akademi University.

Scheppele, Kim Lane, and Karol Edward Soltan. 1987. The Authority of Alternatives. In *Authority Revisited: NOMOS XXIX,* ed. J. Roland Pennock and John W. Chapman, 169–200. New York: New York University Press.

Schlosberg, David. 1999. *Environmental Justice and the New Pluralism: The Challenge of Difference for Environmentalism.* Oxford: Oxford University Press.

————. 2003. The Justice of Environmental Justice: Reconciling Equity, Recognition, and Participation in a Political Movement. In *Moral and Political Reasoning in Environmental Practice,* ed. Andrew Light and Avner deShalit, 77–106. Cambridge, Mass.: MIT Press.

Schlosberg, David, and John S. Dryzek. 2002. Political Strategies of American Environmentalism: Inclusion and Beyond. *Society and Natural Resources* 15 (9): 787–804.

Selle, Per, and Kristin Strømsnes. 1998. *Membership and Democracy: Should We Take Passive Support Seriously?* Bergen, Norway: Department of Comparative Politics, University of Bergen.

Serrano, Isagani R. 1994. *Pay Now, Not Later: Essays on Environment and Development.* Manila: Philippine Rural Reconstruction Movement.

Shelton, Dinah L. 1993. Environmental Rights in the European Community. *Hastings International and Comparative Law Review* 16: 557–582.

Sidel, John T. 1999. *Capital, Coercion, and Crime: Bossism in the Philippines.* Stanford, Calif.: Stanford University Press.

Skinner, Quentin. 1981. *Machiavelli.* Oxford: Oxford University Press.

———. 1990. The Republican Ideal of Political Liberty. In *Machiavelli and Republicanism,* ed. Gisela Bock, Quentin Skinner, and Maurizio Viroli, 293–309. Cambridge: Cambridge University Press.

———. 1992. On Justice, the Common Good and the Priority of Liberty. In *Dimensions of Radical Democracy,* ed. Chantal Mouffe, 211–224. London: Verso.

———. 1998. *Liberty before Liberalism.* Cambridge: Cambridge University Press.

Skodvin, Tora. 2000. The Intergovernmental Panel on Climate Change. In *Science and Politics in International Environmental Regimes: Between Integrity and Involvement,* ed. Steinar Andresen, Tora Skodvin, Arild Underdal, and J. Wettestad, 146–180. Manchester: Manchester University Press.

Smith, Steve. 1993. The Environment on the Periphery of International Relations: An Explanation. *Environmental Politics* 2 (4): 28–45.

Somsen, Han. 1996. *Francovich* and Its Application to EC Environmental Law. In *Protecting the European Environment: Enforcing EC Environmental Law,* ed. Han Somsen., 146–149. London: Blackstone Press.

Strange, Susan. 1996. *The Retreat of the State.* Cambridge: Cambridge Unversity Press.

Summary of Third Global Ministerial Environment Forum (GMEF-3). 2002. *Earth Negotiations Bulletin,* vol. 16, no. 24, February 18. <http://www.iisd.ca/vol16/enb1624e.html>.

Sunstein, Cass. 1997. *Free Markets and Social Justice.* Oxford: Oxford University Press.

Sverdrup, Liv Astrid. 1997. Norway's Institutional Response to Sustainable Development. *Comparative Politics* 6 (1): 74.

Tarrow, Sidney. 1994. *Power in Movement: Social Movements, Collective Action and Politics.* Cambridge: Cambridge University Press.

Taylor, Charles. 1994. *Multiculturalism.* Princeton, N.J.: Princeton University Press.

Taylor, Michael. 1987. *The Possibility of Cooperation.* Cambridge: Cambridge University Press.

Thane, P. 1982. *Foundations of the Welfare State.* London: Longman.

Thomas, Keith. 1983. *Man and the Natural World: Changing Attitudes in England 1500–1800.* London: Allen Lane/Penguin Books.

Thompson, Mark R. 1995. *The Anti-Marcos Struggle: Personalistic Rule and Democratic Transition in the Philippines.* New Haven: Yale University Press.

Thornton, J., and S. Tromans. 1999. Human Rights and Environmental Wrongs. *Journal of Environmental Law* 11 (1): 35–58.

Tiefenbach, Paul. 1998. *Die Grünen: Verstaatlichung einer Partei.* Cologne: PapyRossa.

Toynbee, Polly. 1999. Solar Power Is Clean, Cheap and Catching Fire Abroad. *Guardian*, December 29, 12.

Toynbee, Polly, and David Walker. 2001. *Did Things Get Better?* Harmondsworth, UK: Penguin.

Toyne, Phillip. 1994. *The Reluctant Nation: Environment, Law and Politics in Australia.* Sydney: ABC Books.

Tucker, Richard. 2000. *Insatiable Appetite.* Berkeley: University of California Press.

Turner, B.L. II, R. E. Kasperson, W. B. Meyer, K. M. Dow, D. Golding, J. X. Kasperson, R. C. Mitchell, and S. J. Ratick. 1990. Two Types of Global Environmental Change: Definitional and Spatial-Scale Issues in Their Human Dimensions. *Global Environmental Change* 1 (1): 14–22.

Tyrell, Ian. 1999. *True Gardens of the Gods: Californian-Australian Environmental Reform, 1860–1930.* Berkeley: University of California Press.

United Church of Christ Commission for Racial Justice. 1987. *Toxic Wastes and Race in the United States: A National Report on the Racial and Socio-Economic Characteristics of Communities with Hazardous Waste Sites.* New York: United Church of Christ.

United Nations Development Programme, United Nations Environment Programme, World Bank, and World Resources Institute. 2003. *World Resources 2002–2004: Decisions for the Earth: Balance, Voice and Power.* Washington, D.C.: World Resources Institute. <http://pubs.wri.org/pubs_pdf.cfm?PubID=3764>.

United Nations Economic and Social Council. 2002. *Implementing Agenda 21, Report of the Secretary General.* E/CN.17/2002/PC.2.

United Nations Environment Programme. 2001. Multilateral Environmental Agreements: A Summary. Background Paper Presented by the Secretariat at the First Meeting of the Open-Ended Intergovernmental Group of Ministers or Their Representatives on International Environmental Governance. UNEP/IGM/1/INF/1.

United Nations General Assembly. 1997. *Programme for the Further Implementation of Agenda 21.* Adopted by the Special Session of the General Assembly, July 23–27. A/RES/S-19/2.

United States Environmental Protection Agency. 1992. *Environmental Equity: Reducing Risk for All Communities.* Washington, D.C.: Government Printing Office.

United States General Accounting Office. 1983. *Siting of Hazardous Waste Landfills and Their Correlation with Racial and Economic Status of Surrounding Communities*. Washington, D.C.: Government Printing Office.

van Tatenhove, Jan, Bas Arts, and Pieter Leroy. 2000. *Political Modernisation and the Environment*. Dordrecht: Kluwer.

Victor, David G., Kal Raustiala, and Eugene B. Skolnikoff, eds. 1998. *The Implementation and Effectiveness of International Environmental Commitments: Theory and Practice*. Cambridge, Mass.: MIT Press.

Viroli, Maurizio. 1995. *For Love of Country*. Oxford: Clarendon Press.

Vogler, John. 1999. The EU as an Actor in International Environmental Politics. *Environmental Politics* 8 (3): 24–48.

———. 2000. *The Global Commons: Environmental and Technological Governance*. Chichester, UK: Wiley.

———. 2003. Taking Institutions Seriously: How Regime Analysis Can Be Relevant to Multilevel Environmental Governance. *Global Environmental Politics* 3 (2): 25–39.

Von Weizsäcker, Ernst, Amory Lovins, and Hunter Lovins. 1998. *Factor Four: Doubling Wealth, Halving Resource Use*. London: Earthscan.

Walker, R. B. 1991. Fauna and Flora Protection in New South Wales 1866–1948. *Journal of Australian Studies* 28 (March): 17–28.

Walpole, Peter, Gilbert Braganza, John Ong, and Celine Vicente. 1994. *Upland Philippine Communities: Securing Cultural and Environmental Stability*. Manila: Environmental Research Division, Manila Observatory.

Waltz, Kenneth N. 1979. *Theory of International Politics*. Reading, Mass.: Addison-Wesley.

Wapner, Paul. 1995a. Politics Beyond the State: Environmental Activism and World Civic Politics. *World Politics* 47: 311–340.

———. 1995b. The State and Environmental Challenges: A Critical Exploration of Alternatives to the State System. *Environmental Politics* 4 (1): 44–69.

———. 1997a. Environmental Ethics and Global Governance: Engaging the International Liberal Tradition. *Global Governance* 3: 213–231.

———. 1997b. Governance in Global Society. In *Global Governance: Drawing Insights from the Environmental Experience*, ed. Oran R. Young, 65–84. Ithaca, N.Y.: Cornell University Press.

Watts, Robert. 1987. *The Foundations of the National Welfare State*. Sydney: Allen and Unwin.

Weale, Albert. 1992. *The New Politics of Pollution*. Manchester: Manchester University Press.

Weber, Stefan. 1991. Environmental Information and the European Convention on Human Rights. *Human Rights Law Journal* 12 (5): 177–185.

Weinzierl, Hubert. 1993. *Das grüne Gewissen. Selbstverständnis und Strategien des Naturschutzes*. Stuttgart: Weitbrecht.

Weiss, Edith Brown, and Harold K. Jacobson, eds. 1998. *Engaging Countries: Strengthening Compliance with International Environmental Accords.* Cambridge, Mass.: MIT Press.

Weiss, Linda. 1998. *The Myth of the Powerless State: Governing the Economy in a Global Era.* Cambridge: Polity.

Wells, Michael, and Katrina Brandon, with Lee Hannah. 1992. *People and Parks: Linking Protected Area Management with Local Communities.* Washington, D.C.: World Bank.

Wendt, Alexander. 1992. Anarchy Is What States Make of It: The Social Construction of Power Politics. *International Organization* 46: 335–370.

———. 1999. *Social Theory of International Politics.* Cambridge: Cambridge University Press.

White, Damian. 2002. A Green Industrial Revolution? Sustainable Technological Innovation in a Global Age. *Environmental Politics* 11 (2): 1–26.

White, Stuart, ed. 2001. *New Labour.* London: Palgrave.

Williams, Bruce A., and Albert A. Matheny. 1995. *Democracy, Dialogue, and Environmental Disputes.* New Haven: Yale University Press.

Wilson, John, Jane Thomson, and Anthony McMahon. 1996. *The Australian Welfare State: Key Documents and Themes.* Melbourne: Macmillan.

World Commission on Dams. 2000. *Dams and Development: A New Framework for Decision-Making. The Report of the World Commission on Dams.* London: Earthscan.

World Commission on Environment and Development. 1987. *Our Common Future: The Report of the World Commission on Environment and Development.* Oxford: Oxford University Press.

World Commission on Protected Areas. 1997. *Proceedings: Parks for Peace— International Conference on Transboundary Protected Areas as a Vehicle for International Cooperation.* September 16–18.

World Conservation Union (IUCN). 1990. *Parks on the Borderline: Experience in Transfrontier Conservation.* Gland, Switzerland: IUCN.

World Conservation Union (IUCN) and World Bank. 1997. *Proceedings: Large Dams— Learning from the Past, Looking at the Future.* April 11–12.

Worldwide Fund for Nature. 2001. UK Must Work Harder to Reduce CO2 from Transport. January 10. <http://www.wwf.org.uk/News/n_0000000300.asp>.

Wynne, Brian. 1982. *Rationality and Ritual: The Windscale Inquiry and Nuclear Decisions in Britain.* Preston, UK: British Society for the History of Science.

Young, Iris M. 1990. *Justice and the Politics of Difference.* London: Routledge.

———. 1996. Communication and the Other. In *Democracy and Difference: Contesting the Boundaries of the Political,* ed. Seyla Benhabib, 120–135. Princeton, N.J.: Princeton University Press.

———. 2000. *Inclusion and Democracy.* Oxford: Oxford University Press.

Young, Oran R. 1989. *International Cooperation: Building Regimes for Natural Resources and the Environment.* Ithaca, N.Y.: Cornell University Press.

──── . 1990. Global Environmental Change and International Governance. *Millennium* 19 (3): 337–346.

──── . 1994. *International Governance: Protecting the Environment in a Stateless Society.* Ithaca, N.Y.: Cornell University Press.

Young, Oran R., ed. 1997. *Global Governance: Drawing Insights from the Environmental Experience.* Cambridge, Mass.: MIT Press.

──── . 1999. *The Effectiveness of International Environmental Regimes: Causal Connections and Behavioral Mechanisms.* Cambridge, Mass.: MIT Press.

Young, Oran R., with Arun Agarwal, Leslie A. King, Peter H. Sand, Arild Underdal, and Merrilyn Wasson. 1999. *IDGEC Science Plan.* International Human Dimensions Programme on Global Environmental Change. Report 9. Bonn: IHDP.

Young, Oran R., Mark A. Levy, with Gail Osherenko. 1999. The Effectiveness of International Environmental Regimes. In *The Effectiveness of International Environmental Regimes: Causal Connections and Behavioral Mechanisms,* ed. Oran R. Young, 1–32. Cambridge, Mass.: MIT Press.

Young, Stephen. 2000. The United Kingdom: From Political Containment to Integrated Thinking. In *Implementing Sustainable Development: Strategies and Initiatives in High-Consumption Societies,* ed. William Lafferty and James Meadowcroft, 245–273. Oxford: Oxford University Press.

Zurn, Michael. 1998. The Rise of International Environmental Politics. *World Politics* 50: 617–649.

Cases

International Court of Justice. Joined cases C-6/90 and C-9/90. *Francovich v. Italian Republic* (1991) ECR I-5357.

International Court of Justice. Case C-236/92. *Comitato di Coordinamento per la Difesa della Cava v. Regione Lombardi* (1994) ECR I-483.

Joined Cases C-46/93 and C-48/93. *Brasserie du Pêcheur* and *Factortame III* (1996) 1 CMLR 889.

Contributors

John Barry is reader in politics and deputy director of the Institute of Governance, Public Policy and Social Research at Queens University, Belfast. He has written extensively about normative aspects of environmental politics. His publications include *Rethinking Green Politics: Nature, Virtue, Progress* (1999); *Environment and Social Theory* (1999); *Citizenship, Sustainability and Environmental Research* (2000), with John Proops; and he has co-edited *Sustaining Liberal Democracy: Ecological Challenges and Opportunties* (2001), with Marcel Wissenburg; *The International Encyclopedia of Environmental Politics* (2001), with Gene Frankland; and *Europe, Globalization and Sustainable Development* (2004), with Brian Baxter and Richard Dunphy.

Raymond Bryant is reader in geography at King's College, London. He has written extensively on political ecology and the political economy of natural resource use. His books include *The Political Ecology of Forestry in Burma* (1997); *Environmental Management: New Directions for the Twenty-First Century* (1997), with Geoff Wilson; *Third World Political Ecology* (1997), with Sinead Bailey; and *Making Moral Capital: Non-Governmental Organizations in Environmental Struggles* (2005).

Peter Christoff teaches and coordinates environmental studies in the School of Anthropology, Geography and Environmental Studies at the University of Melbourne. Formerly the assistant to the Commission of the Environment in Victoria, he is on the board of Greenpeace Australia-Pacific and vice-president of the Australian Conservation Foundation.

Ken Conca is an associate professor of government and politics at the University of Maryland and director of the Harrison Program on the Future Global Agenda. His research and teaching focus on global environmental politics, political economy, environmental policy, North-South issues, and peace and conflict studies. He is the author or editor of several books on global environmental politics, technology, and international political economy, including *Green Planet Blues: Environmental Politics from Stockholm to Johannesburg* (2004), *Environmental Peacemaking* (2003), *Confronting Consumption* (2002), *Manufacturing Insecurity: The Rise and Fall of Brazil's Military-Industrial Complex* (1997), and *The State and Social Power in Global Environmental Politics* (1993).

John Dryzek is professor of social and political theory in the Research School of Social Sciences at the Australian National University. His books include *Democracy in Capitalist Times* (1996), *The Politics of the Earth* (1997), *Deliberative Democracy and Beyond* (2000), and *Postcommunist Democratization* (2002), with Leslie Holmes.

Robyn Eckersley is a senior lecturer in political science at the University of Melbourne. She has written extensively on environmental politics and green political theory, including *Environmentalism and Political Theory: Toward an Ecocentric Approach* (1992), the edited volume *Markets, the State and the Environment: Towards Integration* (1995), and *The Green State: Rethinking Democracy and Sovereignty* (2004).

Tim Hayward is a reader in the School of Social and Political Studies at the University of Edinburgh. He is author of *Ecological Thought: An Introduction* (1995), *Political Theory and Ecological Values* (1998), and *Constitutional Environmental Rights* (2005). He has published journal articles on environmental and political philosophy and has co-edited *Justice, Property and the Environment: Social and Legal Perspectives* (1997), with John O'Neill.

Christian Hunold is associate professor of political science in the Department of History and Politics at Drexel University, Philadelphia. His articles on environmental politics and democratic theory have appeared in *German Politics & Society, Governance, Environmental Politics,* and *Political Studies.* He is a co-author of *Green States and Social Movements: Environmentalism in the United States, United Kingdom, Germany, and Norway* (2003) and is currently writing a book on issues of justice and democracy in U.S. radioactive waste disposal policy.

Karen Lawrence received a Ph.D. degree in 2002 with a dissertation on negotiated conservation as social change in Northern Palawan, the Philippines. She has worked with community-mapping methodologies in the Philippines for more than eight years. She has been involved in national and regional policy dialogue in Asia that seeks meaningful involvement of local people in resource management. She has transferred forest management planning processes based on community mapping to communities in Cross River State, Nigeria, while also conducting consultancy work in Cambodia.

James Meadowcroft is professor of political science in the School of Public Policy and Administration, Carleton University, Ottawa. He publications include *Implementing Sustainable Development: Strategies and Initiatives in High Consumption Societies* (2000), with William Lafferty; *Planning Sustainability* (1999), with Michael Kenny; and articles on environmental governance and sustainable development. He is an editor of the *International Political Science Review* and an associate editor of the *Journal of Political Ideologies.*

Matthew Paterson is an associate professor of political science at the University of Ottawa. He works on the intersection between global political economy and environmental politics. His main publications developing these interests are *Global Warming and Global Politics* (1996) and *Understanding Global Environmental Politics: Domination, Accumulation, Resistance* (2000). He is currently working on the political economy, cultural politics, and environmental politics of cars.

David Schlosberg is an associate professor of political science at Northern Arizona University, where he teaches political theory and environmental politics. He is author of *Environmental Justice and the New Pluralism* (1999) and co-author (with Dryzek, Downes, and Hunold) of *Green States and Social Movements: Environmentalism in the United States, United Kingdom, Germany, and Norway* (2003). His articles have appeared in *Environmental Politics, Political Research Quarterly, Political Studies, PS,* and *Society and Natural Resources.*

Steven Slaughter teaches international relations at Deakin University, Burwood, Australia. His Ph.D. dissertation was titled *Public Power in a Globalising Age: A Critical Analysis of Liberal Governance.* He has taught at Monash University, Royal Melbourne Institute of Technology, and the Australian National University. His research interests include international relations, globalization, global governance, international ethics, and political theory.

John Vogler is a professor of international relations at Keele University, U.K. He is also convenor of the British International Studies Association Environment Group and served on various Economic and Social Research Council committees, including that for the Global Environmental Change Programme. His main interests are international environmental cooperation and European Union external policy, and he is currently reconsidering regime analysis under the heading "taking institutions seriously." He is working, with Charlotte Bretherton, on a study of EU external policy for the Palgrave European Union Series. His publications include *The Global Commons: Environmental and Technological Governance* (1995; 2000); *The European Union as a Global Actor* (1999), with Charlotte Bretherton; and *The Environment and International Relations* (1996), with Mark Imber.

Index